WALKING LOCH LOMOND
AND THE TROSSACHS

About the Author

Ronald Turnbull is seen here in the eye of the Argyll Needle, just below the summit of the Cobbler. Among his experiences in the Lomond and Trossachs he includes a bivvy-bag night at the summit of Ben Ledi when he woke up covered in sleet, and a crossing of all eight of the Luss Hills in one November day. Researching this book he has enjoyed in particular revisiting those intricate Crianlarich Hills, and the area's two big views, from Ben A'an and from the Dumpling (alias Duncryne).

He has won awards for his writing – the Outdoor Writers and Photographers Guild Award for excellence six times, in four different categories; and also for his walking – the Fell Running Association's Long-distance Trophy for a journey over all the 2000ft hills of southern Scotland. He is based in Dumfriesshire.

Other Cicerone guides by the author
The Lowther Hills
Walking in the Cairngorms
Three Peaks, Ten Tors
Ben Nevis and Glen Coe
The Book of the Bivvy

Photo by Matt Scase

WALKING LOCH LOMOND AND THE TROSSACHS

by

Ronald Turnbull

2 POLICE SQUARE, MILNTHORPE, CUMBRIA LA7 7PY
www.cicerone.co.uk

© Ronald Turnbull 2009
First edition 2009
ISBN: 978 1 85284 530 8

A catalogue record for this book is available from the British Library.

All photographs are by the author unless otherwise stated.

Acknowledgements

Alois Stukavec and Virginia Kearse (Munroist) added to the enjoyment of the hill days here, and Matt Scase was very good-natured when it came to posing on awkward boulders.

The National Park Ranger Service, the National Trust for Scotland and the Forestry Commission have done (and are doing) good work in looking after and improving these heavily used paths. Special thanks to Steven Kenney and Babs Robertson who went out of their way to clear up the expanding firing range on Route 47 four days before the manuscript for this book went to Cicerone Press.

Thanks to Harveys of Doune who kindly supplied me with all of their most recent mapping at two different scales.

Advice to Readers

Readers are advised that, while every effort is made by the author to ensure the accuracy of this guidebook, changes can occur during the lifetime of a particular edition. Please check the Cicerone website (www.cicerone.co.uk) for any updates before planning your trip. It is also advisable to check information on such things as transport, accommodation and shops locally. Even rights of way can be altered over time. We are always grateful for information about any discrepancies between a guidebook and the facts on the ground, sent by email to info@cicerone.co.uk or by post to 2 Police Square, Milnthorpe LA7 7PY.

Front cover: Ben More (left), the highest point of the National Park, with its sister hill Stob Binnein, seen from Beinn Tulaichean. The two are crossed on Route 17

CONTENTS

Mountain Warning

Mountain walking, particularly scrambling or in winter, can be a dangerous activity carrying a risk of personal injury or death. It should be undertaken only by those with a full understanding of the risks and with the training and experience to evaluate them. While every care has been taken in the preparation of this book, the user should be aware that conditions can be highly variable and can change quickly, thus materially affecting the seriousness of a mountain walk.

Therefore, except for any liability which cannot be excluded by law, neither Cicerone nor the author accepts liability for damage of any nature (including damage to property, personal injury or death) arising directly or indirectly from the information in this book.

To call out the **Mountain Rescue**, phone 999 from a landline. From a mobile, phone 999 or 112: these should connect you via any available network. Once connected to the emergency operator, ask for Mountain Rescue – you will be connected to the police, who co-ordinate the MR teams.

The Cobbler, at only 884m, is still mainland Scotland's toughest summit, reached by an exposed Grade 2 scramble (Route 61). The mica schist is uncomfortably smooth, especially when damp. The left-hand walker here has preferred a roped ascent. Having reached the summit, both are now (in theory at least) qualified to lead Clan Campbell

N

▲ Map Key

☐	ground above 1050m/3500ft
☐	ground above 900m/3000ft
☐	ground above 750m/2500ft
☐	ground above 600m/2000ft
☐	ground above 450m/1500ft
☐	ground above 300m/1000ft
☐	ground above 150m/500ft
☐	ground below 150m/500ft

Contour intervals chosen to feature the Munro and Corbett levels at 3000ft and 2500ft.

▲   a Munro

△   other summit of interest: on overview maps, a Corbett

P   parking (typically at walk start)

◻   building

🏠   bothy

♖   castle

⬭   loch

〜   river, stream

motorway

major road

minor road

unsurfaced track

railway

route

variant or adjacent route

Overview map (pages 12–13)

estate boundaries (see Appendix 2)

estates (see Appendix 2 for full names)

National Park boundary

route location

town, village

Route symbols on OS map extracts

route 1

route 2

routes follow same path

variant

linking routes

start point

finish point

start/finish point

direction of walk

For OS symbols key see OS maps.

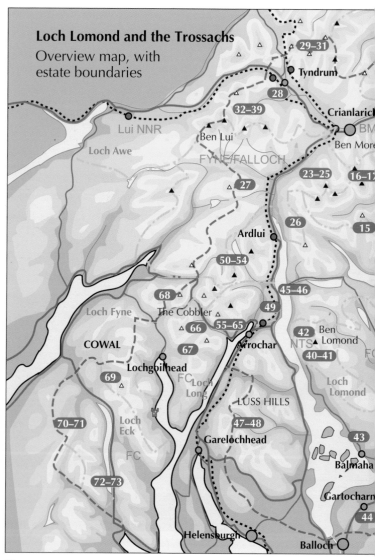

Loch Lomond and the Trossachs

Overview map, with estate boundaries

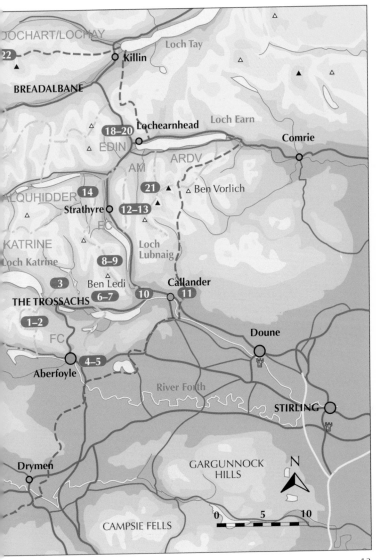

Heading up the Cobbler's east corrie (Route 57) with the North Top (the 'Cobbler's Wife') overhead

INTRODUCTION

Loch Lomond and the Trossachs are the beginning of the big hills of the Scottish Highlands. And given that they stand in the front doorway, it's only right that they are the friendly and welcoming ones. Instead of huge crags and airy, scary ridges, here are small paths that weave uphill among boulders and little lumpy outcrops. The Munros (3000ft or 914m mountains) are not easy anywhere, but here in the south they are that little bit less serious.

So it makes sense that these hills, first in geography for those approaching from the cities of the south, are also, for many Scottish hill-goers, first in time. The Munro tick-list will often start off on the most southerly of them all, Ben Lomond. Rowardennan car park is large, and has a handy shelter hut. Ben Lomond's path is as wide, and as well used, as a town shopping street – but a lot more sociable and friendly. Chaps with chainsaws have cleared the gloomy spruce from the lower slopes, so straight away you see the spreading waters of Loch Lomond and feel the cool mountain air. The path will offer views of the much-sung loch all the way up – at least, until the cloud closes in. And across the otherwise gentle slope runs one small crag, as a first footfall on the crinkly grey mountain rock. It's the schist of the southern Highlands, wrinkled like the hide of an elderly rhinoceros, and like that rhinoceros friendly on the whole but with the occasional nasty moment. Unlike the rhino, the grey schist breaks down into a fertile soil that gives lots of grass, a sprinkling of tormentil and bedstraw, and in special lime-rich corners the tiny gardens of alpine rarities.

Nobody, we suppose, would clamber over a rhino, however elderly. And the schist, slippery when wet and well endowed with wild flowers and other green shaggy matter, tends also to form knobs and excrescences rather than high crags. It is not great for scrambling or climbs – the Cobbler, with its fine routes and rock-tower top, is an atypical oddity. Otherwise there's a loose ridgeline on Ben Lui, some scrappy crag on Beinn a' Chroin, and small unserious scrambly moments almost anywhere you please.

But the walker attempting that first-ever Munro is probably quite pleased about the lack of scrambling on Ben Lomond. As you emerge at the kissing gate onto the open hill, the loch spreads ever wider, with islands casually flung about in it by a preoccupied glacier. One of the little ferryboats chugs along the shoreline, its passengers well waterproofed and hunched under the drizzle. Or it's a different day and they're wondering

15

*A clear winter's day on An Caisteal gives a panorama over most of the National Park.
At the left, Ben Lomond (Routes 40–42), then Loch Lomond lies under mist.
Above nearby Beinn Chabhair (Route 24) are the Arrochar Alps (Routes 50–54).* ▶

why the sunshine isn't also warm, as the breeze of the boat's passage flutters their T-shirts.

Opposite, the hills of Arrochar give the impression of being somehow more mountainous than where you are just now. Their name 'Alps' is an exaggeration, for here are no sharp shapes high against the clouds. It's just that the skyline of Arrochar is excessively crinkly; a whole lot of ruggedness is happening over there. The Cobbler is referred to by the pedantically proper as Ben Arthur. By whatever name, its convoluted wee crags offer genuine mountain rock: more, a corner of them forms the actual highest point of the hill. So that the Cobbler, not even a Munro of 3000ft, proves to be the most difficult summit anywhere on the UK mainland.

But here on Ben Lomond the big and busy path winds upwards. The grass is comfortable, if perhaps a little damp. The view behind gives, at any moment you may need it, an excuse to stop and gaze.

Apart from the water, and the mountains opposite, the glory of that downward view is in the oak trees.

Nothing sets off the smooth grass slopes and the silver-grey loch at their base half so well as the knobbly grey rocks bursting out all over the upper slopes. Nothing – apart from the lush oakwood foliage bursting out all over its base. Wild oakwoods once covered those lower slopes, and inside them lurked even wilder MacGregors and the occasional wolf. Sheep nibbled the saplings and stripped the slopes to bare grass. But in recent years more and more of the dreary spruce is being chopped down, and the wild oakwoods are rising again.

So around the lochs and along the riversides are paths where the wild flowers grow, and you glimpse water between the tree trunks. This is the Trossachs: originally a single oakwood hump at the end of Loch Katrine, the name has colonised the whole eastern end of the National Park. 'Trossachs' now is shorthand for the rough, rugged Highland landscape experience, as invented in the late 18th century by Sir Walter Scott. For those who walk long but low, the West Highland Way, in its loveliest section, runs along the eastern side of Loch Lomond. Gentler

◀ *Distant three-peaked Beinn Bhuidhe, outside the National Park, lies above the Corbett Meall an Fhudhair (Route 27). On the right are the four summits of Ben Lui (Routes 32–39).*

walks are found from all the villages, through plantations and woodland to rocky viewpoints and waterfalls. Even so, by the standards of anywhere further south, any walk here will be a bit rugged. This is, after all, the homeland of Rob Roy MacGregor, the red-headed renegade who resisted the government for half his life and was celebrated by Sir Walter Scott.

As well as the lochs and oak-woods, 'Trossach' implies a sort of midget mountain. From Ben Ledi and Ben Venue down to Ben A'an, these hills are tough but tiny, each carrying enough crag to clothe a hill of double the size.

Oakwood wanders and mini-mountains: but when it's time to get serious, there are some high-altitude hills as well. For its final quarter hour, Ben Lomond gives a taste of real Scottish mountain ground, as the ridgeline narrows, and drops on the right

The National Park has two mountains called Ben Vorlich. This is the one above Loch Earn (Route 21), not the one at the head of Loch Lomond (pictured on page 199).

Bluebells and River Forth on the Fairy Knowe at Aberfoyle (Route 5)

to an untrodden corrie. But it's on the Arrochar Alps, and above Crianlarich, that you savour the special sort of hill found here in the south. Ben More, the high point of the park, is a tough mountain, steep on every side; but the rambling range to its west, from Cruach Ardrain to Beinn Chabhair, mixes grass and rock for a day of rugged ridges and wide views. This is ridge-walking of a friendly sort, as the path winds among knobs and terraces of the crinkly schist rock. And in the northwest of the area, Ben Lui is a full-sized mountain in both altitude (1130m, Scotland's 28th) and seriousness.

With their easy access, convenient shops and accommodation, and public transport by road, rail and water, these slightly less savage mountains make an excellent introduction to the Scottish Highlands. From Lomond's bonnie banks to the Hill of the Fairies, from Arrochar Alps to lowly Ben A'an, and whether you take the high road or the low, here is some of Scotland's best – and best-loved – hill country.

WALKING CONDITIONS

For **low-level walking**, Scotland until recently has offered only the plod through the bog or the smooth and stultifying forest road through the spruce. Here in the National Park this is gradually getting better. Commercial plantations are being cleared and natural oakwoods restored. Footpaths are being improved – sometimes over-improved into smooth and rather boring bike tracks, but even those are immeasurably better than the bog and brushwood they replace.

In the Trossachs in particular, the footways used daily by Rob Roy and enjoyed by Sir Walter Scott and the Wordsworths are re-emerging from under the Christmas trees. The West Highland Way, along the east side of Loch Lomond, is even better if you arrive romantically on a lake ferry.

The **mid-level hills** here are particularly rewarding. Because they are close to the cities, and rise rockily out of lovely lochs, they have helpful, followable paths. Ben Venue is probably Scotland's best-loved low hill (although conceivably Arthur's Seat in Edinburgh might steal that title); but with it come Conic Hill and the Luss Hills, and Ben A'an.

Even away from their paths, these smaller hills are grassy rather than harshly heather. This is down to overgrazing by the clansmen's cattle and then by sheep – but the result is that you can wander solitary in remote corners of Cowal, working your own route across unvisited small mountains, with crags around to add seriousness, but without the vegetation hell you'd find elsewhere in the Highlands. The southwest of the area is the place to look imaginatively at the map and experiment with hill routes of your own invention. The Luss hills are relatively gentle, excellent for a first-ever attempt at a self-guided walk; the Lochgoilhead and Cowal ones are more severe.

The Luss Hills offer gently grassy walking with outstanding views of Loch Lomond. Just above Luss village on Beinn Dubh (Route 48).

Mountains of 750m and upwards are conventionally distinguished as **Munros** (above 914.4m or 3000ft) and **Corbetts** (750–914m, or 2500–3000ft). Over the Highlands as a whole, it's the Munros that are pathed and peopled, and that makes them actually easier than the slightly lower Corbetts. Here, however, the Corbetts are as well walked as the higher ones; and deservedly so. Ben Ledi is every bit as good as Ben More. The Cobbler (884m) is arguably the finest hill south of Glen Coe (I shall argue with anybody who says it isn't). So in this book the 'mountain' designation starts at 750m.

WHEN TO GO

April is still winter on the summits, but low-level routes already offer good walking then and in May. The

leaves are breaking and birds are at their noisiest. Low-level routes are also excellent in October as the birch leaves turn gold.

May and June are enjoyable at all altitudes. July and August can be hot and humid, with less rewarding views and midges infesting the glens. West Highland midges can be pretty grim; the trick is to keep moving, and when you stop, stop high.

Midges hang on until the first frost, normally some time in September. October often brings clear air and lovely autumn colours. In between times there'll be gales. Over Ben Lomond and the southern approaches to the Arrochar Alps there are no access restrictions during stag stalking. Elsewhere, from mid-August (sometimes July) to 21 October, responsible access includes avoiding disturbance to deer stalking. The northern part of the area is covered by three Hillphones schemes, where recorded phone messages warn you, around 24 hours in advance, of which hills' deer are under attack (see Appendix 2).

Winter is a time of short days and foul weather. Snow can lie on the high tops from December to April. Well-equipped walkers skilled in navigation and with ice axe love the winter most of all, for the alpine-style ascents of Ben Lui and the 100km views through the winter-chilled air.

SAFETY IN THE MOUNTAINS

Safety and navigation in the mountains are best learnt from companions, experience, and perhaps a paid instructor; such instruction is outside the scope of this book. For those experienced in hills further south, such as Snowdonia or the Lake District, these hills are only slightly larger but noticeably more rugged.

The international mountain distress signal is some sign (shout, whistle, torch flash or other) repeated six times over a minute, followed by a minute's silence. The reply is a sign repeated three times over a minute, followed by a minute's silence. To signal for help from a helicopter, raise both arms above the head and then drop them down sideways, repeatedly. If you're not in trouble, don't shout or whistle on the hills, and don't wave to passing helicopters.

To call out the rescue, phone 999 from a landline. From a mobile, phone either 999 or the international emergency number 112: these will connect you via any available network. Reception is good on most summits and ridges, and on hillsides that happen to have line of sight to Crianlarich or Arrochar. Sometimes a text message to a sensible friend can get through when a voice call to the rescue service can't.

Given the unreliable phone coverage, it is wise to leave word of your proposed route with some responsible person (and, of course, tell that person when you've returned safely). Youth hostels have specific forms for this, as do many independent hostels and B&Bs.

The following signals are used to communicate with helicopters

Help required:
raise both arms
above head to
form a 'V'

Help not required:
raise one arm above
head, extend other
arm downward

On the north ridge of An Caisteal (Route 23), looking to Ben Lomond

Being lost or tired is not sufficient reason for calling the rescue service, and neither – in normal summer weather – is being benighted. However, team members I've talked to say not to be too shy about calling them: they greatly prefer bringing down bodies that are still alive...

There is no charge for mountain rescue in Scotland – teams are voluntary, financed by donations from the public, with a grant from the Scottish Executive and helicopters from the Royal Air Force and Royal Navy rescue services. You can make donations at youth hostels, TICs and many pubs.

MAPS

Some people enjoy exploring in mountains that are poorly mapped or not mapped at all. They should stay

away from the Loch Lomond and The Trossachs National Park, as it has been excellently mapped – four times over. The mapping in this book is from the Ordnance Survey's Landranger series at 1:50,000. For lower-level walks this book's mapping may well be all you need. For mountain walks, however, it's advisable to have a larger map that shows escape routes (and the other glen you end up in when you come down the wrong side of the hill).

The 1:50,000 Landranger mapping covers the area on sheets 56 (Loch Lomond), 57 (Stirling & Trossachs), 50 (Glen Orchy) and 51 (Loch Tay). The Crianlarich Hills (Parts 3 and 4) are awkwardly on the shared corner of all four maps.

For detailed exploration of crags and corries and pathless boulder slopes you will be helped by the extra contour detail at 1:25,000 scale. The Harvey maps are ideal; they are beautifully clear and legible, mark paths where they actually exist on the ground, and do not disintegrate when damp. They also overlap conveniently. Five Harvey sheets – Arrochar Alps, Crianlarich, Ben Lomond, Ben Ledi, Ben Venue – cover the National Park apart from Cowal (Walks 70 to 73) and the Luss Hills (Walks 47 and 48).

The Harvey maps mark fences and walls on the open hill, but not on the lower ground; so if you're planning complicated valley walks you may prefer the Explorer maps, also at 1:25,000 scale. They are bulkier and less robust than the Harvey ones, and the contour lines are less legible, but if Harvey hadn't done it better, they'd be excellent maps. Sheets 364 (Loch Lomond North) and 365 (Trossachs) cover most of the ground, with 347, 360 and 363 for outlying western and southern walks.

Harveys also offer the *Loch Lomond and The Trossachs National Park Outdoor Atlas* at 1:40,000 scale. It's spiral bound to fit into a map pocket, and has useful overlap between the pages. Compared with the four Landranger maps it's slightly lighter in weight, appreciably more detailed, and half the price. Not everybody will like it, but I've used it for researching and walking the routes in this book.

The relevant maps (LR = Landranger; Expl = Explorer) are listed in the information box which appears at the start of each route.

In good winter conditions Ben Lui is the best. The south ridge (Route 33) with Ben Lomond and the Arrochar Alps behind.

COMPASS AND GPS

A compass is a very useful aid in mist, even if your skills only extend to 'northwest, southeast' rather than precision bearings. Magnetic deviation is about 4° West: to convert a map bearing to a compass one, add 4. The crystals of magnetite found on Cruach Tairbeirt (see Appendix 1) are too small to affect navigation: it's you that's wrong, not the compass!

GPS receivers should be set to the British National Grid (known variously as British Grid, Ord Srvy GB, BNG or OSGB GRB36). GPS readings are normally good within 20m, and I have given 8-digit (10m accuracy) grid references at various tricky points such as where you turn down off a ridge. I have recorded these on the hill, checking for plausibility against a 1:25,000 map afterwards. I have found

GPS less reliable on steep slopes, such as the corrie of Ben Lui, with a smaller sky in sight, and hopeless in Loch Lomond's woods; so such readings should be regarded with some caution. Somewhere on the device, if you press the correct buttons, you can find the degree of inaccuracy. The GPS readings are supplementary; the book is designed for use without a GPS receiver.

WHAT'S IN THIS BOOK

This book suggests the most straightforward routes to each of the area's 21 Munro summits of 3000ft (910m) and over, but seeks out also the wilder and less walked-on ways around the back. It covers the slightly smaller but equally worthwhile hills in which this area is especially rich, from the

In midsummer you either keep moving or wear a midge net. Marshalls on the West Highland Way Race at Beinglas campsite

A walker reaches her final Munro summit on Stuc a' Chroin above Loch Earn (Route 21)

Cobbler to the Luss Hills and Ben Ledi. For days of storm and wind, for snowy ones when you didn't bring your ice axe, for when you just don't feel like dragging your legs up another 600m ascent, here too are the walks of the woods and watersides.

Each of the **Munros** has its well-worn 'standard route'. That will be the quickest and most convenient – and fairly straightforward – way up, but usually not the most interesting. I have pointed out those routes in the preambles, and they are listed in several guidebooks, including Steve Kew's *Walking the Munros Vol 1* (Cicerone – see Appendix 4). However, I've concentrated on what I consider the most rewarding routes for each hill. These may also be a little more demanding,

as they seek out the steeper scenery and avoid the flat Landrover track.

Among less-high hills, here are routes up all but three of the area's 20 **Corbetts** (2500–2999ft/762–914m) as well as Meall an Fhudair, outside the boundary by 400 metres. Some of the **Grahams** (2000–2499ft/610–761m) are rough and comparatively unrewarding. Here are walks onto just 13 of the available 27, including Ben Venue, five of the Luss Hills, and Beinn Mhor of Cowal.

For the very finest hills I have left the choice to you. **Ben Lui**, the **Arrochar Alps**, **the Cobbler**: these are hills you will want to ascend lots of times, by many different routes, or ranges where only you can decide how much, once you're up, to do.

25

Camp in Coire an Lochain of Ben Lui. Such lightweight, traceless wild camping is now a legal right in Scotland

The type of walk is indicated as follows:

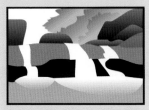

Low level
Forest and riverside walks below 500m

Mid level
Moorland and foothills below 750m

Mountain
Mountain walks above 750m

For these I have given a 'summit summary', with the standard route and the adventure around the back, the slightly rocky scramble and the long, long walk in from somewhere else altogether. **Ben Ledi**'s various routes are spread between two sections of the book, but there's a Ben Ledi summary map in Part 1.

There are no icons for difficulty and length with these routes – they are all mountain routes requiring appropriate skill and care.

HOW TO USE THIS BOOK

The headers at the start of each route should be self-explanatory. The walk-type icons are shown in the panel to the left; the difficulty ratings are explained on page 28. The length ratings correspond with the **approximate times** in the main headers: one square indicates a route that could take up to 2.5 hours, two squares up to 4 hours, with the full five squares for walks of over 8 hours. The approximate times are based on 1 hour for 4 horizontal km or for 400m of height gained, with extra time where the ground is particularly steep or rough. They'll be about right, including brief snack stops, for a moderately paced party. There are no length squares in the Summit Summary routes as these are only half routes (and mostly uphill only).

Where a bus or train can be used to link the two ends of a linear route, or to facilitate going up one route and coming down another, I've noted this

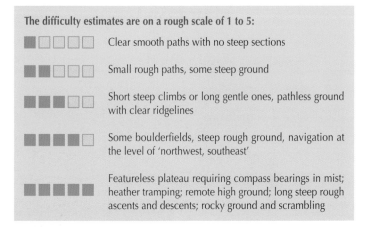

The difficulty estimates are on a rough scale of 1 to 5:

Clear smooth paths with no steep sections

Small rough paths, some steep ground

Short steep climbs or long gentle ones, pathless ground with clear ridgelines

Some boulderfields, steep rough ground, navigation at the level of 'northwest, southeast'

Featureless plateau requiring compass bearings in mist; heather tramping; remote high ground; long steep rough ascents and descents; rocky ground and scrambling

at the routes concerned. Other public transport information is in Appendix 3.

In old numbers, 600ft was a vertical distance, while 200yds was horizontal. I've used a similar convention, so that 600m is an altitude or height gain, while 600 metres (with 'etres') is along the ground. When going up or downhill diagonally, 'slant up left' means in a direction to left of straight up. So if straight up the slope is north, 'slant up right' would be northeast. I

use 'track' (rather than 'path') for a way wide enough for a tractor or Landrover.

Finally, the 'standard route' up a hill is the convenient and well-trodden one featured in guidebooks like Steve Kew's *Walking the Munros*. It's usually the shortest, and because it's so well used, also the easiest. Sometimes it is also the best and most interesting. But to avoid 90 per cent of other hill-goers, simply stay off the standard route.

Ben Narnain sunset (Routes 52 & 53)

THE EAST

PART ONE
TROSSACHS

Bilberry ground at the back of Ben Ledi: looking back to Stuc Odhar (Route 6)

The mountains of this book arrange themselves in a great three-quarter circle whose centre is blocked by Loch Lomond. The book could have started at Ben Lomond and gone clockwise, but the opposite direction makes sense, historically at least. For the Trossachs are where it all begins. The twisty oak trees and small but incomparably rugged hills around them, along with the eight lochs, meant that those who had already learned to like the Lake District were going to just love this side of Loch Lomond. Sir Walter Scott was the first landscape guide. The Wordsworths visited the Trossachs twice on their Scottish expedition of 1803. Behind them came the crowds.

And the crowds are still here, ferried up and down Loch Katrine, and treading the busy peaks of Ben A'an and Ben Ledi. They are quite right to come. The hills look out over the misted Lowlands. With spruce plantations gradually being removed, the flourishing oakwoods at the 'true Trossachs', the patch at the foot of Loch Katrine, are gradually recolonising the wider area between Lomond and Loch Lubnaig. And the fairies still lurk in the green darkness below the branches of Aberfoyle.

1 Ben Venue (shorter)

Length
■ ■ ■ ☐ ☐

Difficulty
■ ■ ■ ☐ ☐

Start/finish	Ben Venue car park, Loch Achray NN 505067
Distance	11.5km/7 miles
Ascent	700m/2300ft
Approx time	4½hr
Max altitude	Ben Venue 729m
Terrain	Smooth paths to forest top, then pathless hill and rough path
Map	LR 57; Expl 365; Harvey *Ben Venue*

Ben Venue is small but surprisingly rocky, and is deservedly the second most popular hillwalk in this area (personally I prefer it to Ben Lomond, the area's Number One). The straightforward up and down by Gleann Riabhach is good in itself. The upper glen is spectacular, so that if you use the South Ridge ascent, and the Gleann Riabhach path just for the descent, you do miss out a little.

However, Ben Venue does call for a detailed exploration, so an unfrequented ridgeline is here offered for the ascent. Route 2 gives the wider Ben Venue some more of the attention it deserves.

The former start for Ben Venue was along the road to Loch Achray Hotel and up forest tracks behind it (past a quirky sign giving Ben Venue 2763ft of height, a mysterious extra 370ft). But the Forestry Commission has created a tarmac-free and much nicer route with blue waymarkers.

Or else follow the right-hand path, also with tricoloured markers, and then turn right. ◄

From the back of the car park, **start** by the left-hand path (tricoloured waymarks) for 400 metres to a junction where you turn left. ◄

The path, with a blue/green marker, heads downhill towards Ben Venue and crosses duckboard to a road junction. Take the lane to the left ('Private Road') for 800 metres, when a path on the left leads across a charming footbridge and up to a forest track. Turn right (signposted for Ben Venue) and after 300 metres turn left up a wide path with vehicle-obstructing boulders.

The path rises between tall trees, to the top end of a forest track. Turn up right here, on a well-built path, running up to join another forest road. Turn left, and in 300

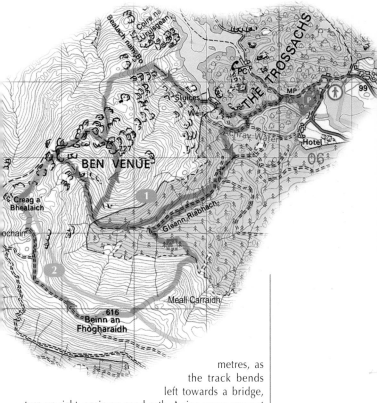

metres, as the track bends left towards a bridge, turn up right, again on good path. A sign warns you not to descend other than by the ascent path, as the path emerges to a clear-felled area and another forest road.

Cross the forest road and continue ahead on the good path. After 800 metres this re-enters forest (though

31

*Summit ridge of
Ben Venue*

these trees too look ready for the chop any time now). In another 1.5km the path emerges onto open hill. For the first few steps, a boardwalk lifts you above the peat. After that, as far as the Forestry Commission is concerned, you're on your own (apart from one decrepit waymark post much higher up the hill). Continue by the main path (and eventual descent route) ahead, or else by the untrodden ridge up on your right.

• Gleann Riabhach path
The path runs up the corrie ahead, sometimes quite steep and sometimes a bit peaty, to a sprawling cairn in a **col at 580m**. Here turn right on a path that's initially steep and loose but then gets nicer. Where the path dips into a small col, look out for a side-path turning left, for only this takes you to the actual summit. It winds up among the rocks of the crest to the **summit cairn** at 729m (NN 474062). In the next col, the bypass path rejoins, and climbs steeply with a crag above it to the **trig point** at 727m (NN477061). The trig point is in ruins, probably struck by lightning – however it's an even better viewpoint than the true summit.

• South ridge

Having emerged from the forest top, continue for 100
metres before turning back up right onto the ridgeline
above. Thus you bypass the very bottom of the ridge,
which is a vertical outcrop. Head up the ridgeline above:
a short rise on steep grass and then hummocky. There's a
path for the final rise to the ruined **trig point** at 727m.

Descent by Gleann Riabhach path

From Ben Venue's ruined **trig point** (727m), take the worn
path that runs down below a crag to the first col. Now
keep up right for the true summit (729m) or take the bypass
path contouring round to the left. Follow the rejoined path
down into a **col (580m)** with a sprawling cairn. The path
continuing up ahead goes to Kinlochard, so turn down
left into the corrie, with the new path, at first not obvious,
soon becoming wide and worn. It runs down the rocky
little valley to the boardwalk and the forest top.

Having descended to the forest road top, you could
instead of turning left continue directly downhill past
Loch Achray Hotel: slightly shorter, and an easier finish
by starlight. Otherwise, return via the charming footbridge. At the final path junction, take whichever path
you didn't use on the outward walk for the last 400
metres to the car park. ▸

For those with two
cars or a chauffeur,
from Achray to
Kinlochard via Ben
Venue is a popular
crossing.

*Ben Venue above
Trossachs woodland.
Birch and oak are
growing back into
the gaps left by clear-
felling a commercial
softwood plantation*

33

2 Ben Venue (Achray Horseshoe)

Length

Difficulty

Start/finish	Ben Venue car park, Loch Achray NN 505067
Distance	15km/9½ miles
Ascent	900m/3000ft
Approx time	6hr
Max altitude	Ben Venue 729m
Terrain	Grassy hill, tracks and a very rugged descent
Map	LR 57; Expl 365; Harvey *Ben Venue*

This wide horseshoe of Gleann Riabhach turns Ben Venue into a richly varied adventure. There's a peaty ridgeline, with wide views in the moments when you're not stumbling over a tussock, but which suddenly gives way to a surprising high-altitude track and a peculiar building complete with ricketty balcony. After that comes the rocky ascent of Ben Venue itself.

But the real interest is reserved for the descent. From various points on the upper hill you look down on Loch Achray. Attempting to follow your eyeline down towards it from any of them will get you onto very nasty ground with hidden crags. Don't attempt this in mist unless your navigation is very confident. The route-finding would be easier taken uphill – as you can see the crags – but the ruggedness of the heather makes this option unpleasant.

Either of the lines of Route 1 make less romantic but also less demanding descents.

Start along Route 1 to the noticeboard warning of unsafe descents (NN 491055). ◄ In clear fell immediately above, turn left up the forest road. It crosses a large stream, and in another 300 metres ends at a turning area. A much rougher path continues ahead, slanting up to a conspicuous little outcrop, where it turns uphill to just below the top of the felled plantation. At a junction, turn back right to reach the very top of the tree stump zone (NN 486045).

Head steeply up a rocky knoll just above, then up the slope to the minor top **Meall Carraidh** (NN 485042). Cross rough ground southwest to the derelict fence that marks the ridgeline. Follow this westwards over **Beinn an Fhogharaidh**, with a few peat hags to work through. ▸ When a small pool is on the right-hand (north) side of the fence, cross through the fence to find a grassy track just below. This runs easily along the ridgeline. Before Stob an Lochain, it forks: head up right to the cairned summit, and the strange small building on its southern side, a disused fire-watchers' hut.

'Foghar' is harvesting; the hill is 'Ogharray'.

Beware of the track leaving **Stob an Lochain** as it spirals, so that you may find yourself returning along your path of arrival. Instead keep north, following a few fenceposts over two very minor summits. At the second one, **Creag a' Bhealaich**, turn down northeast for a rugged ridgeline towards Ben Venue. In the **580m col**, you reach a sprawling cairn.

Keep ahead on the well-worn Ben Venue path. It's initially steep and loose but then gets nicer. Where the path dips into a small col, look out for a side-path turning left, for only this takes you to **Ben Venue's summit**.

On Ben Venue: looking back up the descent route above Loch Katrine. The route goes up to right of the stream cave, then leftward up the grassy dip to the col on the summit ridge.

It winds up among the rocks of the crest to the cairn at 729m (NN 474063). In the next col, the bypass path rejoins, and climbs steeply with a crag above it to Ben Venue's **trig point** at 727m (NN 477061). The ruined trig point is an even better viewpoint than the true summit.

See Route 1 for the simpler descent route.

◄ **Descent** Return down the steep crag-base path for just 100 metres, to the col before Ben Venue's true summit (NN 4762 0617). Now a little stream valley leads down to the right, just west of north, towards Loch Katrine. Soon slabby rocks are passed on your right, but when the slope opens out, keep on down the stream to the top of its little gorge (NN 4763 0661). Here head down to left (west) of the gorge, to cross the stream below its cave waterfall (NN 4762 0672). ◄

See picture on the previous page.

Now bear away to the right, north, to cross a second stream beside a rowan tree (NN 4765 0694). A small path starts here. Keep the same direction to a wide, wet col just around the corner (NN 4775 0705). Turn down right, into the top of a steep stream notch leading down towards two islands at the head of Loch Katrine. Your navigation problems are now over, though those of some very steep ground are about to start.

Traces of path lead straight down the notch, aiming directly for a fenceline far below. Where a stream starts to form, the path keeps on slopes to right of it, marked by one or two small iron posts. Eventually you reach a fence corner at the foot of the steep ground.

Go through a fence gap, to find a clear path running to the right below the side-fence. It leads down into and through a little grassy valley. In another 100 metres, take a ladder stile on the left, and turn right, downhill, on a path that bends round left to the dam of **Loch Katrine**.

Cross the dam, and take the tarred lane ahead near **Achray Water**; it becomes the one used at the start of the outward walk. Just before it joins a road, turn right on the boardwalk path with waymarks. Where it divides, both branches lead quickly to the car park.

Start/finish	Ben A'an car park, Loch Achray
	NN 509070
Distance	6.5km/4 miles
Ascent	450m/1500ft
Approx time	3hr
Max altitude	Ben A'an 454m
Terrain	Good but steep path up; rough
	small path down
Map	LR 57; Expl 365; Harvey *Ben Ledi*

Length

Difficulty

Some might suppose that Ben A'an, with only a few metres of drop separating it from the higher Meall Gainmheich, wasn't a hill at all. They would be wrong! Seen across Loch Achray, Ben A'an is a miniature mountain, and from the path by Allt Inneil it may well remind you of the Matterhorn. Below the crags the path is steep, but well repaired. The summit is, quite simply, one of the scenic spots of Scotland; the view is across to Ben Venue, downward onto oakwoods, and all the way along Loch Katrine.

Many will be content to return down the well-built path. The alternative descent route gives further views along Katrine, but is small, rough, and quite steep, followed by a pleasant ramble back alongside the water.

Start across A821 on a path signed for Ben A'an. It is rugged and ascends steeply, to cross **Allt Inneil** by a foot-bridge. Soon above this it levels, recrosses the stream on stepping-stones, and gives an intimidating view of Ben A'an directly ahead.

The path emerges from the birches at a patch of level grass with boulders for sitting on. Here it bends right and ascends steeply beside a stream and to right of Ben A'an's rocky cone. At the stream top, ignore eroded short cuts up left. The good path circles round to the col joining Ben A'an with the main slope behind, and turns left to the rocky summit of **Ben A'an**.

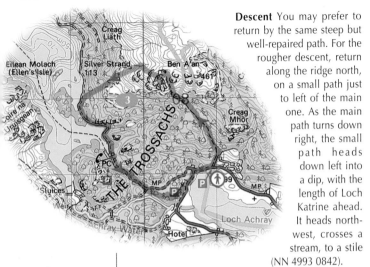

Descent You may prefer to return by the same steep but well-repaired path. For the rougher descent, return along the ridge north, on a small path just to left of the main one. As the main path turns down right, the small path heads down left into a dip, with the length of Loch Katrine ahead. It heads north-west, crosses a stream, to a stile (NN 4993 0842).

Ben A'an from woodland behind the Ben Venue car park

If you cross the stile you'll just have to recross below. So head down to left of the fence to the top corner of a plantation. The path continues to left of the tall plantation

fence, recrossing the stream, into oak woods. It is steep and rough, and in places wet and peaty. It drops onto the tarred track alongside **Loch Katrine**, arriving beside a cattle grid.

Turn left alongside the loch – the track was blasted out with gunpowder, but in Walter Scott's time this was a path suspended from the crags with heather ropes. Pass through the car park at the **ferry pier** onto the entrance road. After 800 metres, where a tarred lane turns off right, turn half-right onto a duckboard path. This runs east through open woodlands. Where it divides, the right-hand branch has better views up to Ben A'an but both reach the car park for Ben Venue. Turn left along A821 to a junction, and right for 250 metres to Ben A'an's car park.

4 Aberfoyle to Menteith Hills

Start/finish	Aberfoyle Riverside car park NN 521009 (or David Marshall Lodge NN 519015)
Distance	16km/10 miles
Ascent	700m/2300ft
Approx time	6hr
Max altitude	Craig of Monievreckie 400m
Terrain	Two thirds paths and tracks, one third rough ground over the hills
Map	LR 57; Expl 365; Harvey *Ben Venue*

Length

Difficulty

The extreme northern edge of the Lowlands is formed of a layer of tough conglomerate (puddingstone) rocks, bent into an upright position by the movement of the Highland Boundary Fault. These rocks form the abrupt ridgeline of the Menteith Hills (as well as Conic Hill, four of the Loch Lomond islands and Callander Craigs). From its heathery, peaty vantage you look south across the Lake of Menteith to the Lowlands, and north across Loch Venachar to the Highlands. ▶

◀ You also look down on the woods and plantations of the Queen Elizabeth Park. The well-laid trails around David Marshall Lodge give relaxing walking under birch and oak and by small waterfalls. The junction of forest and hill here is also the joining point of Highland and Lowland, with a glimpse of the strange ocean-bottom rocks of the Highland Border Complex.

The start from the David Marshall Lodge makes the walk slightly shorter, but you'll have to pay for your parking. Skip straight to the second paragraph below.

Start from Aberfoyle up the A821 (Callander). Take steps up left past the Bowling Club to short-cut the road's big bend. At the top of the village, turn right up stone steps (not the bike path that turns up right 30

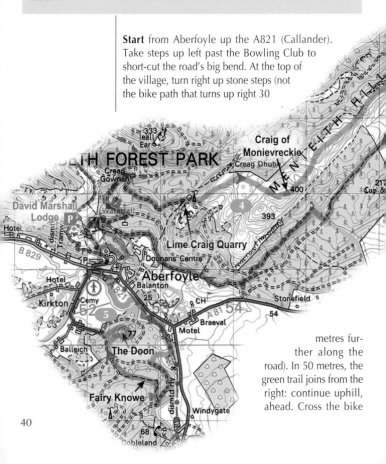

metres further along the road). In 50 metres, the green trail joins from the right: continue uphill, ahead. Cross the bike path onto a path signposted for the **David Marshall Lodge**, 300 metres away on a hilltop. Pass to left of the lodge and head down to the small lake beyond. Bear right, around the foot of the lake, to its northeast corner.

At the northeast corner of the **lake** is a signboard with various maps. A path turns away from the lake, with four-coloured waymarkers. Follow it ahead, past the end of a boardwalk. At the next junction, as the Red Trail forks off left, follow the remaining three colours forking right. The path drops to the foot of the **Little Fawn Falls**.

Cross the footbridge below the falls (signed as Bike Path 7) to a rough track, and turn left up this, with blue/red marker posts. In 400 metres turn back left, still with blue/red markers, to pass another small waterfall over on your left. In another 400 metres is a four-way track junction.

Turn sharp right, southwest and slightly downhill, with blue waymarkers. The track levels for a while, then climbs to the top of the forest, where it ends. Immediately above is the former **Lime Craig Quarry**, cut into the very edge of the Lowlands. The back wall is reddish conglomerate, whose cobbles, where broken, show discoloured quartzite washed out

Lime Craig Quarry. Right, serpentinite, ocean-floor rock, caught up in the Highland Boundary Fault. Left, Lowland puddingstone, in its natural state above, quarried below.

of a now-non-existent mountain range. The lower rocks, to left and right, are quite different: reddish black where weathered, pale green when freshly broken. ◀

A steep path runs up to left of the quarry, then turns right, to a gateway gap above. A viewpoint overlooking the David Marshall Lodge is just ahead, but turn left alongside an old fence on a faint, wet, path northeast. The path soon edges up right to follow a small ridge just above. With a forest visible ahead, turn right alongside two decayed fences side-by-side, towards the highest point of the hill. After 800 metres southeast, climb a heathery bank then turn left on a small path to the trig point (400m) on **Craig of Monievreckie**.

The decayed fence follows the ridgeline northeast. The path heads away to right of the fence to start with but soon rejoins it. Follow the ridgeline for 3km, with two sharp dips along the way. With trees ahead, the fence ends at the top of low crags.

Slant down left, then back right along the foot of the crags, with an old wall hidden in bracken just below. Head downhill through patchy bracken, some of it unpleasantly thick, for 300 metres, to reach a well-used path. This runs back southwest, along the base of the ridgeline. After 1km it enters forest at a stile. In another 1km, after a gate, it reaches the beginning of a forest road.

This track runs ahead to Braeval car park, but for better views turn off right on a path with yellow-topped waymarkers. This heads up to a higher forest road, and follows it left (southwest) with views of the Lake of Menteith. After 1km, turn down left (yellow marker) then to the right (red/green markers). In 200 metres, a path down left (red/green marker) would lead to **Braeval car park** but stay on the main track (red markers).

The track runs along the top of Aberfoyle golf course. A fork left is signed for Aberfoyle but bear right on the track that re-enters woodland and becomes the Blue Trail. After 800 metres, the Blue Trail forks down left on a path signed for David Marshall Lodge, to cross a footbridge just below. Go up the short rise beyond to a signpost.

This is serpentinite, originally a fragment of ocean bed snatched up between the two moving continental blocks. See further pictures of the quarry in Appendix 1.'

- **For David Marshall Lodge** Turn right. After 200 metres, as the bike path bends left, keep ahead, uphill, towards the lodge. Below the lodge, both directions have multicoloured waymarkers: left leads up to the lodge, right contours round to the lake and car park.

- **For Aberfoyle** Turn left, signposted as the Oak Coppice Trail. Green-top posts mark the path that rambles back towards the golf course before bending to the right, downhill. It passes above houses of Aberfoyle to rejoin the outward route.

5 Aberfoyle Fairy Knowe

Start/finish	Aberfoyle Riverside car park NN 521009
Distance	7km/4½ miles
Ascent	100m/300ft
Approx time	2hr
Max altitude	Doon Hill 77m
Terrain	Waymarked paths
Map	LR 57; Expl 365; Harvey *Ben Venue*

Length ■ □ □ □ □

Difficulty ■ □ □ □ □

This hill, so regularly formed, so richly verdant, and garlanded with such a beautiful variety of ancient trees and thriving copsewood, was held by the neighbourhood to contain, within its unseen caverns, the palaces of the fairies: a race of airy beings, who formed an intermediate class between men and demons, and who, if not positively malignant to humanity, were yet to be avoided and feared, on account of their capricious, vindictive, and irritable disposition.

'They ca' them,' said Mr Jarvie, in a whisper, 'Daoine Schie, whilk signifies, as I understand, men of peace – meaning thereby to make their gude-will.'

Walter Scott in *Rob Roy* (1817) was describing Doon Hill, his information coming from *The Secret Commonwealth*, the detailed account of fairy lore ▶

43

◀ published by the Aberfoyle minister Robert Kirk in 1691. The Revd Kirk has an official gravestone in Kirkton graveyard, but actually was snatched away in 1692 while walking on the Doon.

Don't believe in fairies? Neither do I. This is still a great little walk of riverside and woodland, particularly fine in bluebell time.

From Aberfoyle's Riverside car park, **start** along the tarred Riverside Walk downstream, with the **River Forth** on your right. In 300 metres you can either cross the small stream ahead, or else follow the tarred path left to a tarmac cycle way, turn right over the stream, and at once right again on a community path, to rejoin the River Forth.

The grass path continues downstream for 500 metres, then joins the tarred cycle way. As the river bends away again, take a stile on the right to follow a fisherman's path, again rejoining the tarred cycleway. In another 400 metres, just after a small bridge, turn right on a gravel path with green waymark post. This crosses the **River Forth** to a forest track.

Turn left, now following yellow waymark posts. Turn off left onto a riverside path that leads to a small car park called **Lemahamish** (NS 529991). There's a path map here.

Double back right on a forest road past a barrier, then turn up left (blue/yellow waymarks) to cross **Fairy Knowe**. The path drops to a junction of forest roads. Keep ahead, downhill, to another junction. Again keep ahead, with a green waymark, across a bridge. The track rises to a signpost, and a red waymarker, indicating the path up to the right onto **Doon Hill**. ◀

Slightly to right of the upward path, a red waymark shows the descending one. At the hill foot it meets a track where you turn left, then right on the continuation of the track you arrived on.

The track runs into **Kirkton** village. Keep ahead on a street, past the graveyard supposedly containing the earthly remains of The Revd Kirk, that leads to the bridge of the Forth at Aberfoyle.

The summit is decorated with votive offerings, some apparently left by adults. Most of them dangle from the summit pine, inside which the spirit of Revd Robert Kirk is supposedly captive.

Votive offerings at the summit of Doon Hill.
The spirit of Revd Robert Kirk is imprisoned within this tree.

SUMMIT SUMMARY: BEN LEDI

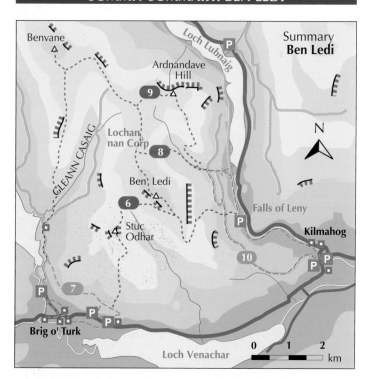

BEN LEDI

Low routes

7   Finglas Woods

10 Kilmahog: Lowland to Highland

Ben Ledi routes

6   Ben Ledi and Benvane from Brig o' Turk

8   Ledi from Lubnaig

9   Ardnandave Hill to Ben Ledi

Start/finish	Little Drum car park, Loch Venachar head NN 548062
Distance	21.5km/13½ miles
Ascent	1350m/4500ft
Approx time	8¾hr
Max altitude	Ben Ledi 879m
Terrain	Hill paths and some pathless hillside
Short cut	Omitting Benvane saves 1km and 300m, about 1¼hrs
Map	LR 57; Expl 365; Harvey *Ben Ledi*

Length

Difficulty

Between Stuc Odhar and Ben Ledi is a place of bilberry slopes and schist, a patch of wild country that few visit as it really belongs about 100 miles further north. However, a new path up through Glen Finglas woods is considerably more convenient than driving all the way to Glenfinnan or Creag Meagaidh. The woodland path will just get better over the next few years as the birches grow; the wild ground is only moderately rugged; and it's fun surprising all the people on the busy southeast ridge by suddenly arriving from somewhere else.

Though no Munro, Ben Ledi is the highest point of the Trossachs and gives an outstanding overview of most of the National Park. The sharp-eyed could also spot the sea on both sides of Scotland from here.

With Brig o' Turk as your base, it becomes very natural to continue along the knolly ridge for the horseshoe to include the second of the Corbetts, Benvane. Alternatively, there's a quick track descent by Gleann Casaig. Ben Ledi's more popular route, from Loch Lubnaig, is Route 8.

Start from Little Drum car park (or Lendrick car park 500 metres west). Turn right out of the car park (towards Callander) on a roadside path for 100 metres across a bridge. Then cross onto a path up through woods. It joins a wider track, and runs up through a gate with a bench. It bends left to pass a cairn and another bench – an official

47

Benvane above Loch Lubnaig

viewpoint, and the waymarks now alter from black to purple. The track bends to the right, and then contours back to the left at 230m altitude. After 400 metres a slight descent to a stream is just ahead. Here turn up sharp right, past a waymark post.

The recently opened path has not been used much, and is indistinct, with widely spaced waymarkers. It runs up to right of the stream then slants up slightly leftwards, north, crossing a couple of streams, to exit the woodland at a ladder stile (NN 552080). Continue uphill beside a tiny stream to the ridgeline of **Stuc Odhar**. A few iron fenceposts guide along the southeast ridge to the summit cairn. ◀

Stuc Odhar, pronounced 'oh-arr', is 'Pointed Hill of nondescript dun colour'.

More old fencing guides down the northeastern ridgeline, skirting left of ridgeline hummocks to a col above the ridge foot (530m). Here turn down right in a grassy hollow to cross the top of the **Milton Glen Burn**. Ahead now Ben Ledi is looking very big. A direct ascent leads up broken ground, so slant right, eastwards, up a grassy ramp defined by a streamline. You reach Ben Ledi's southeast ridge at the point called **Meall Odhar** (815m). A large path leads up left to **Ben Ledi's summit**.

A very pleasant ridge path leads northwest then north to Ledi's north top. Here slant down northwest, on a clear

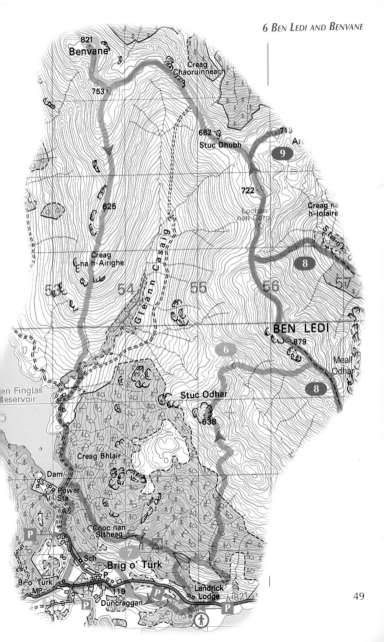

821
Benvane

Creag
Chaoruinneach

753

662
Stuc Dhubh

713
Ar

9

722

Lochan
nan Corp

Creag na
h-Iolaire

625

Stank

Creag
na h-Airighe

8

53

54

55

56

57

Gleann Casaig

BEN LEDI
879

6

Meall
Odhar

8

en Finglas
Reservoir

Stuc Odhar

638

Creag Bhlair

Dam

Power
Sta

Cnoc nan
Sitheag

P

7

Brig o' Turk

119

Sch

P

Lendrick
Lodge

B'o Turk
MP

P

Duncraggan

P

A 821

P

Corp is indeed 'corpse'; this pass was the line of an old corpse road.

Just above this col there's a short-cut track down left into Gleann Casaig. The track does not quite reach the ridgeline, so it's possible to walk past it; however, it is obvious in any glance back from the col just below.

path, to **Bealach nan Corp**. Over the next rise you pass the little Lochan nan Corp. ◀

The path passes just to right of the small hummock of **Biorann na Circe**. Over the next 1km the path undulatingly descends towards a peaty col at 604m. ◀ There are some hags to deal with as you cross this col, before grassy slopes lead up to Point 711m above Creag Chaoruinneach. The path and fence remnants now take a wide swing to the left over **Meall a' Coire Dubh** (753m), avoiding peaty places on the direct line. Near three quartz boulders the path and fence turn right, up to the summit of **Benvane**. Elsewhere in the Highlands this might be spelt Beinn Mheadhoin: it means 'Middle Hill'.

Return along the fence and path to **Meall a' Coire Dubh**. At the corner with the three quartz boulders, keep ahead down the gentle south ridge. Steep ground dropping right (west) appears transversely sliced, and is classic landslip terrain undermined by the glacier of Gleann nan Meann.

At its tip the ridge steepens, down to rough pasture. A fence crosses, with a gate at a convenient point. Go through it and survey the slope below. A wall across the broad ridgeline below is the top of inbye pastures, and you will head for the left-hand end of it. So slant down left, to a fenced-off strip above the river, a drove for sheep. Follow this down to a gate leading down to the river (NN 535096). This is easily crossed in normal conditions, but if it's in spate be aware that there's a waterfall just below (so you'll be safer heading on down the field to the track bridge below at the loch side). Follow a fence up to a gate and a track just above.

Turn down right, through the first of three gates, to the tarred lane above **Glen Finglas Reservoir**. You reach the lane at Ben Ledi Cottage. Follow it down for 500 metres, until a smooth bike path turns up to the left (beige waymark). It climbs briefly to pass through a deer fence, then contours through woods above the fence. After emerging onto open hillside, it dips to a footbridge. A short path down right leads to a waterfall – only worthwhile if streams are full. In another 200 metres the main path turns downhill. Where it splits at a ruined shieling, either fork leads down to a gate into the Woodland Trust's **Lendrick car park**.

Turn left through the car park to a roadside path to Lendrick Steading. Its driveway leads out to the Little Drum car park.

REVERSE ROUTE

This is straightforward apart from the descent from Stuc Odhar, when it is important to find the path down through the woodland. The easiest way to find the ladder stile is to descend southeast from Stuc Odhar alongside the decayed fencing to the first col and then up the short sharp rise just beyond, before turning directly downhill southwest. The ladder stile is at NN 5522 0805 (altitude 475m). Once you've found and followed the descending path and track, after the gate with bench, keep ahead on a path where the track bends away left.

7 Finglas Woods

Start/finish	Little Drum car park, Loch Venachar head NN 548062 (or parking below Glen Finglas dam NN 532073)
Distance	8km/5 miles
Ascent	250m/800ft
Approx time	2½hr
Max altitude	Glen Finglas Woods 250m
Terrain	Good paths, with a steepish climb to start
Map	LR 57; Expl 365; Harvey *Ben Ledi*

Length

Difficulty

On the slopes above Brig o' Turk the Woodland Trust has planted 450,000 native trees and laid out some smooth and easily followed paths. With its wide views of Loch Venachar, ancient oaks and tearoom, this is everything you ask for in a valley walk.

Woodland Trust pathway in Glen Finglas

Start from Little Drum car park (there is additional parking at Lendrick car park 500 metres west, and an alternative start point and parking below Glen Finglas dam, halfway around the walk). Turn right out of the car park (towards Callander) on a roadside path for 100 metres across a bridge. Then cross onto a path up through woods. It joins a wider track, and runs up through a gate with a bench. It bends left to pass a cairn and another bench – from here the waymarks alter from black to purple.

The wide path bends to the right, and then contours back to the left at 230m altitude. After 400 metres is a slight descent to cross a stream (ignore the hill route to Stuc Odhar turning up right here). The path then descends slightly, and passes between two tall gateposts to join a wide, smooth bike track.

ALTERNATIVE

For a shorter walk you could turn down left here, taking either of two branches below, to the valley floor. Turn left through a car park to a path to Lendrick Steading, and head out along its driveway to the Little Drum car park (distance 2.5km/1½ miles, ascent 200m/656ft, approx time 1¼ hours).

Main route Take the bike path contouring ahead. Soon a branch path down left leads to a waterfall just below, worth visiting in rainy weather. The main path ahead contours high above Brig o' Turk, and eventually drops left through a deer fence to join a tarred byway.

Turn down left, soon passing a viewpoint where a clearing carrying power lines gives a view along **Glen Finglas Reservoir**. Steep zigzags lead down to a small car park and the edge of Brig o' Turk. With houses and a school sign just ahead, a path crosses the road. There's a choice.

- **For Brig o' Turk's tearoom** take the signposted path right, following River Turk to the Brig o' Turk itself (the actual stone bridge). The path here runs left alongside the **A821**, then on pavement, through

Brig o' Turk village. At the village end the path is alongside the road for 400 metres, then heads up right onto a low grassy ridge.

- **For woodland without a cup of tea**, turn left through a kissing gate. The path slants up under trees to two field gates – take the kissing gate between them. In 300 metres turn off left, waymarked, on a path that becomes a boardwalk. It runs past a swamp to reach the **A821**. Cross to a kissing gate, and head up onto the low grassy ridge beyond.

The two routes rejoined follow the grassy ridgeline east, entering oakwoods. The path drops to a junction. Here red and yellow waymarks indicate some short woodland walks on the right, but the main path turns left, to **Little Drum car park**.

PART TWO

CALLANDER AND LOCH LUBNAIG

Loch Lubnaig, looking north to Sgiath a' Chaise

Loch Lubnaig is a gloomy sort of place between steep slopes of Sitka spruce. It's a special site for fans of Sue Townsend, whose hero Adrian Mole passes a 'dead boring' holiday in the Strathyre Forest Cabins.

However this is the starting point for the popular route up Ben Ledi, set off up by Adrian Mole's mother and her lover Mr Lucas at 5am after a drunken all-night party. This despite Adrian sensibly pointing out to them that they were 'blind drunk, too old, unqualified, unfit and lacking any survival techniques'. They overcome these disadvantages to complete Route 8 in time for a late breakfast of bacon and eggs.

As well as this literary pilgrimage, Loch Lubnaig offers a very varied group of mid- and low-level walks taking in two impressive waterfalls, the Highland Boundary faultline, and a little-visited Corbett.

8 Ledi from Lubnaig

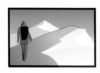

Length

Difficulty

Start/finish	Track end of Strathyre Forest Cabins NN 586091
Distance	9.5km/6 miles
Ascent	750m/2500ft
Approx time	4½hr
Max altitude	Ben Ledi 879m
Terrain	Steep rough hill paths
Map	LR 57; Expl 365; Harvey *Ben Ledi*

Ben Ledi is a fine, upstanding hill whose position right on the edge of the Highlands gives it commanding views to the south; it is high and isolated enough for a mountain panorama in the other three directions as well. 'A handy wee hill' said one middle-aged walker from Glasgow who didn't want to reveal just how many times he'd already been up Ben Ledi. It's not just being so close to the cities that makes this one of Scotland's most popular hills.

Forest felling has cleared fresh views for the lower slopes, and Forestry Commission pathbuilding eases the passage to the 400m contour. After that it gets more rugged: the Stank Glen is an attractively craggy place.

The one disadvantage of this, the favourite Ledi circuit, is its limited car parking. Even on cloudy weekdays this can fill up. Route 10 lets you use instead the spacious car parks at Kilmahog – but this adds 3km to each end of the day (well, Kilmahog is actually in the Scottish Lowlands!).

The following Route 9 gives a wilder way up over Ardnandave Hill: rough moorland instead of a peopled path. Route 6 (in the previous section) is a longer, tougher day that also includes Benvane (see Summary on page 46).

Once across the narrow bridge over Garbh Uisge, turn left for the small parking areas.

Start by walking upstream along the right-hand of two tracks, marked as the Route 7 cycle path. After 1.2km the two tracks draw close together, and a path signed for Ben Ledi switches you across onto the left-hand one. Straight away fork left, uphill, on a track with a red waymarker.

As it nears the **Stank Burn gorge** the track doubles back left, but take the path ahead. It rises, fairly rough, above the river gorge, to a higher bend in the same track. Again take the path uphill above the river. After a slightly longer ascent, you meet that track for the third time. Cross it to where the path continues slightly to the right. Less steeply now, it leads you up to the beginning of the **Stank Glen**'s hanging valley. The dirt track met here is actually a new one, heading north above Loch Lubnaig. ▶

There are two well-made paths up the Stank Glen, one on either side of the stream. The one directly ahead,

The Ardnandave Route 9 turns off here.

The path from the Stank Glen rises up the steep side of Ben Ledi

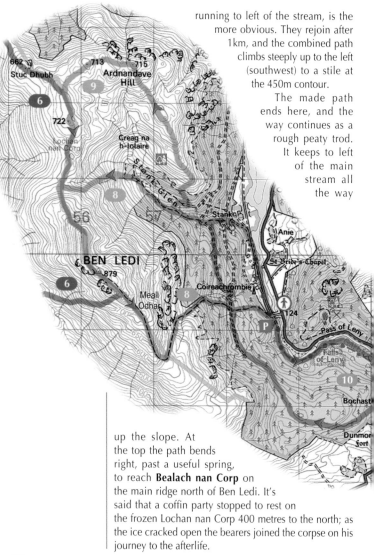

running to left of the stream, is the more obvious. They rejoin after 1km, and the combined path climbs steeply up to the left (southwest) to a stile at the 450m contour.

The made path ends here, and the way continues as a rough peaty trod. It keeps to left of the main stream all the way up the slope. At the top the path bends right, past a useful spring, to reach **Bealach nan Corp** on the main ridge north of Ben Ledi. It's said that a coffin party stopped to rest on the frozen Lochan nan Corp 400 metres to the north; as the ice cracked open the bearers joined the corpse on his journey to the afterlife.

A grassy path follows old fenceposts up to Ledi's **north top** at 852m, a good stopping point short of the busy summit. The last ridge-section, though comfortably wide, is steep on both sides and has an airy feel. A trig point marks **Ben Ledi** summit.

Heading north off Ben Ledi's summit towards Benvane. Crianlarich hills Cruach Ardrain, Ben More and Stob Binnein range along the skyline behind

Descent The path down Ben Ledi's southeast ridge is well trodden and clear. It sets off past a memorial cross mounted on a rocky outcrop. After a sharp drop, it rises slightly over **Meall Odhar** (815m) and then descends towards a broad peaty shoulder at 550m.

As soon as the ridge levels off, the path turns sharply down left, slanting down northwards with views along Loch Lubnaig, and soon with craggy ground above. At 450m is a stile, after which the path is well rebuilt and smooth, but still quite steep. At 220m it crosses a forest road, with blue waymarkers, and descends through plantations to the bridge over Garbh Uisge.

DESCENT BY STANK GLEN

This route has been taken anticlockwise so as to have the steepest ground uphill; and also because the views up the Stank Glen are rocky, while looking down it is depressing woodpulp plantations. However, the descent by Stank Glen is straightforward – apart from the turn-off from the ridge into the corrie. After the slightly undulating summit ridge, the path drops quite steeply right down to **Bealach nan Corp**, which is the first point where there is rising ground ahead. The path turning off to the right here only becomes clear once you reach the top of the steep ground. If you reach **Lochan nan Corp**, a substantial pool 100 metres wide, then you have overshot and must return south for 400 metres.

9 Ardnandave Hill to Ben Ledi

Length

Difficulty

Start/finish	Track end of Strathyre Forest Cabins NN 586091
Distance	13km/8 miles
Ascent	850m/2900ft
Approx time	5½hr
Max altitude	Ben Ledi 879m
Terrain	Rough hillsides and moorland
Map	LR 57; Expl 365; Harvey *Ben Ledi*

A tough, strength-sapping route, quite countrified and wild and inhabited by red deer, that gives great views of Loch Lubnaig and a whole new way of looking at Ben Ledi.

Start as for Route 8 (note parking problems at Garbh Uisge bridge). Follow it up to the lip of **Stank Glen**'s hanging valley.

At this final forest road, don't take the waymarked path opposite, but turn right on the dirt track across the stream. Ignore the second built path turning up left beside the stream, and continue on the smooth track for 200 metres. As it starts to descend, double back left up a grassed-over track. It slants up the corrie side to emerge from the trees onto slopes of long grass and rushes.

Head up right, towards the skyline ridge overlooking Loch Lubnaig. Follow it up northwards, with the vegetation gradually getting less heathery and hampering. The ridgeline widens, and bends round left to the two hummocks of **Ardnandave Hill**.

A short sharp drop leads to a wide, wet col. Head west across two grassy hummocks, to join an old fenceline. Turn left along this, with a small peaty path. In 500 metres it leads to Bioran na Circe. ▶ The path bypasses to left of the small summit hump. The path drops to pass **Lochan nan Corp**, and then crosses a gentle grassy hump to Bealach nan Corp.

Here the path from Stank Glen joins from the left. The path and old fenceposts lead up south onto **Ben Ledi**'s summit ridge, which is followed to the summit trig point.

Descend by the southeast ridge, as on Route 8 – it also describes the descent by Stank Glen if you prefer that.

'The Hen's Little Pointed Stick' – probably not indicating that the poultry uses a walking pole, but suggesting, untruthfully, that the hill is a pointy one.

Ardnandave Hill, across Loch Lubnaig

10 The Whole Kilmahog: Lowland to Highland

Length

Difficulty

Start/finish	Kilmahog car parks NN 608082
Distance	10.5km/6½ miles
Ascent	170m/600ft
Approx time	3hr
Max altitude	Bochastle Hill 240m
Terrain	Dirt track and paths
Map	LR 57; Expl 365; Harvey *Ben Ledi*

The Highland Line is defined by geology. The rocks change suddenly from brown Lowland sediments to the tough grey schist. Kilmahog, no doubt to its great disappointment, is outside the Highlands by just a few hundred metres.

But this isn't merely a walk to the Highlands and back (a feat that could also be achieved by walking the A85 to the 40mph sign at the north edge of the village...) Clear-felling has given the timber track a fine outlook up Loch Lubnaig. And the walk back through birchwoods is a riverside delight, more especially when heavy rains have made the Garbh Uisge noisy enough to drown out the traffic on the main road opposite.

The walk intersects both of the eastern paths up Ben Ledi, and can be used as a preamble to it when the Garbh Uisge car park is full up (see map on page 58).

Start from the National Park's Kilmahog car park on the east side of the A821 (or from the Forestry Commission one above the road 200 metres into the walk). Cross to the west side, where the Route 7 cycle path continues ahead – the return part of this walk. For now, turn left on a fenced path that turns up away from the road into a car park. At the far end of this, a dirt path rises to join a forest road.

Follow this as it zigzags uphill. As it does so, it passes a roadstone quarry, which exposes the lumpy

The Falls of Leny

puddingstone (or 'conglomerate') that shows that we are as yet still in the Scottish Lowlands.

The trees rise on either side as the dirt road passes through the slight col behind **Bochastle Hill**, but it then emerges into clear-felled ground. In 500 metres, as the road bends left, a cutting exposes the grey schist of the Highlands. The track re-enters trees, and in another 800 metres a path descends from the left, and plunges into the trees down on the right – both branches being way-marked with blue posts. The downhill path could be used to shorten the walk. ▶

This path is used by Route 8 descending Ben Ledi's south ridge.

Keep ahead on the track, which crosses a stream and then forks. The lower fork ahead could be taken, but the left branch, doubling back uphill, is more interesting. It soon bends back to the right, and then descends gently through cleared ground.

When you see a well-built path forking up left, look for the descending path, on the right, just before it. Both are waymarked in red. ▶ The path is rough and quite steep, above the **gorge of Stank Burn**. It meets a corner of the lower forest road, but continues ahead downhill above the stream. Finally it emerges onto a lower bend of the forest road.

This red-waymarked path is Route 8, heading up to Stank Glen and Ben Ledi.

63

Head down the forest road until it levels, then take a short path on the left to join a tarred track (the Route 7 cycle path). Follow it ahead, with the wide **Garbh Uisge** river on your left, for 1.2km, to a crossroads with a bridge on your left. ◄

Here the short-cut path arrives from above, out of the trees.

Don't cross the bridge, but take the Route 7 cycle-path on downstream past car parks onto a wide, firm bike path. After 1km it passes the pier of a railway bridge that once crossed the river, and the path is now wider and smoother, being on the old railbed. Just after this, at a stone table, a rough path leads down left to follow the riverbank for views of the **Falls of Leny**. (The railinged walkway opposite might offer better views, from a convenient car park on the A85; but both car park and walkway have been barricaded off, so we west-bankers have the better of it.)

You can now rejoin the smooth cycle path, or remain on rough little paths alongside the river. After 1km, with houses on the opposite side, river and railbed converge and the rough paths rise back onto the cycleway just before it crosses a small stone bridge. Follow the cycle path for the last 800 metres to the A821.

ROCK NOTES (SEE ALSO APPENDIX 1)

The brown 'puddingstone' is conglomerate of Old Red Sandstone or Devonian age (400 million years old). It is also seen at Conic Hill (Route 43), at Doon Hill (Route 5), on Callander Craigs (Route 11) and the Menteith Hills (Route 4). The great Caledonian mountain range, formed at the collision of Scotland with England, was then decomposing. The smooth pebbles within the puddingstone were probably an outwash fan below the mountains.

At the roadstone quarry you can see some of the pebbles cut open. Many are of dark andesite lava with pink or white feldspar crystals. Others have irregular white blobs, former bubble-holes refilled with calcite mineral. When the Caledonian mountains formed, the volcanoes were on top and so were the first to get eroded away. Their only remnants are these pebbles – and two bits that sank and so escaped erosion, Ben Nevis and the mountains of Glencoe.

The rock that forms the northern edge of the Lowlands: conglomerate (puddingstone) of the Old Red Sandstone, from the roadstone quarry on Bochastle Hill. The pebbles within it are dark rhyolite lava, some with feldspar crystals, one with gas-bubble holes that have filled up with white calcite. Other pebbles are of near-white quartzite. All were washed down out of Highland mountains that no longer exist.

The grey rock on the north side of the Highland Boundary is noticeably different. It contains no embedded pebbles, it has a slaty cleavage (or tendency to break in slices), and the white quartz within it is bent and broken about. This is Dalradian schist, about three times as old as the puddingstone. The schist was already mangled and old before Scotland and England ever met: the collision mangled it even more to make the deep roots of the new mountain chain.

Around 100 million years after the puddingstone eroded out of the mountains, the combined Scotland–England bit of continent was being stretched north-to-south. The earth's crust broke at Kilmahog, with the northern rocks being pulled away and up, and the southern sliding downwards. Thus the less ancient puddingstone rocks to the south were brought down alongside ancient schist of the mountain roots to the north. Another 300 million years of erosion, plus a final scrub from the Ice Age, has left the two contrasting rocks standing side by side.

On Bochastle Hill you can contrast the lumpy-looking Lowland hills, such as Meall Garbh directly opposite, with the stronger lines of Ben Ledi. On the return part of the walk, the Falls of Leny are in grey slaty schist. In fact, the road cutting of the A85, just before the northern 40mph limit of Kilmahog, is still showing the grey Highland rocks. An exploration of the Garbh Uisge might show the actual fault line between the two. The strange rocks along the actual boundary can be examined on Route 4 (Aberfoyle to Menteith).

11 Callander: Falls and Crags

Length
■ ■ □ □ □

Difficulty
■ □ □ □ □

Start/finish	Callander woods NN 634082
Distance	7km/4½ miles
Ascent	300m/1000ft
Approx time	2½hr
Max altitude	Victoria monument 343m
Terrain	Good paths, very minor road, rough path onto Callander Craig
Map	LR 57; Expl 368; Harvey *Ben Ledi*

This is a walk of pleasant woodlands, an impressive small gorge, and a viewpoint reached without undue effort. Callander Craig, when you get there, is made of lumpy puddingstone: it's the same stuff as Doon Hill at Aberfoyle and Conic Hill above Loch Lomond, and belongs to the Devonian or Old Red Sandstone age. Thus Callander is revealed as being a Lowland town, if only by about 2km.

The exciting footbridge across Bracklinn Falls was washed away in 2005, but may eventually be replaced.

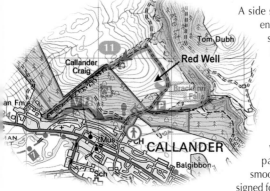

A side street at the Lowlands end of Callander is opposite the Roman Camp Hotel and is signed for Bracklinn Falls. It runs up to a car park on the left. **Start** by continuing on foot up the road, past a signpost for a golf course walk, to another car park. Here the wide, smooth path on the right is signed for Bracklinn Falls. After almost 1km it descends earth steps to **Bracklinn Falls** in their impressive gorge.

Return to the tarred road, and continue uphill, emerging from the woods. A signposted path on the left leads in 100 metres to the **Red Well**.

Return to the lane, continuing uphill then level across grassy moorland. As the road bends sharply right, a stony path is on the left under trees. It winds up to a fence corner, and follows the fence onto **Callander Craig**. A conical cairn marks the summit.

The mildly rugged path continues southwest along the top of the crags. Where it dips to a footbridge, a side

Better than Irn-Bru:
the chalybeate waters
of Red Well. Its orange
water is cheaper than
Irn-Bru, Scotland's soft
drink supposedly made
from girders

path down left has a red waymarker and would be a short cut back to the car park. The main path continues along the crag tops, then down in zigzags under fir trees, before bending left to approach the top edge of the town. Here the path turns slightly uphill, then works around and up through beechwoods to cross a footbridge (NN 629084).

Ignore a small path turning down right, but take the main path ahead (southeast then east). It widens and runs gently downhill into the car park.

12 Glen Ample

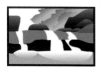

Length

Difficulty

Start	Ardchullarie More, Loch Lubnaig NN 584136
Finish	Edinample Bridge NN 602224
Distance	10km/6 miles
Ascent	220m/700ft
Approx time	3hr
Max altitude	Pass top 350m
Terrain	Mostly rough track, two sections of sometimes rough path
Map	LR 57 & 51; Expl 365; Harvey *Ben Ledi*
Local travel	Bus C60, see below
To Lochearnhead car park	
	Add 2.5km/1½ miles

Glen Ample is a natural and pleasant through route between Loch Earn and Callander, used long before the A84(T) was a gravel pebble lodged in some planner's brain. Although forest plantings deface both sides of the valley, the track runs through natural woodland alongside the river before emerging into the bleak upper glen.

The modern tarmac alternative carries four buses daily (service C60, Kingshouse Travel) between Loch Earn and Loch Lubnaig. The convenient walk plan is to park at Lochearnhead, and ask the bus driver to let you down at the spacious lay-by on the east side of the road at Ardchullarie More.

If using cars parked at both ends of the walk, note that there is very limited parking at Edinample Falls, so that it's often more convenient to use the big free car park at Lochearnhead. This means walking 1.5km of the South Loch Earn road. It has fine views across the loch, but is narrow with blind corners. That said, most of the afternoon traffic is walkers off Ben Vorlich, who may offer lifts.

If walking this southwards, you'll probably want a northbound bus up Loch Lubnaig. The best place to flag it down is a lay-by (west side of the road) 1km south of Adrchullarie More.

There's a lay-by (mentioned above) on the east side of A84 beside the track foot. **Start** up the **Ardchullarie** track but fork left of a garage with a large 'footpath' sign. A rough path runs uphill, slants left over a stream, and joins a forest road at the 250m contour.

Turn left along the track, which soon rises steeply to the forest top and a gate. It continues for 600 metres, then after the crossing of **Eas an Eoin** becomes a rough path, passing above a ruined shieling (summer pasture house).

Silvery phyllite rocks of the Edinample Falls at the north end of Glen Ample

Map continues opposite

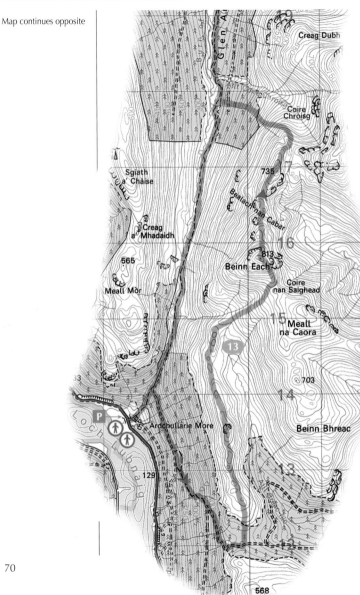

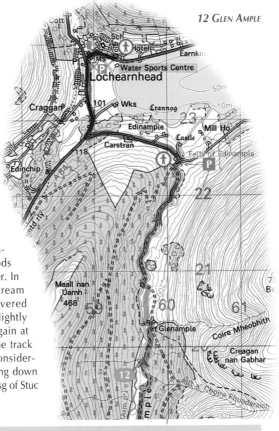

Keeping just up to right of the boggy valley floor, the path reaches its high point after 800 metres and starts to descend **Glen Ample**.

In another 1km it becomes again a rough track. After a gate with ladder stile, it enters plantations, passing through woods to right of the river. In 500 metres, a stream outwash has covered the track: head slightly uphill to find it again at the other side. The track then fords the considerable stream coming down out of Coire Chroisg of Stuc a' Chroin.

> **Note** If this crossing should be impossible, force a way up through the plantation for 250 metres to a forest road, which has a culvert. A faint track left leads straight back down to the lower track; but if streams are very full, stay on the ugly upper one to avoid another ford further on.

The track becomes green wheelmarks across an open field, then fords the stream from Coire Fuadarach before a final 500 metres of woodland to **Glenample farm**. At

Map continued from p70

the point where the track enters the farm compound, follow a waymarked path down left, to pass alongside the river to a stile onto the farm's entrance track. Follow the track downstream for 1.5km, to waterfalls in strangely silvery rocks. These are phyllite, a less-altered form of the standard grey schists. The waterfalls continue beside the track down to **Edinample Bridge**.

Turn left along the single-track road, to reach A84 just south of **Lochearnhead**.

13 Beinn Each from Loch Lubnaig

Length

Difficulty

Start/finish	Ardchullarie More, Loch Lubnaig NN 584136
Distance	15.5km/9½ miles
Ascent	850m/2800ft
Approx time	6hr
Max altitude	Beinn Each 811m
Terrain	Tracks, 1km of heather, grassy slopes and a ridgeline of grass and rock knolls
Map	LR 57; Expl 365; Harvey *Ben Ledi*

Beinn Each is an obscure hill. It's not visible from any road, and even from surrounding hills it's overshadowed by big Stuc a' Chroin immediately to the north. From Ben Ledi it stands unnoticed immediately in front of the bigger hill. And from anywhere else, it's masked by the tree-covered lump of Sgiath a' Chaise.

On just one day a year Beinn Each becomes a busy place. The Stuc a' Chroin hill race, out of Strathyre, effortlessly surmounts that dull Sgiath a' Chaise, crosses Beinn Each, and mounts the ridgeline to Stuc a' Chroin. Then it returns across deep Glen Ample, and surmounts for the second time (and this time with rather more effort) Sgiath a' Chaise. That race almost achieves the obscure bagging feat of a Graham (2000ft-er), a Corbett and a Munro all in one morning. But it bypasses the Sgiath by 200 metres, and turns back at a cairn just short of Stuc a' Chroin's top. So the only actual hill achieved is Beinn Each – and by a tough and rather unrewarding route, at that.

However, without the hill race I doubt I'd have discovered the 2km of ridgeline northwards from Beinn Each. It's a charming line of little crags, and rocky drops, and a peaty path that weaves among all the ups and downs.

This route gives a way up Beinn Each that's less assertively tough, although it does have its heathery bit. It then savours the excellent little ridgeline, before a long stroll home along Glen Ample. Tough types will enjoy the continuation to Stuc a' Chroin, by a considerable extra climb and some more rugged ridgeline. They would descend by Route 21 to Glenample farm before an even longer trek south along Glen Ample. Hillrunners will check into Strathyre on the Saturday before the May Day bank holiday. The race has 5000ft of ascent and a record time a few seconds under 2hrs.

There's a lay-by on the east side of A84 beside the Ardchullarie track foot. **Start** up this track but fork left of a garage with a large 'footpath' sign. A rough path runs uphill, slants left over a stream, and joins a forest road at the 250m contour.

Turn right along the level-running forest road. After 1km it passes below broadleaf trees and a swampy area. At it bends slightly downhill, turn left up a grassed-over old track. This slants uphill, through an old gate in deer fencing, and reaches a higher forest road at 375m.

Turn left, up this track, which immediately bends back right above the trees and rises to cross the wide ridgeline above. At its highest point turn off left (north) along the ridge.

At first this has been ploughed for failed tree plantings, and is deeply heathery. It soon gets rather less nasty as the ditches are left behind and a little height is gained. Over **Meall Gobhlach** the way becomes grassy with a trace of path. From the ridge's final knob, Meall Liath, bear right across a wide peaty col just below, and head up grassy slopes to the southeast ridge of Beinn Each. A small path, and old fencing, lead up to the summit of **Beinn Each**, with its very small inobtrusive cairn. ▶

'Each' is pronounced 'AY-ach', and means horse.

Descent What now appears as the continuing ridgeline, with path, actually leads down west into Glen Ample. Bear right, down what seems to be the right flank, on a smaller path that soon doubles back right onto the real north ridge. It zigzags down briefly northeast, then contours to the left, right across the ridge, to descend to left of crags to the foot of Beinn Each's steep summit cone.

The ridgeline with its small path continues with many small humps and bumps and craggy outcrops, to the unnamed (and when I visited last, uncairned) 735m rise at its northern end. Follow the small path down to the right, into **Bealach Glas**. ◄ Turn down left, keeping to right of the stream that flows northwest out of the col. Follow the stream down as the slope steepens: there are traces of path among the heather. A decaying gate in deer fence leads to the tree gap alongside the stream. Go down, still to right of the stream, to a forest road. Unfortunately, this ends just to your left. So head to the right for 20 metres, to a heathery tree gap descending to the valley floor.

> The path here continues up Stuc a' Chroin ahead.

The stony outwash of the stream has covered the lower track here, but head down left to find it in grassland above the river. Follow it up **Glen Ample**. In 1.2km, after a gate in deer fence, the track becomes a rough path. It leads through the pass and down towards more plantations, where it becomes a steep descending track. A large 'right-of-way' sign marks the right turn down the steep path which was used on the upward walk and which leads down to Ardcullarie More.

Note Where the Glen Ample track becomes path at **Eas an Eoin**, NN 590150, shepherds' wheelmarks run up the south side of the stream towards the col northeast of Meall Liath. For those with an urgent requirement to bag Beinn Each, this appears more comfortable than the standard line from the high point of the path 500 metres further north.

Looking back to Beinn Each from Point 728m

14 Hill of the Fairies, Strathyre

Length

Difficulty

Start/finish	Strathyre NN 561168
Distance	10km/6 miles
Ascent	550m/1800ft
Approx time	4hr
Max altitude	Beinn an t-Sidhein 572m
Terrain	Steep, rough paths
Map	LR 57; Expl 365; Harvey *Ben Ledi*

Beinn an t-Sidhein (Ben Shian) translates as 'Hill of the Fairies'. The crag and heather of its summit ridge has a lot of atmosphere and wide views. Even the plantation on its flank is more interesting than most, as the spruce has been allowed to grow huge.

Start at Strathyre's main car park, just south of the village centre. There's a path map right at the back of the car park, close to a reconstructed broch. You'll follow the Blue Trail to Ben Shian summit.

Go up behind the signboards, and turn right on a bike path (former railway) beside **River Balvag** to a street. Turn left, over the river, and at a junction head left (towards the school) for a few metres to the foot of a waymarked path. This leads up to a forest road at the 200m contour. Turn right for 100 metres to the continuing uphill path. At once, a fork left is a short-cut path, but the main path to the right is better built in zigzags up the steep wood.

At a higher track (320m altitude) turn left following the blue waymarker. The track contours, becoming a rough path. After 300 metres, at the junction with the short-cut path, blue waymarkers indicate the path slanting uphill ahead. After crossing a stream, it heads up through young self-seeded spruce onto the open hill.

The path bends right, climbing quite steeply to the base of the first rocky top. Turn right up the final few metres to its cairn (**An Sidhean** 546m). It's a fine viewpoint and, though not the true summit, many make it their destination.

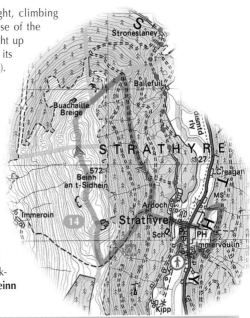

Return briefly down the rocky knoll, and turn right (north) on a small, rather wet, heather path. It heads across a stile, then climbs slightly onto the higher ridge. After 400 metres it passes to left of a small cairn in the heather marking the true summit of **Beinn an t-Sidhean** at 572m.

Beinn an t-Sidhean, the 'Hill of the Fairies', seen across Loch Lubnaig

Descent In the next, wet col, you start to see old iron fenceposts marking the route. The path climbs a little to cross another fence, then descends gently north, still with occasional old fenceposts, to the knoll **Buachaille Breige** (NN 546187) overlooking forest on the right.

Head down northeast to the corner of a more recently decayed fence. Follow this down ahead. Soon it joins a decayed fence with a wall: follow this down ahead, still northeast. Where it enters trees, part the branches to discover a rough path. This runs down alongside the decayed fencing to a junction of forest roads.

Both roads to the right are waymarked as Green Trail. The upper runs across some cleared slopes and would offer some views, but the lower is the quick way down, gently descending for 1.5km. At a junction, take the slightly rising track ahead, and in 600 metres turn down left on the ascent path, to the lane into **Strathyre**.

Note For a bonus mile through mixed woodland, head into Strathyre and cross the **A84**. Head up past a pub car park to a Red Trail waymarker. Slant up left to a war memorial, and turn left, briefly downhill. Pass to right of a tennis court to cross a footbridge. At a path fork, bear right; the path ascends beside a stream then crosses it by a footbridge. It then heads up under spruce to a forest road.

Turn right, with a red waymarker. The track has views across to Ben Shian. After 600 metres you pass below some modern cup-and-ring marked rocks, and then cross a stream. A wide path turns downhill beside the stream, to reach the **A84** directly opposite the car park.

PART THREE

BALQUHIDDER AND LOCHEARNHEAD

On Beinn a' Chroin (Route 16), looking at Ben Lomond (Route 40)

The tiny road that bumbles along the back of Balquhidder is tiresome for the driver, although passengers with strong stomachs will appreciate the lovely views of Loch Voil. Presumably it's this challenge to the stomach and the suspension that keeps the Inverlochlarig car park comparatively quiet. So the surrounding hills add to their considerable charm the bonus of small or absent paths and not too many other people.

Of the days spent researching this book, the long one over the Munros north of the glen was the most enjoyable of all. The combination of grassy paths, little craggy outcrops, and huge views was enhanced by the perfect February weather you see in the photographs.

This is classic Highland hillwalking. If Lomond and The Trossachs is your introduction to the game of Munro-bagging, then here is what you have to look forward to, another 280 times, over the rest of your life. And above Loch Earn, Route 21 over Ben Vorlich and Stuc a' Chroin makes another classic outing over two Munros. Enjoy the hills here, and that's your weekends sorted for the next 15 years...

15 Stob a' Choin

Length
■ ■ ■ □ □

Difficulty
■ ■ ■ ■ □

Start/finish	Car park east of Inverlochlarig NN 446184
Distance	13.5km/8½ miles
Ascent	850m/2800ft
Approx time	5½hr
Max altitude	Stob a' Choin 869m
Terrain	Track, steep grassy hillsides
Map	LR 56 & 57; Expl 364 & 365; Harvey *Loch Lomond*

North of the Trossachs and south of Rannoch Moor is the country of Breadalbane. It's a country of big green hills, many of which are featureless and, to all but the most ardent, somewhat unexciting. Stob a' Choin (Dog Peak) is typical of 'good' Breadalbane. Its top is rocky and complicated; meanwhile its sides, though steep and high, are comfortably grassy. Around 5km of valley ramble offers a warm-up, and a view of the impressive northern slopes. The hill's western slopes are a test for the legs, but for descent there's a knolly ridge that's pleasantly gentler, at least until you get down to the last slopes to the footbridge.

This hill should not be confused with Beinn a' Chroin, on the north side of the glen, nor with Beinn a' Choin, 8km to the southwest. Then again, it also isn't Stuc a' Chroin, 20km to the east.

Start along the track up the glen, passing the buildings of Inverlochlarig. After 2km a footbridge is on the left, below Stob a' Choin's steep northern slopes. This footbridge will be the return route. However, you will be crossing this same river, without benefit of bridge, another 2km upstream. If it's in spate cross the footbridge, and use the descent route for the upwards walk also.

Otherwise, continue up the track. After 1.5km the main track fords the **Ishag Burn** that comes down off Cruach Ardrain: a side-track takes a rough bridge 200 metres downstream. In another 1.5km, and through two

Approaching Stob a' Choin along the Inverlochlarig track. The footbridge used on the descent is just ahead

gates, the track fords another stream, **Allt a' Chroin**. Now take a gate on the left, and cross the grassy valley floor to River Larig. In normal conditions this can be crossed on boulders.

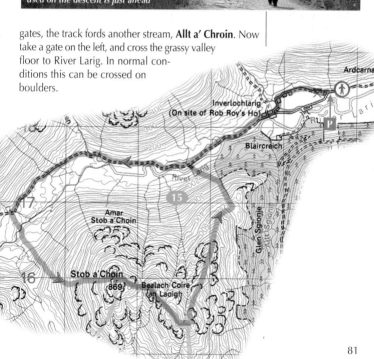

Head up the steep face of Stob a' Choin, slanting round right to reach the slightly less steep western slope. Even so, the grass is almost alarming: one damp patch and you might slide right down to the bottom. This hillside mostly consists of damp patches…

At around 700m the slope is interrupted by small outcrops; weaving among these gives grass of a less alarming angle. As the slope eases off, it's worth heading up left for the small northern summit, which has views right down into the valley. The main summit of **Stob a' Choin** is just 2m higher and 100 metres southeast. The cairn stands on a tiny outcrop that overhangs on its west side.

Descent Occasional iron fenceposts mark a way east down the next steep descent. Keep to right of the main upper crag and weave among the smaller ones into the col **Bealach Coire an Laoigh**. Fenceposts and a rough little path lead up the next steep rise. (Rock exposed in the scrambly path is silvery phyllite.) The fencing leads to the right, over grassy humps, to **Meall Reamhar**. ◄

Meall Reamhar is 'Fat Hump'. An outlier of Creag Mac Ranaich, on Route 20, has the same name.

Head east for 100 metres onto a lower hummock. Finding the descent ridge might now be awkward in this knolly ground, but there are some more old iron posts to guide you. Descend north, soon on a well-defined ridge with an intermittent path. Follow it down, with one steep step requiring care, to the 450m contour. Here follow the old fence down to the right to the head of a grassy valley, where it meets a tall deer fence marking the top edge of plantations. Head down the green valley alongside the fence. At its foot, go over a low gate ahead onto open slopes. Slant down left, northwest, on grass and rushes, to the footbridge over River Larig.

Turn right and follow the track for 2km, past **Inverlochlarig** to the car park.

Start/finish	Road end near Inverlochlarig farm NN 446184
Distance	19km/12 miles
Ascent	1550m/5200ft
Approx time	9hr
Max altitude	Cruach Ardrain 1046m
Terrain	Small paths, pathless grassy hillsides (some quite steep), good track to finish
Map	LR 56 & 57; Expl 364 & 365; Harvey *Crianlarich*

Length

Difficulty

The rambling range to west of Ben More is, when approached from the south, the Braes of Balquhidder; or when approached as they mostly are from the north, the Crianlarich Munros. By either name, from Cruach Ardrain to Beinn Chabhair, they typify what the southern Highlands are all about. Here are no huge and intimidating crags, nor the endless grass slopes of Perthshire to the east, but the perfect mix of both. Small wiggly outcrops of schist interrupt steep-sided ridges, with a small path winding along on the grass between the rocks.

Route 23 in the Crianlarich section is typical of this less-difficult and friendlier form of Munro-bagging. That route takes in Beinn a' Chroin along with An Caisteal, and the standard route to Cruach Ardrain is from the same direction. A car park on A82 1km south of Crianlarich is the 'standard' startpoint for Cruach Ardrain. However, this approach from the south gives more of a wilderness experience, with a smaller car park, and pathless wandering in the gap between the main Munros. Taken this way, the hills are quieter and more challenging. But from either side, it's the same satisfying mixture of grass and rock, for a day of rugged ridges and wide views.

Start along the road's continuation track past **Inverlochlarig farm**. Pass to right of the buildings to a bridge over the large Inverlochlarig Burn. Immediately across it turn right over a stile signed for Beinn Tulaichean and Cruach Ardrain. Head up, initially through mud, to

The south slope of Beinn Tulaichean, with a view to Ben Lomond

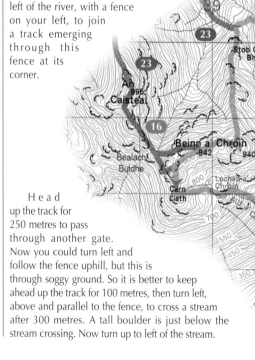

left of the river, with a fence on your left, to join a track emerging through this fence at its corner.

Head up the track for 250 metres to pass through another gate. Now you could turn left and follow the fence uphill, but this is through soggy ground. So it is better to keep ahead up the track for 100 metres, then turn left, above and parallel to the fence, to cross a stream after 300 metres. A tall boulder is just below the stream crossing. Now turn up to left of the stream.

Slog uphill all the way up the stream. Above its top, a crossing fence at about 500m altitude has a gate at the convenient point. Keep uphill northwest until the angle eases, and a pleasant ridgeline forms for the last kilometre to the top of **Beinn Tulaichean**.

A clear baggers' path heads down the easy angled ridge roughly northwest. It continues up the ridge opposite. At a knoll with a small outcrop at its top (1000m, NN 407211) the path turns right, along the summit ridge to the cairn of **Cruach Ardrain**.

Return to the 1000m knoll. Here another baggers' path descends right (towards Grey Height and A82), while straight down ahead leads onto steep broken ground. So return leftwards down the ridge towards Beinn Tulaichean. Halfway down to the col, at about the 900m contour, turn back to the right and slant down westwards, over steep grass, to reach a gently angled platform.

The wide ridgeline towards Beinn a' Chroin is typical of the 'rough' schist ground. There are many tiny crags, rock blocks, dips and hollows, all covered in comfortable grass and peaty holes. Head down southwest to a lower platform, where you pass to left of the bare rock hummock **Stob Glas**. The continuing ridgeline again leads to crags, so once past Stob Glas find a stream running down to the right (**An Teanga**, 'the Tongue'). Head down the lumpy spur to left of the stream, northwest, until the slope eases at 600m. Now you can slant down left, southwest, to cross the valley between the two mountains.

Head up the slope opposite to gain the crest of Beinn a' Chroin's north spur. Here there is a small path, running up to just before the first, 940m, **east top**. In mist it's quite important, and also quite difficult, to distinguish Beinn a' Chroin's various tops – this eastern one was until recently believed to be the actual summit.

Just below the east top the path turns right to run along the lumpy crest, west then northwest. It drops into a dip, where it passes to right of the highest line and has a 2m scramble step. The path continues roughly west for 500 metres to the small cairn on the 942m top (NN 387185). This is bare rock with a short drop just behind its cairn, and is now surveyed as **Beinn a' Chroin**'s true summit.

Continue west to the **west top**, at 938m, marked by a cairn and a distinctive blocky rock (NN 385185, pictured opposite). A rock lump alongside it is actually higher than the cairn. ◀

A note at the route's end gives a diversion here to An Caisteal.

From this summit, the main path continues along the crest towards yet a fourth top, also 938m (NN384184). This, the **southwest top** of Beinn a' Chroin, is the last of them, with steeply dropping ground beyond.

Descent From it head south, down a gentle ridge, with occasional steepenings where you must ramble sideways to avoid outcrops. At the col before Carn Liath

The boulder marking Beinn a' Chroin's west summit (938m)

either descend directly left, east, to the peaty **Lochan a' Chroin**, or keep ahead over Carn Liath before descending to the lochan. This is an engaging secret spot even though the lochan itself is soggy-edged.

Descend to right of the outflow stream. Below the lochan, the headwall of **Coire a' Chroin** is craggy, so some care is needed here in descent. The spur to right of the stream leads to a crag top. Descend to left of this crag, on steep grass, while further to your left the stream descends rocky steps. Where the slope levels off, cross the stream and descend now to its left, as the spur to its right descends to another crag, a blackened overhang. At this level the stream itself has some fine waterfalls, though they are only seen when looking back uphill. Keep on all the way down open slopes to left of the main stream, past more waterfalls. Eventually at a fence corner head down between the fence (left) and the stream (right), to reach the track below.

Turn left along the track, soon passing through the gate at the foot of the fence just followed downhill. After a second gate, the main track fords the stream of **Ishag Glen** (between Beinn a' Chroin and Beinn Tulaichean). A side-track leads to the bridge just downstream. Continue along the track, which eventually leads through a muddy farmyard and past houses to the bridge at **Inverlochlarig**.

Note It is possible to include An Caisteal in this already energetic day, though care is needed as crags lie across the descent line to the Bealach Buidhe pass. The best way is from Beinn a' Chroin's **west top**, identified by the boulder pictured on the previous page. Slant down to the right, west, gently downhill around the hill flank. Keep below the main outcrops. Faint paths lead to a pathed grassy gully down to the right, to emerge on steep slopes below the rock band. Keep slanting down west to gain the broad col **Bealach Buidhe**.

The path opposite climbs up talus slope initially. Then the pleasant ridge with ridgetop hollows, rock blocks, and scrambly outcrops alongside the path leads to the summit of **An Caisteal**.

Return to **Bealach Buidhe**. This time avoid the rock band ahead by a grassy ramp up its right-hand end. The path climbs quite steeply among rocks and up the grassy ramp slanting to the right. It then contours across the western steep slope of the mountain with crags above. After about 200 metres it turns sharply left, uphill, and zigzags up to a 2m scramble on good holds but somewhat exposed. Further erosion of the overlying grass may soon extend the scrambling here. Above this it emerges on a grass platform (cairn). Cross this to another short rise eastwards, to pass through a notch onto the summit plateau. Just to your right is a small, uncairned knoll at 938m, the **southwest top** of Beinn a' Chroin.

---

17 Stob Binnein and Ben More from the south

Length

■ ■ ■ ■ □

Difficulty

■ ■ ■ □ □

Start/finish	Road end near Inverlochlarig farm NN 446184
Distance	16km/10 miles
Ascent	1600m/5400ft
Approx time	8hr
Max altitude	Ben More 1174m
Terrain	Grassy slopes and hill paths
Map	LR 57 & 51; Expl 365; Harvey *Crianlarich*

Ben More, the Big Hill, is indeed the biggest in this book. That doesn't necessarily make it the best. Ben More is steep on all sides, all the way up. Once up, there's nowhere to go but back down – steeply back down. The normal approach is from the north, at Benmore Farm. The 'steeply down' is then to the aptly named Bealach-eadar-dha Bheinn, the 'Pass Between Two Hills', after which there's a second steep ascent to the twin peak, Stob Binnein. After returning to the bealach, a rough path is forming around the flank of Ben More and down into Benmore Glen.

If you require to place yourself on every Munro summit in the minimum possible time, then that is the way to do these two. Just supposing the relentless up and down and up doesn't damage your knees, then you'll gain useful exercise and some fitness, plus two more ticks for your list.

If, on the other hand, you would actually like to enjoy these two shapely summits, then Stob Binnein on its south side has a slim and elegant ridgeline. After the airy promenade of Na Staidhrichean, your knees are rested enough to cope with the steep down-and-up-again to Ben More. A craggy little side corrie on Stob Binnein's northeastern side, then the descent ridge is a gentle stroll that no knee could object to – until you get down to Meall Monachyle and the 600m contour, anyway.

And what of that tick-list? Well, you get not only the two Munro summits, but the two subsidiary tops as well.

Start by crossing the road to a stile marked 'Stob Binnein'. A path, a bit eroded in places, heads up to left of a stream, becoming quite steep. At 550m a fence crosses, with a stile. The path bends left then contours back right, the worst steepness now over. There is a last view down to the car park, and also along Loch Voil. Cross a stream (last water) then head up onto a shoulder called **Stob Invercarnaig**, with a steeper climb to the first false top, at 890m.

Now a gentle and very pleasant ridge, becoming quite narrow, leads to **Stob Coire an Lochain** (whose lochan, to the southeast, has filled itself in). ▶ It continues northwest, with a steepish climb up the final cone to the summit of **Stob Binnein**.

A bigger path leads down north, becoming rather steep – in early spring this spur can hold refrozen snow,

The nice ridge is Na Staidhrichean, possibly meaning 'the Staircase'.

*On Na Staidhrichean,
the southern ridge of
Stob Binnein*

unsuspected when the mountain is seen from the south. Cross the wide col **Bealach-eadar-dha Bheinn**. The ascent path opposite is initially again rather steep, a bit left of the direct line out of the col. At 1000m the slope becomes less steep. The final moment to the summit is defended (on the path line) by a 2.5m scramble up an inwards corner in a rock wall. It has good holds and is not exposed but is steep – a walk round to the right will avoid the step. **Ben More** summit has a trig pillar and, just beyond, a cairn overlooking Crianlarich.

Descent Return to **Bealach-eadar-dha Bheinn**. The descent into the corrie to the east is rather steep and holds snow; the easiest line slants down left, northeast, out of the col. Cross the corrie floor southeast below the craggy slope of Creagan Dubha – it's drier if you keep close under the crags. Then rise a little to cross the open **Coire Each**, and gain the col east of Stob Coire an Lochan. Aim for the low point of this ridge; short-cutting to Meall na Dige leads to crags. At the wide crest, turn left on a small path, threading among low outcrops to the summit of **Meall na Dige**.

From Meall na Dige head southeast down a gentle ridge with a small path. At its end, it tips up to **Meall**

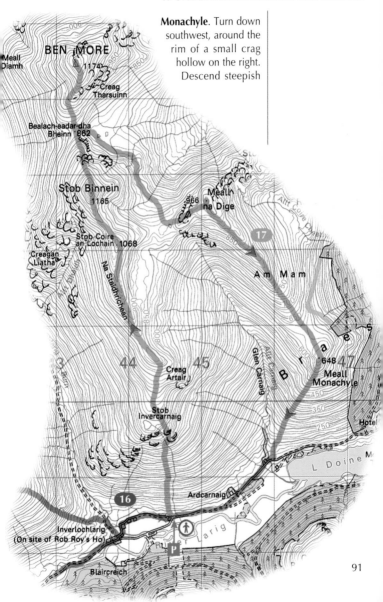

Monachyle. Turn down southwest, around the rim of a small crag hollow on the right. Descend steepish grass slopes, which become tussocky at the very foot. A wall crosses at the 250m contour. Head for the right-hand (western) end of this where it has a gate. A green track runs down beside (to left of) a small river Allt Carnaig to the valley road.

Turn right over a bridge and follow the road to the car park.

18 Glen Ogle Rail Trail

Length

Difficulty

Start/finish	Lochearnhead NN 593238
Distance	16km/10 miles
Ascent	170m/600ft
Approx time	4½hr
Max altitude	Glen Ogle head 280m
Terrain	Smooth track and rough path
Map	LR 51; Expl 365; Harvey *Ben Ledi*
Part walk:	Edenchip end – 8km/5miles, 60m/200ft Ascent, 2¼hr
Part walk:	Glen Ogle only – 10km/6 miles, 150m/500ft Ascent, 3hr

The Ogle Trail proper is a walk of 10km, up Glen Ogle by the old railway that's now a cycle path, and down by the old military road. The railway runs along an impressively steep hillside decorated with two rockfalls and a high viaduct. The military road winds by streamsides and through little woods. This would be completely charming, except for the traffic noise from the A85 that, regrettably, uses the same convenient pass as the railway and the old soldiers did.

The extension around Edenchip that starts the walk uses more cycle paths and old railways, through woods and over another impressive viaduct. It is quieter, both in road noise and in people on and off bicycles. Each half of the walk can be enjoyed on its own.

Start at the large car park in Lochearnhead, and follow the pavement across the river (footbridge alongside) to the **A84**. Turn left along pavement past the village shop. After 800 metres, at the end of the village, turn right up a lane towards the church.

Follow the lane to its top. Before a bridge over an old railway, turn off left on a smooth path to join the Route 7 cycle path. Keep ahead on this, along the old railbed. The cycle path passes through ash woods, then crosses a high viaduct, before reaching the **A84**. The path runs alongside this, crossing a side road to Edenchip. Then it bends to the right, into woodland. After 1km it joins a section of old road alongside the A84. It follows this briefly, before turning off right across soggy moorland.

Straight away it crosses a cattle grid and small bridge. In another 150 metres, as the cycle path bends left, turn off right through a field gate. An old green path runs northeast, becoming a grassy track as it passes to right of a reedy lochan. The track joins a wider one at some derelict sheds and cattle feeders.

Bear left, on what is the higher of Lochearnhead's two abandoned railway lines. The smooth track crosses

Lochearnhead and Glen Ogle. The old railway can be seen crossing the flank of Creag Mac Ranaich, left

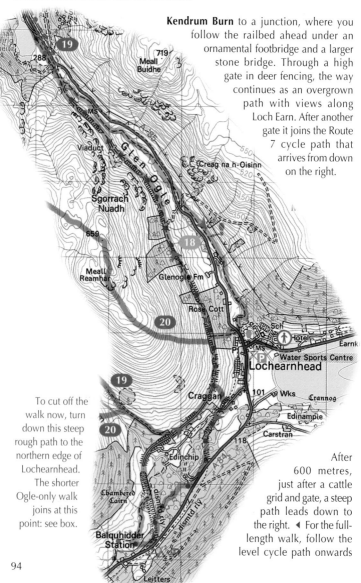

Kendrum Burn to a junction, where you follow the railbed ahead under an ornamental footbridge and a larger stone bridge. Through a high gate in deer fencing, the way continues as an overgrown path with views along Loch Earn. After another gate it joins the Route 7 cycle path that arrives from down on the right.

To cut off the walk now, turn down this steep rough path to the northern edge of Lochearnhead. The shorter Ogle-only walk joins at this point: see box.

After 600 metres, just after a cattle grid and gate, a steep path leads down to the right. ◄ For the full-length walk, follow the level cycle path onwards

94

along the steep side of **Glen Ogle**. It passes through the rockfall that put a sudden stop to the railway service in 1960, then crosses a viaduct. In another 1.5km it reaches the head of the glen.

Just after the path becomes tarmac, take a stile on the right signed as the old military road. The small, rough path crosses a wooden footbridge and at once bears left to join the damp, grassy track of the old road. The next stream bridge is an ancient stone arch.

The path is narrow and in places rather wet, but clear, as it runs down the valley. It passes along below the viaduct, and then reaches a stream outwash. Contour across this, to find the path again on the further side, descending through rushes. Soon it passes under alder trees to join the stream briefly. Then it rises to the left, runs beside the **A85**, and then crosses it at a signboard.

A waymark indicates the path continuing opposite. It runs above the road to a stile. Cross a grassy field to another stile, and turn uphill to ford a stream. The path runs along the valley side to pass above a shed of **Glenogle farm**. After a pleasant wood it runs down to join the river. It soon crosses a long footbridge, and follows the river's right bank downstream through one field, until a tall kissing gate leads out onto the A85 at the northern edge of **Lochearnhead**.

Turn left between the piers of an abandoned railway bridge into the village.

SHORTENED WALK: GLEN OGLE ONLY

Start at the large car park in Lochearnhead, and follow the pavement across the river (footbridge alongside) to the A84. Turn right for 250 metres, to pass between the stone piers of a former railway viaduct. Turn left on a track signposted 'Glen Ogle Trail', but at once fork off right on a waymarked path. After a stile and a tall gate, this zigzags up steeply through birch scrub to join the old railway line above.

Turn right on the Route 7 cycle path along the steep side of Glen Ogle, following the second part of the full walk.

19 Kendrum and Ogle Circle

Length
■ ■ ■ ■ □

Difficulty
■ □ □ □ □

Start/finish	Lochearnhead NN 593238
Distance	22km/14 miles
Ascent	550m/1800ft
Approx time	6½hr
Max altitude	Kendrum/Dubh pass 600m
Terrain	Smooth tracks
Map	LR 51; Expl 365; Harvey *Ben Ledi*

In terms of the going underfoot, this could be the easiest route in this book. But the Landrover track takes you into high remote moorland, to pass between two cragged mountains. If you don't see red deer up here then you've been unlucky. On the descent there's a gorge so slot-like and gloomy you can hardly see into it at all. The forest road has been improved by clear-felling, offering for the next few years views to the corner of Loch Tay.

For the final part of the walk, you could choose the Glen Ogle railway, which is smooth and scenic (and at least some of the cyclists flying past you from behind will be polite enough to use their bells). Or there's the other leg of the Ogle Trail, the old military road, which is rough enough to bump the route up from 'easiest in the book' to getting two (out of five) difficulty blobs in the headings above.

Start at the large car park in Lochearnhead, and follow the pavement across the river (footbridge alongside) to the **A84**. Turn left along the pavement past the village shop. After 800 metres, at the end of the village, turn right up a lane towards the church. ◀

The car park here is marked for church use only.

Around 100 metres further up the lane, take a gap on the right and go up a faint path through grass. Across a former railway line, the now clearer path slants up to the left. It goes up through birch scrub to a bend on the Route 7 cycle path. Head up this, to reach the upper of Lochearnhead's two abandoned railway lines.

Turn sharp left, through a gate in a high deer fence, on a path along the overgrown railbed. After a couple more gates, this becomes a well-used track. Where the trackbed heads under a stone bridge ahead (numbered 98), turn up left on a grassy track, and cross the bridge to join an uphill track.

With the cragged face of Creag Mac Ranaich ahead, the track runs up **Glen Kendrum**. After 3km it fords a branch of the burn, and slants up into the moorland pass between Creag Mac Ranaich and Meall an t-Seallaidh. ▶

The horseshoe route of these two is Route 20.

Through the wide moorland col, the track descends **Gleann Dubh**, with small waterfalls in the stream alongside on the left. After 3km the track bends left towards a ford, but here fork off right on a faint old track that stays to right of the stream. After a waterfall, the stream is in a deep slot, not easy to see into until its foot just above the forest plantations. At a ramshackle gate the track enters the plantations.

After 150 metres, fork up right on a track running level. This becomes surfaced and used by vehicles, and passes through a clear-felled area to meet a smooth,

In Glen Kendrum, with Creag Mac Ranaich ahead

97

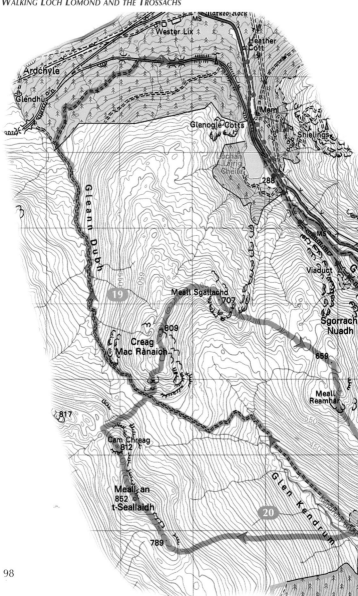

level-running track that is again the abandoned railway. Turn right on this for 2km, where it is alongside the A85 at its car park at the very top of Glen Ogle.

Keep ahead, alongside **Lochan Lairig Cheile**, with Route 7 cycleway now joining the railbed. The path is tarmacked through a cutting. At the end of this you have a choice.

- A ladder stile on the left lets you continue down the rough path of the **old military road**, the second half of **Route 18**.

- **For a quicker finish**, keep ahead down the railbed. After 1.5km it crosses a viaduct. In another 2.5km, just before a gate and cattle grid, a steep path with a waymark post turns down left. It zigzags down through scrub, to reach A85 at the northern edge of **Lochearnhead**.

Length
■ ■ ■ ■ □

Difficulty
■ ■ ■ ■ ■

20 Twa Corbetts

Start/finish	Lochearnhead NN 593238
Distance	17km/11 miles
Ascent	1150m/3800ft
Approx time	7½hr
Max altitude	Meall an t-Seallaidh 852m
Terrain	Track, grassy hillsides, 1km of rough moorland
Map	LR 51; Expl 365; Harvey *Ben Ledi*

Meall an t-Seallaidh and Kendrum track
17km/10½ miles, 800m/2600ft
Ascent, 6¼hr

Kendrum track and Creag Mac Ranaich
15km/9 miles, 850m/2800ft
Ascent, 6hr

Meall an t-Seallaidh is the 'Hump of the Viewpoint' and Creag Mac Ranaich is the 'Craggy Hill of the Son of Ranaich'. But it's unusual to find two hills of Corbett-height (above 2500ft/762m) lying together in a natural horseshoe, so the summary name I've given this walk commemorates that. (It also alludes to the 'Twa Corbies', two crows in an old Scots ballad who find a dead knight on some boggy moor.)

Meall an t-Seallaidh offers comfortable grassy walking, with just enough rock around to seem serious. Like any reasonably isolated hill of its height (including its neighbour Mac Ranaich) it has fine hill views of Breadalbane and Perthshire. The name may mark the way it offers sightlines down the strategically important valleys: along Loch Earn and southwards to Strathyre.

Creag Mac Ranaich has a steep, craggy face whose ascent turns out easier than expected. Its more effective defence, indeed, is the kilometre of flat heathery moorland to be crossed on its southeastern spur. Once on Meall Reamhar (the Fat Hump) the reward is more grassy going, with an outlook straight down onto Lochearnhead.

The track of Route 19 runs between the two hills, and can be used for a one-hill expedition to either. Meall an t-Seallaidh becomes a reasonably easy ascent; Mac Ranaich, with its steep climb, heather crossing, and quite steep descent, is more demanding.

Start at the large car park in Lochearnhead, and follow the pavement across the river (footbridge alongside) to the A84. Turn left along the pavement past the village shop. After 800 metres, at the end of the village, turn right up a lane towards the church. ▶

The car park here is marked for church use only.

Around 100 metres further up the lane, take a gap on the right and go up a faint path through grass. Across a former railway line, the now clearer path slants up to the left. It goes up through birch scrub to a bend on the Route 7 cycle path. Head up this to reach the upper of Lochearnhead's abandoned railway lines.

Turn sharp left, through a gate in high deer fence, on a path along overgrown railbed. After a couple more gates, this becomes a well-used track. Where the track-bed heads under a stone bridge ahead (numbered 98), turn up left on a grassy track, and cross the bridge to join an uphill track. ▶

For Mac Ranaich on its own, continue up this track to its top.

The track runs alongside a plantation for the first 700 metres. Around 200 metres later, a wet green track down left gives a way through the bracken to an informal ford of **Kendrum Burn**. Go up grassy slopes westwards, which is slanting slightly to the right, crossing a couple of the streams on the way up. At the wide flat plateau, turn right and follow occasional posts of an old iron fence up the rising spur. **Point 789** has a cairn with quartz lumps in it. A short descent leads to the continuing rise to the trig point on **Meall an t-Seallaidh** summit. ▶

The 'Hill of the Viewpoint' is pronounced Melon Telly (wittily disparaging the TV set that's the viewpoint of too many of us today).

The fencing leads on gently downhill to a col with a small pool. A slight rise northwards leads to **Cam Chreag**. From it the old posts lead northwest to a steep but grassy and short descent to a col (741m). (Just down left of this col there's a lochan about 100 metres long with horsetail growing out of it.) From the col turn right, northeast, down a grassy hollow. From its foot you can slant out right, to

On Creag Mac Ranaich, Meall an t-Seallaidh behind

minimise the moorland crossing, to the track that passes through the wide col between the two mountains. ◀

For a quick exit, simply turn right, down the track, to rejoin the outward route. Those aiming for Mac Ranaich on its own arrive up the track now.

While descending from Meall an t-Seallaidh, you will have surveyed your route up Creag Mac Ranaich. Turn right on the track as it runs roughly level through the wide pass, then go downhill 150 metres towards Glen Kendrum. A stream trickles under the track: 20 metres up it is a pointed boulder (NN 5431 2472). Go up past this boulder and between two small crags into a steep grassy hollow in the hill face. Bear slightly left and slant up north, passing a large flat-topped boulder like a small shed. Continue slightly left and north, to pass up to left of a rock tower. Continue on the same line, to arrive at the summit plateau at a small col with a bog pool (NN 5435 2511).

Head up northeast to the **south summit** (808m), whose cairn has a rounded quartz boss alongside it. A small path leads north, across a col with a small lochan, and up a rocky step to the **Creag Mac Ranaich**'s main summit. (Its cairn has a quartz streak running past it, but no rounded boss.)

Descent Grassy ridge, with crag drops on the right, leads north over one hump, then northeast over another, and finally east to **Meall Sgallachd** with its small cairn.

Meall Sgallachd means 'Bald-headed Hump'.

◀ Go down a few steps to a peaty col. The direct ridge-line ahead (southeast) leads to some crags, so turn left and descend grassy slopes northeast. As the angle eases, head back to the right to reach the peaty col before the moorland crossing.

Cross moorland humps southeast, until you can gain the grassy slopes of Point 659m (654m on Harvey map). Pleasant walking leads to the cairn on **Meall Reamhar** and down southeast, with a steep descent to the shoulder at 580m. A line of old fencing leads down towards Lochearnhead, on slopes that get more heathery until the fencing dives into deep patches of bracken.

Head down left of the first bracken patch, rejoining the fence below. When it again dives into bracken, slant down to the right for open grassland – you'll have to pass through about 50 metres of bracken to get there. Slant back left towards the fence. Birch trees mark the old railway line across the slope below: aim to reach it at the same point as the descending fence.

Turn briefly left along the railway line's cycle path, at once crossing a cattle grid. Now a waymarked path leads steeply down to the right. It zigzags through birch scrub to the northern edge of **Lochearnhead** village.

21 Ben Vorlich and Stuc a' Chroin

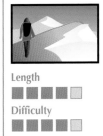

Start/finish	Ardvorlich House, East Lodge NN 633232 (or Edinample Bridge NN 602224)
Distance	18km/11 miles
Ascent	1150m/3800ft
Approx time	7½hr
Max altitude	Ben Vorlich 984m
Terrain	Hill paths, with a steep rather rocky climb (avoidable) to Stuc a' Chroin
Map	LR 51 & 57; Expl 365; Harvey *Ben Ledi*

Length
■ ■ ■ ■ ☐

Difficulty
■ ■ ■ ■ ☐

These two Munros above Loch Earn make a fine mountain day. Stuc a' Chroin means 'Peak of Danger', and the name is appropriate: the direct ascent from the col is steep and broken ground, where the path is somewhat ▶

◀ exposed, and careful route choice is needed to avoid short sections of bare rock. Alternatively, the bare rock can be sought out for one of the rare scrambling opportunities in this part of Scotland (Grade 1, depending on choice of route). Alternatively, the descent line can be used to bypass the difficulties altogether.

◀H◀

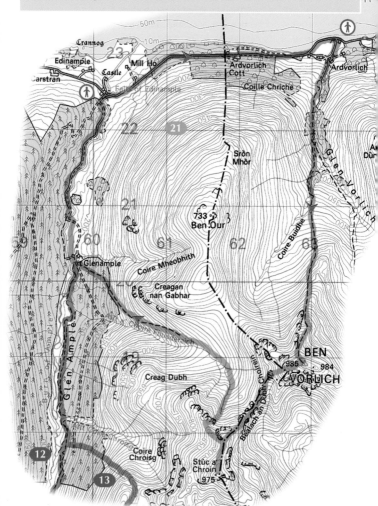

Start at **East Lodge** if you're concerned about nightfall, as the 3.5km of road alongside Loch Earn will thus be at the end of the walk (but if you start at Edinample, you may well be offered a lift along the road by other hillwalkers).

From the bridge where the Loch Earn side road crosses Ardvorlich Burn, a track runs up to the right. It keeps left of the burn for 400 metres, then crosses towards **Ardvorlich House**. But at once turn left on the stony track now to right of the burn. The track runs uphill, south, gradually rising away from the burn and becoming a rebuilt path on the open hill. It is clear all the way to the final steepening and **Ben Vorlich**'s summit trig point. ▸

The southeast summit 200 metres away is 1m lower according to OS mapping.

From the trig pillar, descend the southwest ridge, on a small path, weaving among small outcrops, to the levelling of the **Bealach an Dubh Choirein**. ▸ Head along the col towards the steep rocky face of Stuc a' Chroin.

At the foot of the steep section, the path bears left, then back right above a boulderfield along the base of the rocks. It splits into many branches, with short scrambling sections on some, up to the grassy plateau and the cairned 961m north summit. A path leads south across the slight dip to the main 975m summit of **Stuc a' Chroin**.

Here you could avoid the scrambling ahead by contouring out to the right, on a small path, to a rough zigzag path ascending southwest onto the northern spur of Stuc a' Chroin.

Descent Return north, to take a faint path skirting just below and left of the 961m **north summit**. Briefly descend the northwest ridge to its levelling at 850m, then head right, northeast, down a hollow by an eroding zig-zag path. At the foot of the steep slope, the path reaches a small stream.

Note This path contours north around the corrie, just below the Bealach an Dubh Choirein, then north around the flank of Ben Vorlich, onto its northwest ridge. From there it could be used for a descent over Ben Our to Ardvorlich.

Slant down to the left, descending into and working around the head of **Coire Fuadarach**; this is on shaggy grass, comfortable in descent. Eventually meet a quad bike path and turn down left. Soon it becomes an alternately grassy and stony track down the northern side of the corrie.

Follow the track down to a gate into a plantation (NN 603198, ladder stile on the left). The track leads on down through trees, until it reaches a gate in deer fence just above **Glenample farm**. Don't go through, but follow waymarks down to the left, outside the deer fencing, to cross a lower track, and reach a third track at a small stream. Turn right, towards Glenample farm, for 20 metres, then left on a path around the deer fence. Fence and path bend right, and the path runs alongside the Burn of Ample, to a stile onto the access track below the farm.

Turn left, across the river, and follow the track downstream to waterfalls in silvery phyllite rocks, and **Edinample Bridge**.

The scrambly path on the ascent of Stuc a' Chroin

THE NORTH

PART FOUR
CRIANLARICH TO INVERARNAN

On An Caisteal (Route 23), looking along the Crianlarich Hills to Ben More

This northern arc of the National Park is neither Lomond nor Trossach. It's the ancient earldom of Breadalbane, whose name means 'the high ground of Scotland'. Here are the steep, featureless hills of the Southern Highlands. They may be, in places, a little bit boring; but they are big. The best ones have rocky knobs on: An Caisteal and Beinn Chabhair. The others offer high-altitude grassland where you can stride out under the skylarks.

By the end of this section we're looking down Loch Lomond (Troisgeach on Meall an Fhudair has the classic view). But the book must next wander northwards to the northern borders of the National Park, and Ben Lui. If the view down Loch Lomond is just irresistible, the Arrochar Alps and the loch's west side are Parts Seven and Eight, with Ben Lomond in Part Six.

22 Meall Glas and Sgiath Chuil

Length

Difficulty

Start/finish	Auchlyne NN 510295
Distance	25km/15½ miles
Ascent	1600m/5300ft
Approx time	10hr
Max altitude	Meall Glas 957m
Terrain	Track, grassy slopes and ridges
Map	LR 51; Expl 365

Although swept into the National Park, these hills are typical of the terrain north of the A85 making up Section 2 of Munro's Tables. They are grassy and rounded, with what rock there is being splintered schist. At the same time they are steep, and not particularly small. These hills are quite fertile, with varied wild flowers growing on the soggy slopes. They are particularly appreciated by sheep. Walkers, on the other hand, may find them a little less exciting.

The pleasure here is in unconstrained high-level striding. The ridge rambling eastwards for 5km from Sgiath Chuil is bumpy grassland with the bog cotton nodding hypnotically under the cool breeze. And at half-height, the long track accompanying a buried aqueduct gives more fast untroubled travel, with views across the valley to the slightly more shapely mountains of the Crianlarich range. Otherwise, it's two Breadalbane Munros, and glad to get them done.

Villagers ask you not to park on their mown verges within Auchlyne itself. There's verge parking immediately east of the settlement. For large cars, parking on A85 at the Auchlyne turn-off adds 1.5km to each end of the walk.

Auchlyne has a bridge at either end. **Start** at the bridge over Auchlyne West Burn at the western edge of the village. A track heads uphill to right of the burn. It zigzags up to the 400m level. ◄ Continue left on the main track, soon descending to pass an intake on Auchlyne West Burn, then heading up alongside it. The track contours on eastwards below Sgiath Chuil, and ends at an intake dam on **Allt Riobain**.

Here note the side-track on the right, which can cause confusion when descending at the end of the day.

Cross the stream, and head up damp grassland to its left. Ahead, northwest, is a vestigial corrie under the summit of Meall Glas. The back of the corrie is slightly craggy so head up the spur to left of it, directly to **Meall Glas** summit. ▶

Descent A path heads down east along the broad ridge, skirting to left of a sub-summit (908m, or 911m on Harveys) then climbing slightly to the trig point on **Beinn Cheathaich**. Direct descent east from here is very steep, so head down a gentle spur northwards for about 10 mins (to 850m), then slant down to the right towards the broad, peaty col. A small stream provides a narrow grass strip across the rough ground of the col.

Head straight up the slope opposite until it steepens at 750m. A craggy patch is directly above. Head up to

Gaelic is an unfanciful language at times: Meall Glas is 'Grey Hump'.

Heading east from Meall Glas

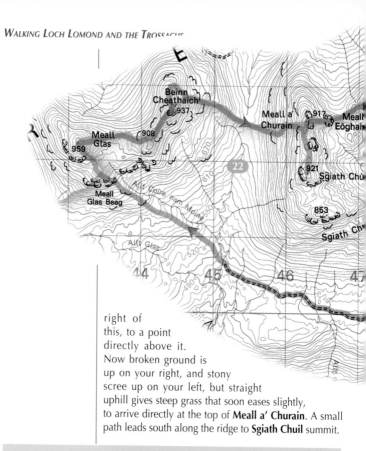

right of
this, to a point
directly above it.
Now broken ground is
up on your right, and stony
scree up on your left, but straight
uphill gives steep grass that soon eases slightly,
to arrive directly at the top of **Meall a' Churain**. A small
path leads south along the ridge to **Sgiath Chuil** summit.

Note From here there's a short cut off the hill if you want it, by way of Sgiath Chrom. Directly behind Sgiath Chuil's cairn, zigzag down left then back right to avoid a small crag, then head south onto Sgiath Chrom. A grassy spur leads down east, then grass slopes southeast to rejoin the aqueduct track.

But for the full Breadalbane-style grassy ramble, from Sgiath Chuil summit return north to **Meall a' Churain** and continue for 100 metres to a slightly lower knoll just beyond. Descend east, steeply at the very top, but

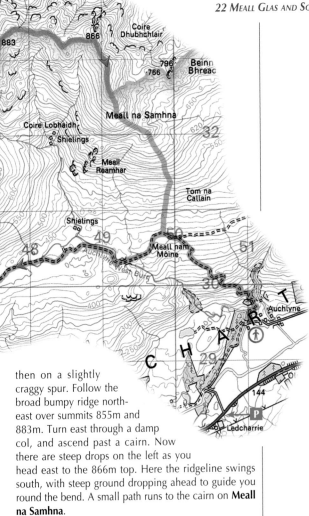

then on a slightly craggy spur. Follow the broad bumpy ridge north-east over summits 855m and 883m. Turn east through a damp col, and ascend past a cairn. Now there are steep drops on the left as you head east to the 866m top. Here the ridgeline swings south, with steep ground dropping ahead to guide you round the bend. A small path runs to the cairn on **Meall na Samhna**.

Descend southeast to a small knoll at 728m (NN 496320). From here, head down due south, hoping to reach the aqueduct track at its high point above the small hump on the moor **Meall nam Moine**. ▶ Follow the

Translated it already: Meall nam Moine means 'Hump on the Moor'.

track downhill to the left, soon passing the junction with the side-track. (However, if you descend slightly further east, you'll reach that side-track. Unlike the main track, this runs level around the hill. So if you turn left and then find yourself contouring level for more than a couple of minutes, you're on the side-track and should now turn back west to the junction.)

The track leads pleasantly down again to **Auchlyne**.

23 An Caisteal Horseshoe

Length

■ ■ ■ ■ ☐

Difficulty

■ ■ ■ ☐ ☐

Start/finish	A83 below Keilator NN 369238
Distance	14km/9 miles
Ascent	1100m/3700ft
Approx time	6½hr
Max altitude	An Caisteal 995m
Terrain	Grassy slopes and pathed ridges
Map	LR 50; Expl 364; Harvey *Crianlarich*

Caisteal is 'Castle', and refers to the rocky lump north of the summit that shows so well from the roadside. Chroin is 'Danger', though this hill is about as risky as any other of its height. These are not particularly proud or outstanding summits, and no huge crags surround them. Even so, they are among my favourites in the Southern Highlands. What I like is their green and friendly ridgeline, dodging among rocky outcrops, occasionally offering a short scramble to those who want one. Even the grass and rushes up Sron Gharbh aren't too severe; the charming ridges continue on all the way over Beinn a' Chroin; the only downer is at the end, with 2km of soggy path alongside River Falloch.

This route is of the sort I sometimes slightly deride, being the standard baggers' way up these two hills. Small paths guide you all the way, and on those paths will be people. But people and paths are *nice* things, surely! For a wilder, more remote side of these hills, see Route 16, which approaches from Balquhidder.

Rocky ridge south of An Caisteal; Beinn a' Chroin behind

A lay-by, part of the former road, is on the south side of the A82 opposite the corner of plantations. **Start** over a stile into a field. The path has some wet bits – returning at the end of the day it'll seem, by comparison, like a very firm dry path.

The path joins a track for a bridge under the railway and then another over River Falloch. Follow the track past felled plantations on your left to a gate. Here a rough path turns off to the right into bog, or you can continue for 150 metres to where the track levels, and head up to the right through grass and rushes. Reasonably comfortable rough grass leads up onto **Sron Gharbh**. The 'Rough Nose', but *sron* is the usual Gaelic for what English calls a hill shoulder.

Here a path runs along the ridgeline, dodging around the occasional outcrop. **Twistin Hill** gives 2km of attractive walking. A slight scramble crosses a crevasse-like landslip notch in the ridge. The Castle at 950m can be scrambled along its crest, or a path runs on the left along the foot of the rocks. A small cairn tops off the Castle. After a slight drop the path continues to **An Caisteal** summit, which has three cairns.

Descent Descend a path south then southeast along the knolly ridge. If the path leads to the top of a 6m steepish down-scramble with rather poor holds, you can turn up right to cross the ridgeline, and find a path below crag round to the foot of the obstacle. The path then descends steeply, slanting right to a wide col, the **Bealach Buidhe**.

A rock band blocks the slope ahead up Beinn a' Chroin. There are various ways to avoid this, including a grassy band slanting up left along the foot of the rock band. But the well marked, and quite exciting, path route will take a grassy ramp up the right-hand end of the rock band.

The path across the Bealach Buidhe could be lost in mist as it splits apart: a compass bearing (147° magnetic) is useful. At the end of the col the path has to get past the end of the rock band; so it climbs quite steeply among rocks and up a grassy ramp slanting to the right. The path then contours across the western steep slope of the mountain with crags above. After about 200 metres it turns sharply left, uphill, and zigzags up to a 2m scramble on good holds but somewhat exposed. Further erosion of the overlying grass may soon extend the scrambling here. Above this it emerges on a grass platform (cairn). Cross this to another short rise eastwards, to pass through a notch onto the summit plateau. Just to your right is a small, uncairned knoll at 938m, the **southwest top** of Beinn a' Chroin.

Head east, on path, to the **west top**, also 938m, marked by a cairn and a distinctive blocky rock (NN 385185, pictured on page 87). Slightly higher is a bare rock beside the cairn.

Continue east to **Beinn a' Chroin** summit (942m, NN 387185), which has its cairn on bare rock with a short vertical step to reach it from this direction. The path then runs down to a dip, with a scramble move down to bog and stream, after which the path passes along down to left of the true col. It then climbs to the **east top**. Just below the cairn the path divides. Turn up right for a few metres to the cairn, which was taken to be the main summit until 2000, when someone noticed a 240m contour ring on the Harvey map 800 metres to the west.

Return for a few steps and take a path heading down roughly north. Ill-defined at first, it soon becomes clear and a bit eroded as it descends the well-defined north ridge. Near its foot this ridge becomes

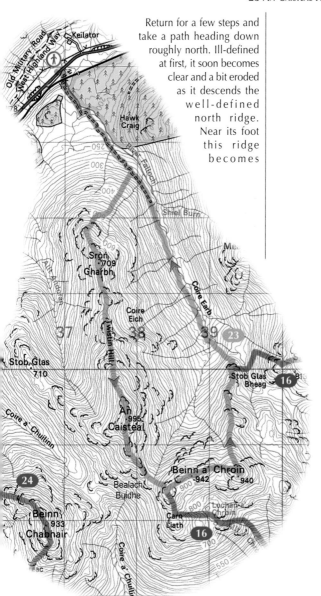

lumpy, and the path winds from side to side, before reaching the grassland of the valley floor.

Here the path bends left, northwest, passing a dead tree to reach a stream crossing above a confluence. It crosses the second stream and heads north, down-valley, to left of **River Falloch**. It is mostly clear, with many boggy bits. After about 2.5km, you reach the start of the valley track, and follow it ahead to rejoin the outward route.

24 Beinn Chabhair

Length

■ ■ ■ ■ ☐

Difficulty

■ ■ ■ ■ ☐

Start/finish	Inverarnan NN 318187
Distance	15.5km/9½ miles
Ascent	1350m/4500ft
Approx time	8hr
Max altitude	Beinn Chabhair 933m
Terrain	Rough path; high grassy moorland, pathless and very undulating
Map	LR 50 or 56; Expl 364; Harvey *Crianlarich*

Standard route up and down
                 12km/7½ miles, 950m/3200ft
                 Ascent, 5½hr

Chabhair is a little awkward to pronounce: it's' Chav-air', with the Scots-type CH on the start of it. There's nothing at all awkward about going up it. The standard baggers' route mounts beside the impressive Beinglas Falls, wanders in along a lively little burn, and then mounts to the knolly ridgeline.

Very nice too. But what a shame to then turn around and come back down the same way. How sad to spend a mere half-hour on that green-and-grey knolly schist ridgeline. A pity to miss the high Lochan a' Chaisteil, set among rock lumps on the high moorland.

Beinn Chabhair, at 933m, is not a big hill. But small is as small does. Make a day of it, rambling among the green hollows, and limp down to Glen Falloch at dusk with a tuft of bog cotton behind your ear.

There's a small pull-off on the main road, but many walkers park at the Inverarnan Inn just to the south. **Start** from Beinglas track foot. Cross River Falloch towards Beinglas campsite, but at once turn right alongside the river and up a field edge. Pass to right of the campsite to reach the West Highland Way at a small information shelter.

Keep ahead across the WH Way and behind some wooden chalets, onto a small uphill footpath. This zigzags up steeply to left of Ben Glas Burn, over an awkward ladder stile. Then it reaches the **Beinglas Falls** (but you get a better view from the car park of the Inverarnan Hotel). After the next ladder stile the path divides, with the lower branch being closer to the stream and prettier, but also encumbered with bracken.

At about 280m the path reaches the boggy hanging valley of the upper burn. It heads upstream, always to left of the burn, and almost always pleasantly, and with a tiny scramble across a side stream. (There are, naturally, one or two small swamps.) After 3km of this upper valley, you reach the outflow of **Lochan Beinn Chabhair**, a wide peaty pool.

Note The 'standard' baggers' path continues briefly to left of the loch, before turning left, up into a grassy gully towards the ridgeline. (The top of this gully is Bealach Garbh, the 'Rough Pass', on the Harvey map.) About halfway up, the path bears up right onto the lumpy ridgeline of Meall nan Tarmachan (719m). Skirting this, it dips into a col, then heads up the ridgeline southwest with many windings and a couple of brief downs on the way up to Beinn Chabhair summit.

For the full-length Chabhair ramble, cross the outflow of Lochan Beinn Chabhair on stepping stones (sometimes underwater, but the stream is small) and cross peaty ground onto **Parlan Hill**, where the going is shorter grass and bare rock. An old fence leads onto the summit plateau. ▶ Descend east towards a broad col, skirting to right of some small crags on the way down.

A cairned knoll is a good point to survey the steepening ahead. Slant up leftwards past the lowest crag, then

The broad col south of Parlan Hill was used by cattle and Rob Roy from Loch Katrine to the drove road at Inverarnan.

back up right above it; or choose your own line – easier ground is found by heading to the left. The ridgeline levels (**Creag Bhreac Mhor**, 742m) then continues with small crags and plenty of grass. A path forms for the last few steps to the cairn of **Beinn Chabhair**.

Descent The much bigger baggers' path continues down the ridgeline ahead, northwest. Ahead, beyond many knolls, you see the rocky hump of Stob Creag an Fhithich and the lonely Lochan a' Chaisteil, and decide whether to go down the quick way instead…

The path drops to cross a col, and 200 metres later passes right to left through another small col with a pool. It then skirts to left (south) of **Meall nan Tarmachan**. ◄ Branch right, off the path, to head west along the undulating ridgeline.

Here you could stay with this path as it descends to the foot of Lochan Beinn Chabhair.

After a first col, the Garbh Bealach, you cross a grassy hump to descend sharply into another col. Ahead and slightly right is the craggy **Stob Creag an Fhithich**. Contrary to appearances, it's only 100m of ascent, and quite easily reached by skirting below its crags to the left and then turning up a grassy ridgeline. It is visited just slightly more often than never, and deserves rather more attention than that.

Descend south-west, passing to left of the rocky hummock of Ben Glas, to **Lochan a' Chaisteil**. Pass along its left-hand shore, and over the cairned hump behind, Meall Mor nan Eag. Descend west, with a few short ascents, and low crags to weave around. Just as the ground cover is getting unpleasantly tussocky, you reach a stony track running across the ridge.

A left turn would bring you quickly to the ascent path – but that path is stony and steep. So it's better to turn

Descending the northwest ridge of Beinn Chabhair, with Ben Lui rising ahead on the other side of Glen Falloch

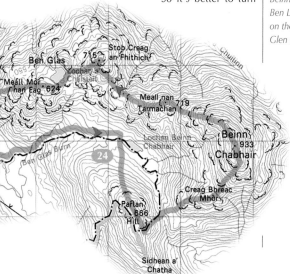

right, on the stony track, which slants down northwards, then descends in wide curves into Glen Falloch. Around 200 metres above the river, it meets the wide, smooth track of the **West Highland Way**. (Another track, which you don't want, is seen lower down below beside the river.)

Turn left on the track, which passes through a gate then drops gently through woods into **Beinglas campsite**.

25 Beinglas Falls Circuit

Length

Difficulty

Start/finish	Inverarnan NN 318187
Distance	5.5km/3½ miles
Ascent	300m/1000ft
Approx time	2hr
Max altitude	Moorland shoulder 330m
Terrain	Rough steep path up, stony track down
Map	LR 50 or 56; Expl 364; Harvey *Crianlarich*

This short but steep walk gives views down Loch Lomond (on the upward section) and up Glen Falloch (on the descent). After the rugged ascent, the gentler track to go down on is a treat. In just one respect it disappoints: the Beinglas Falls (or Grey Mare's Tail) is reached rather high up, avoiding the full thunder and spray of the main waterfall – view these instead from the car park of the Inverarnan Hotel.

There are two small pull-offs just north of Beinglas track end, but most walkers park at the Inverarnan Hotel. **Start** across River Falloch towards **Beinglas campsite**, but at once turn right alongside the river and up a field edge. Pass to right of the campsite to reach the West Highland Way at a small information shelter.

Keep ahead across the WH Way and behind a couple of wooden chalets onto a small uphill footpath. This zigzags up steeply to left of Ben Glas Burn, over an awkward ladder stile. Then it reaches the top of the main **Beinglas Waterfalls**. After the next ladder stile the path divides, with the lower branch being closer to the stream and prettier, but also encumbered with bracken. At about 280m the path reaches the boggy hanging valley of the upper burn. It turns sharp left above a kink in the burn, and in another 200 metres reaches a junction. Here turn off left onto a stony track wide enough for small tractors.

The stony track rises gently northwards across the hill flank, then slants down a wide grassy shelf. Keep to the stony and sunken main track as various grass-and-peat wheelmark tracks run alongside it. The track is well used by shepherds' bikes, and with peat-slop lying over stones is firm but slightly mucky walking. It bends left, downhill,

Beinglas Falls from Inverarnan

and descends in wide curves, through a gateway, down into **Glen Falloch**.

In the wooded glen, 200 metres above the river, the rough track meets the wide, smooth track of the **West Highland Way**. (Another track, which you don't want, is seen below beside the river.)

Turn left on the WHW track, which passes through a gate with stile alongside, and drops gently through woods into Beinglas campsite.

26 Beinglas Falls to Beinn a' Choin

Length

Difficulty

Start/finish	Inverarnan NN 318187
Distance	25km/16 miles
Ascent	1150m/3900ft
Approx time	9hr
Max altitude	Beinn a' Choin 770m
Terrain	Pathless grassy slopes, return along West Highland Way
Map	LR 56; Expl 364; Harvey *Crianlarich* and *Loch Lomond*

Beinn a' Choin is a straightforward up and down from the RSPB car park at Garrison of Inversnaid. Done that way, it's a very ordinary Corbett. However, by perversely starting at the other end, you can make a mountain out of it. A glimpse of a big waterfall, then a long rambling ridge with steep drops to Loch Lomond; and finally, the most interesting 13km of the West Highland Way along the shoreline oakwoods, taking in the hidey-hole of Rob Roy himself.

Choin is from 'con', dog (compare French *chien*). It's not hard to confuse this hill with Stob a' Choin, 8km west above Balquhidder, or with Beinn a' Chroin and Stuc a' Chroin, both named from 'cron', harm or danger.

There are two small pull-offs just north of the Beinglas track end, but most walkers park at the Inverarnan Hotel. **Start** across River Falloch towards Beinglas campsite, but at once turn right alongside the river and up a field edge, passing to right of the campsite to reach the West Highland Way at a small information shelter.

Keep ahead across the WH Way onto a small uphill footpath. This zigzags up steeply to left of **Ben Glas Burn**. At one point it reaches the waterfalls. At about 280m the path reaches the boggy hanging valley of the upper burn. It turns sharp left above a kink in the burn, and in another 200 metres reaches the turn-off left of the path of Route 25. But keep ahead on the main path until you find a convenient point to cross the burn on your right.

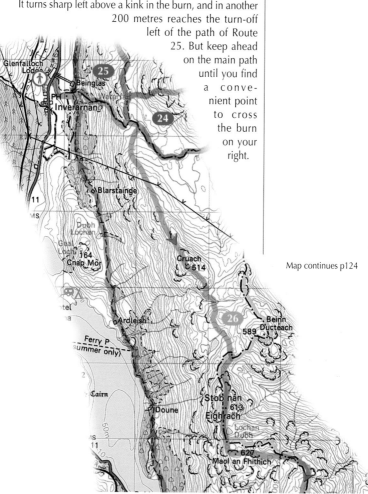

Map continues p124

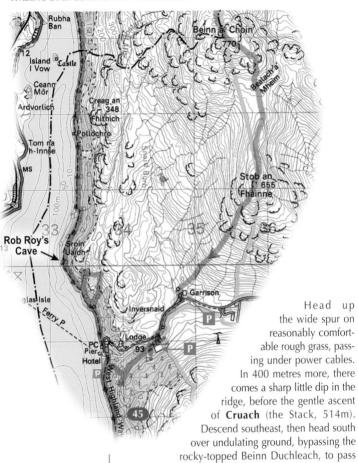

Head up the wide spur on reasonably comfortable rough grass, passing under power cables. In 400 metres more, there comes a sharp little dip in the ridge, before the gentle ascent of **Cruach** (the Stack, 514m). Descend southeast, then head south over undulating ground, bypassing the rocky-topped Beinn Duchleach, to pass just up left of Lochan nam Muc.

Map continued from p123

Immediately behind the lochan you meet a ruined fence, which guides up over **Stob nan Eighrach**, past the hidden Lochan Dubh, and then east over undulations of Maol an Fhithich ('Raven Hump'). After a craggy dip, the ridgeline turns southeast to the cairned summit of **Beinn a' Choin**.

Descend southeast, avoiding small crags, into the peaty Bealach a' Mheim. (Now an old fence takes a line down on the right, which could be followed in mist but bypasses the pretty little ridge to come.) Follow a path trace along the grassy ridge to **Stob an Fhainne**. Descend roughly south to reach the Glen Arklet road near the reservoir dam.

Follow the road downhill, past Garrison farm (where there's a roomy RSPB car park) and past Inversnaid primary school and church until a high bridge across Arklet Water leads up to a car park.

Turn right on a built path through a high deer fence. Where it forks, the right-hand branch is more direct, while the left has a short spur out to **Rob Roy's Viewpoint**, where in breaks in his cattle droving and fleeing for his life he contemplated a long vista down Loch Lomond (or else he didn't and they just called it that). The two paths rejoin above the loch; keep downhill for a few more steps to meet the West Highland Way.

Turn right over two footbridges, the second of them passing above Inversnaid Waterfall. Keep down to left of **Inversnaid Hotel**, and drop to the ferry pier for a view of

Summit of Beinn a' Choin

Though I'm ready to bet the poet just came over from the A82 on the ferry.

the falls, celebrated by Gerard Manley Hopkins. ◄ That ferry plus a bus could now return you to Inverarnan.

Forgetting the ferry, for the best section of the West Highland Way south of the Devil's Staircase, pass along the front of the hotel and through a car park onto a wide track. This shrinks to a path along the lochside. After 400 metres it passes a boathouse shed; in another 50 metres turn up right on the signed RSPB trail. After a climb of more than 200 wooden steps it reaches some open views across the loch and then descends by 200 more wooden steps to rejoin the West Highland Way (or you could just stay on the WH Way, passing a couple of attractive wild campsites).

After another 400 metres, the path passes below a steep little crag then descends sharply. Here a sign back down left is for **Rob Roy's Cave**. Clamber over boulders to a big boulder arch that's Rob's antechamber cavern; but pass this, or pass through it, and clamber over more boulders to the next cave, a complicated hollow under several huge boulders. One entrance is helpfully marked 'CAVE' in high white letters.

Return to the West Highland Way. Its next section is narrow and undulating, and in places mildly rocky, so it's slower and more entertaining than you would expect. After 3km it gets easier, soon passing the bothy at Doune Byre.

Note The passenger ferry to Ardlui followed by a bus or hitchhike would save you the final 4km of the walk, except that the exhausted walker has already missed the 7.30pm final ferry.

At the loch's head the path rises through the col east of Cnap Mor, then slants down through woodland to **Beinglas campsite**.

27 Meall an Fhudair

Start/finish	Glen Falloch farm NN 319197
Distance	15.5km/9½ miles
Ascent	900m/3000ft
Approx time	6½hr
Max altitude	Meall an Fhudair 764m
Terrain	Rocky moorland
Map	LR 56; Expl 364; Harvey *Crianlarich*

Longer route including Beinn Damhain
14.5km/9 miles, 1200m/4000ft
Ascent, 7hr

Length

Difficulty

Meall an Fhudair gets to Corbett-height by a mere two metres (764m/2506ft). And it's more moorland than mountain, a flat place with a lot of glacier-scraped bare rock. Between the rocks are grass and many tiny pools, so the moorland wander is a pleasant one. And the bog myrtle and bracken of the lower ground are passed through on handy hydro-scheme tracks.

The bonus in all this is the classic view from Troisgeach: along Loch Lomond to its Ben. Should the spirit so move you, this is an outstanding place to be half an hour before sunrise – and not just because this leaves the pylons invisible.

Fhudair's summit happens to be 400 metres beyond the National Park's edge. Once there, you have a choice. The convenient way descends to a hydro-scheme track on the north flank. The extended route takes in a hill that's even lower, just as flat, and has if anything even more bare rock. Beinn Damhain is the 'Hill of Stags'. Any of these unvisited hills gives a good chance of deer – the ones I met were actually on Meall an Fhudair.

There's verge parking on A82 near Glen Falloch farm, including on the bridge over Dubh Eas river. **Start** opposite **Glen Falloch farm**, where a locked gate and access sign lead to a roughly tarred track. ▶ The track crosses a high bridge over the railway and climbs in gentle zigzags. Ignore a side-track on the right to a phone mast. Not far above this appears the nice view of Loch Lomond apart from the pylon foreground.

This is the track to left (south) of Dubh Eas, not the newer one to its north.

The track ascends through a gate to a track junction at the 300m contour on **Troisgeach Bheag**. Go straight across and climb rough slopes of grass and outcrops. The ridgeline ascends west, with some rocky outcrops if you keep to the exact crest. Various cairned knolls constitute the summit of 734m **Troisgeach** – the true summit has a small pool just in front.

Continue northwest, crossing flat knolly ground. It's tempting to bypass the next hump, Meall nan Caora, but this saves you nothing as the best ground is along the moor crest. After a small lochan, the ground rises slightly to the summit of **Meall nan Caora** with its small cairn.

The ground now drops quite steeply south-west into a wide

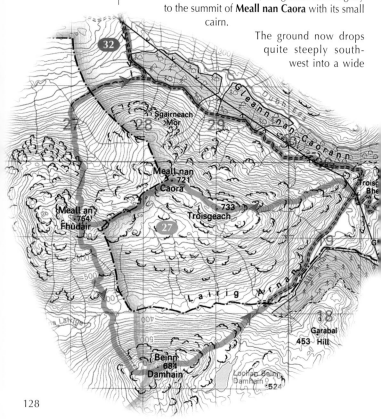

confusing col with many lochans. As it rises again, a small path can be found. The main ridgeline swings west to the shelter-wall cairn at the summit of **Meall an Fhudair**.

Loch Lomond and Ben Lomond, from Troisgeach Bheag

The shorter Caorann track descent

Head down northeast to pass a pool. Continue down grassy slopes, interrupted by the occasional low crag. For shorter vegetation (but rather more crag) keep to the slopes to left of **Coir' an Longairt**, before descending to join its north-flowing stream. At the 330m contour on this there's a small intake dam with concrete footbridge. From here a faint path follows a buried aqueduct, contouring east. (In mist, it would be possible to cross this feature without noticing it, so either follow the stream down to find the dam or, if descending further east, be very alert.)

At the beginning of a huge water-pipe crossing **Gleann nan Caorann**, a smooth track starts. Keep ahead as it contours along the aqueduct line, then slants slightly downhill to the track junction on **Troisgeach Bheag**.

The tough continuation over Beinn Damhain

From **Meall an Fhudair** summit descend gently and then quite steeply south, with no problems despite some crag marks on the map. Cross the wide, open valley of Lairig Arnan to west of its col, and go straight up the steep grass of Beinn Damhain opposite. Head east across the summit plateau to the slight rise and **Beinn Damhain**'s summit cairn.

The slope down east is steep, among boiler-plate slabs: the face is attractively rocky, and with boulder-fields as well, the initial descent is quite slow. Thereafter descend gently northeast to the **Allt Arnan**. There's a small reservoir, and a track bridge just below. The track leads northeast to the junction on **Troisgeach Bheag**.

Heading up from Troisgeach Bheag onto Troisgeach

PART FIVE
TYNDRUM

Plateau of Beinn Chaorach (Route 31)

For many, Tyndrum is a handy stop-off on the A82, a place where it's hard to choose between a tearoom featuring 200 Scotch whiskies and one of the UK's finest chippies. And so it has been (substituting oatmeal for the cream scones and a damp plaid in the heather for the By The Way hostel) since the days of the cattle drovers, Victorian rail travellers and wanderers on the West Highland Way. Many stay, rather fewer head into the hills.

For, despite still being in the National Park, we are now far from the intimate knobbly mountains of the south. Here you need a taste for the wastelands, a weakness for the bleak. East of the village, the Dun Hill and the Sheep Hill lead only to the Crooked Crag and to big Ben Challum.

But grow your legs big by striding up and down these long grass slopes – and you're ready for Ben Lui. Ben Lui, the National Park's finest mountain, is the following Summit Summary.

28 Glen Cononish

Start/finish	Tyndrum NN 329304
Distance	8km/5 miles
Ascent	100m/300ft
Approx time	2hr
Max altitude	300m
Terrain	Forest roads and well-built paths
Map	LR 50; Expl 364 or 377; Harvey *Crianlarich*

Length

Difficulty

This walk is short, sheltered, and easy underfoot. After some dull forest road, Glen Cononish is enjoyably wild, dominated above by Ben Lui and with some ancient pines across its foot. The woodland along the West Highland Way is also enjoyable, despite the rumble of the A82.

Start in Tyndrum centre. Head out towards Fort William and Oban, crossing a footbridge alongside the A82, then turning left along a street signposted as the West Highland Way. At the end of the tarmac turn right on a well-made path waymarked with an acorn as the 'Cattle Creep'. It crosses bog, to a bridge under the Oban railway – the cobbled streambed, normally mostly dry, is the **cattle creep**.

The path heads up beside a stony stream: this is the sterile outwash from old lead mines on Sron nan Colan. The streambed contains chunks of quartz vein, and shattered faultline rocks bound with quartz – there could also be minerals such as grey, cubic galena though I didn't linger in the rain long enough to uncover any.

After 100 metres a waymark points to the left (a path on the right zigzags up through the old workings onto Sron nan Colan). Take this wide path left, above the railway line, to a track above **Tyndrum Lower Station**.

Looking up Glen Cononish from the slopes of Ben Challum

Because the West Highland Railway must climb to 300m under Beinn Odhar, its junction with the Oban line is 8km south, at Crianlarich, and Tyndrum has separate Upper and Lower Stations. My grandfather once found himself in the wrong part

133

of the train after Crianlarich, and managed to leap out at Tyndrum Upper with his rucksack and run down to board the Oban-bound half of the train below.

Turn right, signed for Ben Lui, away from the station just below. The forest road climbs gently, then descends to **Glen Cononish**. At the track 'T' you could ramble up the glen for the views of Ben Lui, before returning downstream. On the right as you follow the valley down is a remnant of ancient Caledonian forest, now fenced to allow regeneration.

The track passes under the railway into scrubby woodland. After 400 metres turn left onto the well-made **West Highland Way** path. In 50 metres pass a small lochan. ◄

The good path continues a little up to left of the stream through regenerating Scots pine and heather. It passes across bare stony ground poisoned by the ore-crushing plant of the lead mines, then enters mature pines to reach the edge of **Tyndrum**. At the first street turn right, to the village centre.

This may be where Robert the Bruce threw away his heavy broadsword when trying to escape from some MacDougalls of Lorne, who caught him up anyway 10 minutes later (see Route 29).

29 Beinn Odhar

Length

Difficulty

Start/finish	Tyndrum NN 329304
Distance	13km/8 miles
Ascent	800m/2700ft
Approx time	5¼hr
Max altitude	Beinn Odhar 901m
Terrain	Grassy slopes, track and path
Map	LR 50; Expl 377

Another 13m (45ft) of altitude would make Beinn Odhar a Munro, with a hundredfold increase in visitors and an eroded path. But Beinn Odhar completely lacks rocky features and doesn't feel much like a mountain. From the north it's an impressive steep cone. But from Tyndrum remains of an old path lead up reasonably angled grass; and the south ridge is a splendidly gentle descent route that wouldn't be out of place as a suburban golf course. A stretch of the West Highland Way completes a day that's far too gentle for something 13m short of a Munro.

Start in Tyndrum centre. Head out towards Fort William and Oban, crossing a footbridge alongside the A82, then turning right up the West Highland Way past the small grocers. The lane becomes a track past a new graveyard, then crosses the railway.

Turn off right, up grassy slopes. On the spur above **Crom Allt** an old green path will be found. While the grassy slopes are comfortable anywhere, the old path aids the ascent for so long as you can keep track of it. At 600m it slants out left onto the southwestern spur, which it follows up to a shoulder at 750m. Here there is a small lochan and tiny stream. Head up a stony slope to the summit of **Beinn Odhar**.

Descending the southeast ridge of Beinn Odhar

Descend southeast, quite steeply at first, to another tiny lochan. Here the ridge eases to give fast, easy walking with a small path. After another lochan and a peaty col, there's a slight ascent to **Meall Buidhe**. The ridge, now slightly rougher, continues south, with a swampy col leading to the final rise with cairn (534m).

Descend southeast, aiming towards Auchtertyre farm, until a fence guides you straight downhill to a footbridge over the railway (NN 350293). Follow another fence down to a stream, with a rough path leading out to the **Auchtertyre** driveway near the A82. Directly opposite, a short path leads to

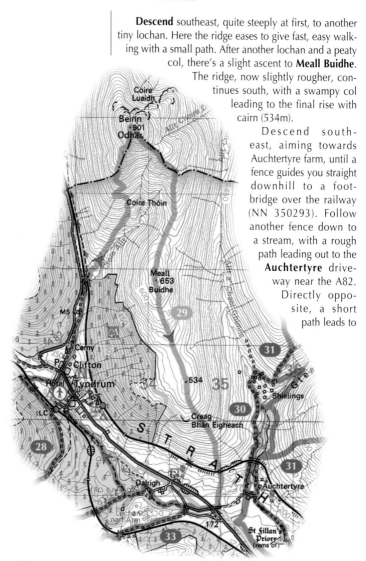

the Holy Pool, used by St Fillan for baptisms but in later centuries for magic dunkings as preliminary to the harsh mental therapy described in Route 30.

Follow the driveway out to the A82, and cross to the tarred path of the **West Highland Way**. It follows the **River Fillan** to a tarred track at White Bridge (where a right turn leads to the Dalrigh car park NN 344291, an alternative start for the walk). Cross the tarred track but not the river, continuing along the north bank on waymarked West Highland Way path. Pass Dalrigh battlefield, site of a small skirmish involving Robert the Bruce in 1306. ▶

Dalrigh means 'Field of the King'.

Near **Dalrigh** houses, turn off left to join a new track, which crosses a wooded side-stream. It bends left through scrubby woodland. After 300 metres turn right on the well-made WH Way path, at once passing a small lochan, possibly the spot where the Bruce threw away his heavy broadsword to aid his escape. The MacDougalls of Lorne caught up anyway at the battlefield a few minutes back down the track. ▶

Bruce lost, but got away to fight again.

The good path continues a little up to left of the stream through regenerating Scots pine and heather. It enters mature pines to reach the edge of **Tyndrum**. At the first street, turn right to the village centre.

30 Auchtertyre Farm Walks

Start/finish	Auchtertyre NN 353289
Distance	6.5km/4 miles
Ascent	150m/500ft
Approx time	2hr
Max altitude	Allt Gleann a' Chlachain 330m
Terrain	The Sheep Walk is a small hill path with a height gain of 150m: the Riverside Walk is on a level path then a track
Map	LR 50; Expl 364 or 377; Harvey *Crianlarich* (riverside walk only)

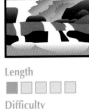

Length

Difficulty

These two paths, and accompanying birchwoods, were created in compensation for the devastation wreaked by the construction of the small Auchtertyre hydroelectric scheme in 2001. With that devastation now completely grown over, the short low-level walks remain as pure profit. The **Sheep Walk** (4km/150m ascent) is enjoyably wild, the path sketchy in one section and fairly wet in another. The **Riverside Walk** (2.5km) would be more delightful without the noise of the adjacent A82 road. During lambing time, mid-April to end May, dogs are not allowed on its field track section.

Both walks start at a car park short of the farm buildings. There's a small café and shop at the farm.

Sheep Walk

Cross the bridge into Auchtertyre farm, and at once turn left at a signpost. In 100 metres, at another signpost beside the first of the **Strathfillan Wigwams**, turn left on a path alongside the river. This passes a small waterfall, into a spruce plantation. Here it drops slightly left to contour the side of the gorge, before turning up steps to a track.

Turn left under the railway viaduct, then turn up right onto the open hill. Marker posts, some red-topped and some plain, mark the faint path that runs up-valley above the top of a plantation. After 1km, the path slants down left to a stile into young birchwood, and continues down towards a substantial footbridge below the confluence of two streams.

For a short cut back, on reaching the right-hand stream (**Allt Gleann a' Chlachain**) you can turn down left to cross that footbridge to the track above, and turn down left. Otherwise ignore the footbridge below, and turn right on a clear path upstream. After a boardwalk section, you reach a footbridge just below the dam of the hydroelectric scheme. Cross and slant up left on the track above.

At a track junction, take the descending track ahead. It crosses the other stream (**Allt a' Chaol Ghlinne**) and bends back left. It runs above the combined stream and back under the viaduct to Auchtertyre.

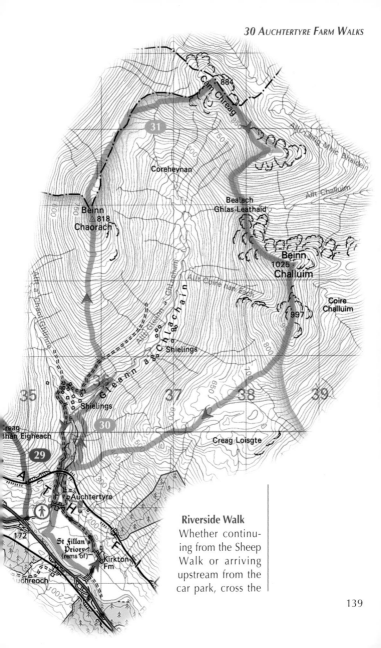

Riverside Walk

Whether continuing from the Sheep Walk or arriving upstream from the car park, cross the bridge into Auchtertyre farm and at once turn right at a signpost. A path runs downstream to **River Fillan**, then turns left alongside the river.

After 1 km you reach the access track of **Kirkton farm**. Turn left to the farm, and follow a West Highland Way signpost to the left just before the buildings. Pass the ruin of **St Fillan's Chapel**.

Note This was a priory established by King Robert the Bruce on the site of St Fillan's original 8th-century cell. Here a radical form of shock therapy was practised on those of unsound mind. They were lashed to a wooden framework and placed in the chapel above the saint's gravestone. The head rested in the chapel font, and St Fillan's heavy brass bell was suspended directly above. Thus the patient passed a therapeutic night, warm under a covering of fresh hay.

Past the chapel, take the track forking left, with WH Way markers. After a couple of fields, it passes into **Auchtertyre farm**.

31 Ben Challum and Two Corbetts

Length

Difficulty

Start/finish	Auchtertyre NN 353289
Distance	17km/10½ miles
Ascent	1400m/4700ft
Approx time	7½hr
Max altitude	Ben Challum 1025m
Terrain	Pathless grassy slopes
Map	LR 50; Expl 377

Ben Challum is a mountain of some majesty, with a steep broken north face. This route approaches it by a natural horseshoe over two Corbetts, the grassy

Beinn Chaorach (appropriately, 'Sheep Hill') and the more rugged Cam Chreag ('Crooked Crag'). This leads to a rocky mountain spur at the back of Ben Challum. The long grass slope that provides the standard up-and-down for Munro-baggers then supplies a comfortable descent.

Start at Auchtertyre farm (Strathfillan Wigwams). ▶ Head on up the track, not turning right into the farm but continuing up to left of the stream, passing under the viaduct of the West Highland Railway.

Route 30 offers alternative ways of starting.

In another 800 metres a stile on the right leads down through a new birch wood to a bridge below the confluence of two streams. Continue up a path to right of **Allt Gleann a' Chlachain**, to a footbridge below a small dam. Cross and head up left on a track. Where this joins a higher track, turn up right for a couple of zigzags. As the track contours off to the right, continue straight up the grassy spur of **Beinn Chaorach** to the trig point on its top.

A gentle ridge leads down northwards, with low posts of a derelict electric fence. In the col you pass the ruins of the electric generator for the fence. Grassy slopes lead up northeast, then east, to **Cam Chreag**. The first knoll of the ridge is the 884m summit.

Follow the bumpy ridgeline southeast, with steep drops on the left and Ben Challum looking large on the right. The final summit (875m, NN 384337) has a quartz vein running up it. Here turn sharp back right, past a couple of pools, to a knoll at the corner of the plateau. Head down a spur, southwest, soon with a ruined fence and wall. As the ground steepens, a line somewhat to right of the fence is slightly easier. Rejoin it in the col, **Bealach Ghlas Leathaid**, 575m.

The fence continues up the steep northwest ridge of Ben Challum. At about 750m it runs into craggy slabs. About 30 metres to right of the fence top a grassy groove runs up the slabs, with a move or two of low-grade scrambling: or the obstacle can be bypassed on steep broken ground further to the right. Above this, another outcrop can also be bypassed on the right.

Now at 800m, the ridge changes its character, becoming smooth and stony to **Ben Challum**'s summit cairn.

Descent Depart southwest, soon picking up the well-worn path. This turns south, and follows a subsidiary mini-ridge to pass to right of the 997m south top. As the ground steepens, the worn path follows old fencing down southwest, to cross a small rise 698m (NN 378305).

At a fence junction just behind this, turn left for 100 metres to a stile on the right. Cross this onto a very small path southwest. It crosses one fence to join a second one. Turn downhill alongside this, with the path gradually fading. At a contouring fence, head straight downhill on rough grass to the viaduct above Auchtertyre farm.

Note The small shop here serves coffee and cakes until 7-ish pm. While the driver enjoys those, those with surplus energy could walk a pleasant 4km of West Highland Way to the pub and chip shop at Tyndrum.

Pass under the viaduct, and at once turn down right at a stile onto a riverside path. Follow this down past a waterfall to **Auchtertyre farm**.

Ben Challum from Glen Lochay.
Route 31 follows the right-hand skyline

Ben Lui is not the highest hill in the Lomond–Trossachs National Park – that's Ben More above Crianlarich. However, it can claim to be the area's finest. Ben Lui is all mountain, rising in five converging ridges to a summit several hundred metres above the rest and visible over half the Highlands. It's no surprise that both gold and garnets are found in its surrounding slopes, for Lui is a jewel of a hill. (For a description and pictures of the garnets that are widespread across Beinn Dubhchraig and Ben Oss see Appendix 1.)

Its impressive northeastern face, the Coire Gaothach ('Windy Corrie'), offers an airy ridgeline on its southern side that's a scrappy scramble in summer, or a fine winter climb. Ben Lui's north face offers a complex and satisfying wild hillwalk, and as outliers it has three more Munros and a Corbett.

While maps use the anglicised spelling, the Gaelic Beinn Laoigh is creeping into fashion. The pronunciation is the same. 'Mountain of the Calves' is a translation (though the reference is probably to deer rather than anything that goes moo).

Ben Lui, with Coire Gaothach on the right face, from the north ridge of Beinn Dubhchraig (Route 33)

143

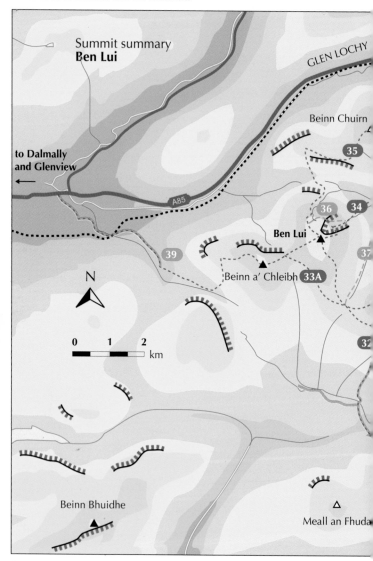

Summit summary
Ben Lui

GLEN LOCHY

Beinn Chuirn

35

to Dalmally
and Glenview
←

A85

34

36

Ben Lui ▲

39

Beinn a' Chleibh ▲ 33A

37

N

32

0   1   2
km

Beinn Bhuidhe ▲

Meall an Fhuda △

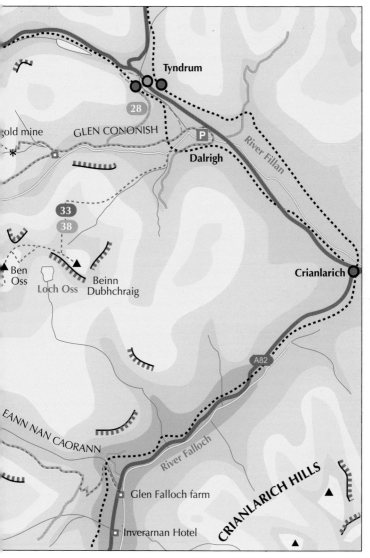

145

The finest route on this fine mountain is the approach over Beinn Dubhchraig and Ben Oss, with a descent by impressive Coire Gaothach and a gentle walk out along Glen Cononish: Routes 33 and 36. Those aiming for all the Munros will add in Route 33A, a dog-leg to Beinn a' Chleibh, an outlying Munro that's a nuisance to do on its own.

So why the other five routes? For the energetic, Beinn Chuirn adds a Corbett and the wilderness flank of the mountain. Coire Laoigh is a gentle and sheltered descent route, especially useful as an escape in bad conditions. Coire Gaothach's south ridge is the scenic but scrappy scramble already mentioned. The final two routes, 32 and 39, create a full backpacking crossing of Ben Lui from Loch Lomond to Loch Awe.

BEN LUI ROUTES

Map
LR 50; Expl 364; Harvey *Crianlarich*

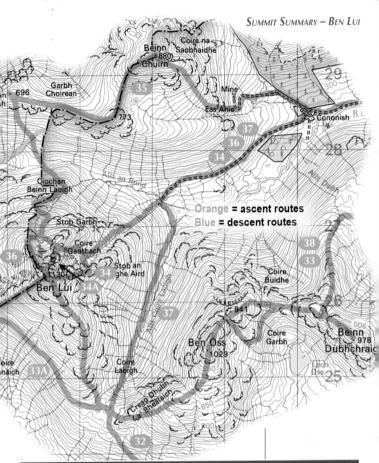

Orange = ascent routes
Blue = descent routes

GLEN LOCHY NOTE

Convenient for the bagging of Beinn a' Chleibh, routes are used from the Oban road in Glen Lochy to the Chleibh/Lui col and direct onto the north-west face of Ben Lui. These involve a dodgy river crossing, a rail crossing discouraged by Network Rail, and steep bog through plantations. These unattractive lines lie entirely outside the National Park, which gives me the perfect excuse to omit them here.

32 From Glen Falloch by the Pipeline Track

Start	Glen Falloch farm NN 319197
Distance up	13km/8 miles
Ascent	1200m/4000ft
Approx time up	6hr
Terrain	Easy track, then grassy slopes

This route is obscure but logical, as a smooth track leads across all the preliminary moorland, plus it's one of only two Lui routes with a view along Loch Lomond. It can be used by walkers on the West Highland Way as a logical-looking (but not at all short) short cut between Inverarnan and Tyndrum – descend by Route 37 or else cross Ben Lui to descend Route 34. It could also be followed by the descent to Dalmally (Route 39) as an early adventure in a backpack trip towards Cruachan and Fort William.

There's verge parking on A82 near Glen Falloch farm, including on the bridge over Dubh Eas river. **Start** opposite **Glen Falloch farm**, where a locked gate with an access sign leads to a roughly tarred track. ◀ The track crosses a high bridge over the railway and climbs in gentle zigzags. Ignore a side-track on the right to a phone mast. Not far above this appears a classic view along Loch Lomond.

This is the track to the left (south) of Dubh Eas, not the newer one to its north.

The track passes under power lines and ascends through a gate to a track junction at the 300m contour on **Troisgeach Bheag**. Turn right on a track that runs high above Gleann nan Caorann, following a buried aqueduct just above. The track turns down right, joining a massive pipeline to cross the valley floor. At the far end of the pipe turn right onto a track that crosses a stream bridge then climbs on, to the 550m contour. ◀ Slant up left, northwest, on grassy slopes rising into the **Lui/Oss col**. ◀ Head up the grassy ridge north, then northwest as the ridge becomes more defined and a path forms, to the airy summit of **Ben Lui**.

Ben Oss could now be included simply by keeping on uphill.

To now include Beinn a' Chleibh, see Route 33A.

The pipeline across
Gleann nan Caorann,
and Ben Lui

33 From Dalrigh by Dubhchraig and Oss

Start	Dalrigh car park off A82
	NN 344291
Distance up	13km/8 miles
Ascent	1550m/5100ft
Approx time up	7hr
Terrain	Small paths

A high ridgeline links three Munros, with a small path and a great view along Loch Lomond. What more could a hillwalker desire? Descend by Route 36, the impressive Coire Gaothach and Glen Cononish, for a classic Scottish hill day. Route 33A extends rather awkwardly over the group's fourth Munro.

Start From Dalrigh car park continue along the overgrown tarmac road with traces of white line and cat's eyes. Cross the West Highland Way and then Drochaid Ban, the **White Bridge**, over River Fillan. At once, as the tarred road bends left, take a track on the right.

Immediately after crossing the railway, turn off right onto a boggy path. This runs alongside the railway then River Cononish to a footbridge over **Allt Gleann Auchreoch** (NN 333284). It continues up to right of the stream through beautiful woods of pine and birch. It passes through a fallen fence with remains of a ladder stile, then through a taller fence above, with a now unnecessary ladder stile still standing on the left. Finally it passes a waterfall in the stream down on your left, before emerging onto open hill.

Ben Lui's summit cone, from the southeast ridge. The right skyline is the top of Route 34, the southern ridge of Coire Gaothach

After crossing a small side-stream two paths continue up Beinn Dubhchraig. It's better not to cross the main stream for a path up the open valley of **Coire Dubhchraig**. Instead stay to right (west) of the stream, on a path continuing up to about 550m then fading. Now head up right, onto a grassy ridgeline. This joins the main ridge of Beinn Dubhchraig 600 metres northwest of the summit, near two pools. Head southeast, past the top of the alternative path, and up the steeper summit cone to the top of **Beinn Dubhchraig**. Here you get that fine view along Loch Lomond.

Return past the two pools. The ridge path runs down west to the Dubhchraig/Oss col, **Bealach Buidhe**. From here you could head on west up the steep stony ridgeline, but a path contours out left (southwest) from the col. After 600 metres it crosses a stream in Coire Garbh at the 780m contour. The path now wanders onto the east face of Ben Oss but nicer is to turn uphill to left of the stream, skirt a boggy plateau patch just above, and continue to left of the stream into a small col on the northeast ridge of Ben Oss. Turn up left on a ridge path to the summit of **Ben Oss**.

Various faint paths follow the wide ridgeline down south. Bend southwest into the wide knolly **Oss/Lui col**. There is a path through the col, easier to spot when descending from Ben Lui. ▶ Head up the grassy ridge north, then northwest as the ridge becomes more defined and a path forms, to the airy summit of **Ben Lui**.

For Beinn a' Chleibh, Route 33A, contour out left now.

33A From Dalrigh by Dubhchraig, Oss and Beinn a' Chleibh

Start	Dalrigh car park off A82 NN 344291
Distance up	15.5km/9½ miles
Ascent	1700m/5700ft
Approx time up	8hr
Terrain	Small paths, and an awkward contour across steep grass

For Munro-baggers, Beinn a' Chleibh is an awkward outlier – and for this book it's not even in the Lomond–Trossachs National Park, the summit lying 150 metres beyond the boundary! But to save a later ascent of some nasty paths out of Glen Lochy, Beinn a' Chleibh can be added onto the previous route by an awkward traverse across the grassy slope of Sgiath Dhubh.

Start Follow Route 33 to the **Oss/Lui col**.

Cross the col, then contour out left onto the south-west slope of Ben Lui. It is steep, grassy, and named as

Descending from Ben Lui towards Beinn a' Chleibh on a winter backpack trip towards Fort William

Sgiath Dhubh (Black Wing) on some maps. Contour along it northwest for 2km, rising slightly towards the 776m col joining Ben Lui to Beinn a' Chleibh.

Note Incised stream valleys run down Sgiath Dhubh, and in mist it is not easy to maintain level here, unless with GPS or altimeter. If you do maintain your level, then it should be easy to recognise the change in the downslope from southwest to south as you arrive below the Chleibh col. If you arrive too high, you'll have to watch out for the fairly clear descending path from Lui, and a more subtle change of slope.

A path follows the well-defined ridge across the Cleibh col (776m), and up to the 916m summit of **Beinn a' Chleibh**. A small pool decorates the summit plateau beyond the cairn.

Return across the Cleibh col, and follow a reasonably clear path uphill. It follows a poorly defined spur, to arrive on Ben Lui's summit ridge at the low point between its northwest summit and its main one. Turn right, crossing a short rocky slab (avoidable on the right) to the main summit.

34 Coire Gaothach Southern Ridge

Start	Dalrigh car park off A82
	NN 344291
Distance up	10km/6 miles
Ascent	1000m/3300ft
Approx time up	5hr
Terrain	Track, steep grass, steep pathed ridge with rocky moves

This ridge can also be considered as the east ridge of Ben Lui. Airy and impressive, it runs from the 800m contour directly to the summit of Ben Lui ▶

◄ 300m above. In summer, it's best regarded as an exciting walk, with a single scrambling move (though even that could be avoided). The crest above the zigzag path does offer more rocky opportunities, but the holds are smooth, sloping and mossy, and some of them are loose. So as a scramble it's one for those with broad minds and experienced fingers.

In good hard snow, or even on well-frozen turf, it's a fine winter route (winter grade I).

Start From Dalrigh car park continue along the overgrown tarmac road with traces of white line and cat's eyes. Just before Drochaid Ban, the **White Bridge**, turn right along the riverside path of the West Highland Way. After 700 metres it reaches a track, with a ford on the left which you can cross if feasible. Otherwise, follow WH Way markers upstream to a track bridge.

Tracks from ford and bridge rejoin to run west, under a railway bridge, and up **Glen Cononish**. Stay on the main track, to pass to right of Cononish farm with its ugly green roofs. The track runs around the southeast slope of Beinn Chuirn and drops slightly to end beside **Allt an Rund** stream.

A path ahead fords the stream, and passes above a stone sheepfold to join a side-stream. The small, steep path goes up to right of this stream all the way into **Coire Gaothach**.

Once in the corrie, the small path for the northern ridge (Route 34A) forks off right but the main path runs up to right of the stream. Above on your left, note a **grass-and-crag hump** that projects from the corrie wall – a scree runnel defines its left, near, boundary angle. The hump will be your route onto the left-hand ridge, but for the time being the path pretends to ignore it, heading up past it well to right of the stream, to peter out at about the 800m level. Contour left across the stream and then across steep grass, rising slightly, to reach the (poorly defined) top of the grass-and-crag hump. Continue leftwards, slightly rising, on a path trace, to reach the level crest of the **Gaothach southern ridge**.

Turn right on the small ridge path, with the ridge soon rising steeply. The steep little path zigzags to left of the crest. You can keep closer to the crest for scrappy scrambling. The ridge steepens to a wall, scrambled on sloping footholds (one of them being loose) or the path is 30 metres to the left.

The ridge levels, widens, and is grassy before rising steeply again. The path moves to the ridge crest for one steep scrambling move, nastily avoidable on a scree runnel down right. Then bouldery clambering leads, in fine style, to the summit cairn of **Ben Lui**.

34A Coire Gaothach Northern Ridge

This ridge can also be considered as the northeast ridge of Ben Lui. It is less interesting than the corrie's southern ridge, as it has no scrambling at all. It may be chosen as a fallback if the southern ridge repels.

Start Follow the previous route into **Coire Gaothach**, and once inside the cosy little corrie, take the path forking up right. It zigzags up to a col southwest of the slight rise of **Stob Garbh.**

Ben Lui's northwest summit looking north towards Ben Nevis

From this col you could drop slightly ahead into the shallow **Coire an Lochain** and cross its rim to ascend Ben Lui's pleasant **northwest ridge** (the descent Route 36, taken uphill). But for the Coire Gaothach ridge, turn up left on the continuing path. It slants out onto the left-hand (southern) face before returning to the crest. This is steep and stony to arrive, suddenly, 30 metres north of the **Northwest Top**. With drops on your left, head around the top of Coire Gaothach to the summit of **Ben Lui**.

35 By Beinn Chuirn

Start	Dalrigh car park off A82
	NN 344291
Distance up	13km/8 miles
Ascent	1450m/4800ft
Approx time up	7hr
Terrain	Grassy hillsides, sometimes steep and rough

The north face of Ben Lui is 600m high, and quite a bit more complex than the map suggests. Making your way up it you could feel like that early party on the Eiger with only a picture postcard of the face for a guide – except that you don't have the picture postcard. But at the crucial entry point (instead of the daring Hinterstoisser Traverse with its irreversible rope moves) a convenient deer path leads sideways between two craggy bits, and above that the line memorised from the hill opposite unfolds without any difficulties. The First Grassfield, the Second Grassfield, lead inexorably to the Waterfall Ramp – except that you get to walk up beside the splashy stuff instead of climbing underwater in a blizzard.

All right, the north face of Ben Lui isn't actually the Last Great Problem in Grassy Hillwalking – but it is just Eigerlike enough to be exciting. Taken with the preliminary Corbett of Beinn Chuirn, followed by the bonus Munros of Oss and Dubhchraig (Route 38 descent) it certainly qualifies you as a hard man or woman, one not cowed by the Calf Mountain.

Start From Dalrigh car park, continue along the overgrown tarmac road with traces of white line and cat's eyes. Just before Drochaid Ban, the **White Bridge**, turn right along the riverside path of the West Highland Way. After 700 metres it reaches a track, with a ford on the left which you can cross if feasible. Otherwise, follow WH Way markers upstream to a track bridge.

Tracks from ford and bridge rejoin to run west, under a railway bridge, and up **Glen Cononish** to Cononish farm with its ugly green roofs. Bear right to avoid entering the farm, then at once turn up right on a track that ascends between two plantations. It zigzags up to the abandoned gold mine, with the **Eas Anie** waterfall above. The track fords the waterfall stream before turning downhill to rejoin the main valley track just west of Cononish. For best photos of the waterfall you'll need to cross the ford, but return across the stream to ascend the steep spur immediately to the right (north) of it. ▶

The spur goes up as grass, then steepens and becomes mixed grass, heather and rock. A very small path may be found. At about the level of the waterfall, two small rock bands cross the spur. Bypass the lower on the left, then slant back right, under the upper rock band. From the

If the waterfall spur is covered in loose snow or is otherwise unattractive, Beinn Chuirn's southeast ridge could be followed from its foot.

One of the waterfalls of Ben Lui's wilderness, the northern flank

spur-crest a mini-rake leads back left through this upper band. Now the ground eases, to join the grassy southeast ridge of Beinn Chuirn.

Crags drop to right of the ridge for the final approach over stony mossland to the cairned summit of **Beinn Chuirn**.

Old iron fenceposts lead down southwest, then south across a wide col to Point 773m (NN 275285). You could descend south from here as the crags marked by the Ordnance Survey are less obstructive than they appear on the map. But it's nicer to head west down a gentle grass ridge for about 1km to a sharp dip. Now turn down left (south) on grassy slopes, passing a few more iron fenceposts. This fence marks the regional boundary as well as the edge of the National Park, though it was ancient and decayed when the park was merely a dream in a bureaucrat's in-tray. It leads down to the wide col at the head of **Allt an Rund**.

The north face of Lui ahead is high and complex. Immediately above are the Ciochan Beinn Laoigh (the rather low-slung 'Tits of Ben Lui'). Slant up left below this crag towards the **Allt Coire an Lochain**. Around 150m (vertical) above you a crag band crosses, with the stream dropping over it in a waterfall. Below this crag, head to the right up the small crag-foot valley, passing below a smaller waterfall, to the little valley's head.

Now a well-marked deer path leads back left along the top of the crag to the smaller waterfall stream. The ground above is now easier. Head up to the left to rejoin the main stream **Allt Coire an Lochain**. Where the stream descends in a small cataract, move out to the right, then rejoin and cross it above the falls and head up to its left to the levelling of **Coire an Lochain** with its small pools. ◀

Turn left across the corrie floor for escape by descent Route 36.

Head up right, onto Ben Lui's pleasant northwest ridge. The ridge is well trodden. It is grassy then becomes slightly rocky with a short scrambling move before arriving at Ben Lui's **Northwest Top**. The highly photogenic but hardly separated Northwest Top was deleted as a Munro Top in 1997. Head round the top of Coire Gaothach to the main summit of **Ben Lui** with its large cairn.

Descent to	Dalrigh car park off A82
	NN 344291
Distance down	11km/6½ miles
Descent	1050m/3500ft
Approx	
time down	3½hr
Terrain	Path by stony ridge and two corries,
	with steep descent into Coire
	Gaothach; then long valley track

This winding way down Ben Lui offers views in various directions, two separate corries, and an alternation of steep sections with short flat bits. It is mostly quite sheltered.

Start From Lui summit follow the pathed ridgeline north-west around the rim of Coire Gaothach, with one small rocky moment avoidable on the left. At the lowest point of the short ridge, a stony path heads down left for Beinn

The scramble moment on Ben Lui's northwest ridge

Route 33A arriving.

a' Chleibh. ◀ But continue ahead bending right, up to **Northwest Top**. It's almost as airy as the true summit.

Continue around the corrie rim for about 30 metres, when a steep spur down right is the corrie's northern ridge. ◀ Here bear left down the pathed northwest ridge. Directly ahead as you descend is Ben Cruachan. On the way down the ridge has a genuine scramble moment, on clean rock with good holds and not exposed.

Route 34A arriving.

At 950m the ridge becomes grassy and less steep. Turn down right, into **Coire an Lochain** with its pools. As a campsite this is breezy even with winds from the south, because of the way Lui projects into the airstream. ◀

On Landranger maps this corrie is unnamed, but marked with a little blue duck.

Cross the corrie rim below the pools, and ease up right to a col on the ridge beyond (Coire Gaothach's northern ridge). In the col, which has a small cairn, you meet a path coming down from the right. Follow it as it descends ahead in zigzags towards **Coire Gaothach**. As it approaches the corrie floor it bends left to join the path in the corrie floor. ◀

Ascent Route 34.

Follow the path as it runs down to left of the stream, dropping steeply out of the corrie. At the valley floor below, it fords the Allt an Rund to the beginning of a bull-dozed track.

Follow the track out along Glen Cononish, passing above **Cononish farm** and alongside River Cononish, to pass under the railway. At a fork, the right branch leads down to a ford, so keep ahead, across a bridge. Where the track turns up left to **Dalrigh** houses, turn off right on the West Highland Way. Follow its waymarks to a ford, and turn left in front of it, for the riverside path downstream to **White Bridge**. Here turn back left on a decayed tarmac road to the car park.

Descent to	Dalrigh car park off A82
	NN 344291
Distance down	12.5km/8 miles
Descent	1000m/3300ft
Approx	
time down	3½hr
Terrain	Grassy ridge, small path, track

Coire Laoigh makes a gentle descent route, and a useful escape from the col between Ben Lui and Ben Oss. The path alongside Allt Coire Laoigh is just large enough to make the walk out a pleasure rather than a trudge.

Start From **Ben Lui**, head down the ridge path southeast. After the levelling at 980m, the ridgeline is less steep and wider, with no particular path. Follow it down south to the **Lui/Oss col**.

Cross the knolly boggy col to its lowest point, just east of a small pool. Descend northwest on a small path found immediately west of a pointy knoll (NN 2745 2465). This gives a comfortably grassy descent, if fairly steep. Descent elsewhere can be more awkward, but not life-or-limb threatening. As the slope eases into **Coire Laoigh** head down to left of the main stream, finding a small but very useful and pleasant path. It runs to left of the stream all the way down the valley below.

As the valley opens out, the wide stream dips to the right past two grassy knolls. Here bear up left across path-less moorland towards the end of a Landrover track. A path forms alongside Allt an Rund stream to a ford and the track's beginning.

Follow the track out along Glen Cononish, passing above **Cononish farm** and alongside River Cononish, to pass under the railway. At a fork, the right branch leads down to a ford, so keep ahead, across a bridge. Where the track turns up left to **Dalrigh** houses, turn off right on the West Highland Way. Follow waymarks to a ford, and turn left in front of it, for the riverside path to **White Bridge**. Here turn back left on the grown-over old road to the car park.

38 Ben Oss,
Beinn Dubhchraig to Dalrigh (descent)

Descent to	Dalrigh car park off A82
	NN 344291
Distance down	15.5km/9½ miles
Ascent	750m/2500ft
Descent	1700m/5700ft
Approx time down	
	6hr
Terrain	Small paths

The steeper routes on Ben Lui are better taken in ascent, in which case the two lower Munro summits will be taken (if at all) on the way down. So this route simply reverses Route 33. At the end of the long day, the descent of Beinn Dubhchraig is long but pleasantly gentle and grassy.

Start From **Ben Lui**, head down the ridge path southeast. After the levelling at 980m, the ridgeline is less steep and wider, with no particular path. Follow it down south to the **Lui/Oss col**.

Pick up the small path again to rise gently east up the opposite slope, then more steeply above, turning north. The ground levels at 1000m, with the cairn of **Ben Oss** 200 metres further on.

Descend the ridge north–northeast on a clear path for 800 metres, to a little col at 910m (NN 289258).

In mist it's easiest to continue over the following ridge hump (941m) and descend steeply east to the **Oss/Dubhchraig col**. In clear conditions it's pleasanter to bypass this hump. The little 910m col is a double one, with a cairn in the first, western, dip. Here turn down right, soon finding a stream and descending to right of it, southeast. Skirt a boggy patch, and just below it, at 810m altitude, find a path crossing the stream. Turn left on this, around the slope and into the **Oss/Dubhchraig col** (Bealach Buidhe).

The small clear path now climbs east to a levelling of the ridge with two pools, then more steeply southeast to the summit of **Beinn Dubhchraig**.

In poor conditions you can simply descend the spur northeast to the fence at the top of plantations, and follow it to the left to join **Allt Coire Dubhchraig.** But pleasanter is to backtrack northeast for 800 metres to the ridge pools, and head down north on a gentle grassy ridge. As the ridge levels off at 650m, slant down to the right (east) to join **Allt Coire Dubhchraig**. A small path is to left of the stream and follows it down through beautiful woodland of birch and pine.

At the confluence with the **River Cononish**, cross a moderately safe footbridge on the right, and follow the river down towards the viaduct of the West Highland Railway. Turn right alongside the railway to join a track which crosses it on a bridge. Follow the track down, alongside the railway at first, to the Drochaid Ban (**White Bridge**) over the River Falloch. Cross it on the tarred lane that leads to the car park.

39 Descent to Dalmally

Descent to	A85 at Corryghoil NN 194275
Distance down	12km/7½ miles
Descent	1200m/4000ft
Ascent	150m/500ft
Approx time down	
	3½hr
Terrain	Pathless grass, forest tracks

The desire to descend Ben Lui to Dalmally will probably only arise in the minds of backpackers heading for Cruachan, Glen Kinglass, Fort William and further. The route is scenic and straightforward, and is the only natural way to acquire the side Munro Beinn a' Chleibh (Hill of the Sword, which is indeed slung on the hip of Ben Lui).

Start From **Ben Lui** drop slightly northwest to the low point at the head of Coire Gaothach, but don't continue towards the Northwest Top. Turn left on a rough path that runs down southwest, rather steeply to start with, on a poorly defined hill spur. Keep ahead on the narrower ridgeline across the 776m Chleibh col, for the gentler rise to **Beinn a' Chleibh**.

Head northwest along the summit plateau for 500 metres, then turn southwest down a gentle ridge to about 700m altitude, before turning down the steep southwest flank. Pass down to left of plantations, and turn into the trees in the gap under power lines. A damp quad bike track is found.

The track dodges left into the trees, then rejoins the power-line gap at a wide, smooth, new forest road. Cross this, and continue downhill under the power lines as they dip towards the **Allt Coire Lair**. Just before this stream is a small wind-powered installation (my notes refer to it, with writerly precision, as a 'thingie'). Here an old track turns off right, into the trees. Follow this down through attractive woodland, past **Succoth Lodge** and under the railway, to turn right on a wider track and reach the **A85** 2km east of Glenview.

THE WEST

PART SIX
BEN LOMOND

Descending the Ptarmigan Ridge of Ben Lomond with Beinn Narnain and Ben Ime above (Route 40)

Ben Lomond by its south ridge is an easy ascent, as easy as any 3000ft-er in Scotland. It has very beautiful views of its loch and, eventually, of the whole of the National Park and north to Ben Nevis; the contrasting views southwards over the Lowland Valley are just as good. Even so, this would not be Scotland's second-most popular hill if it weren't so close to the M9 and Glasgow – and if it weren't for that song about the Bonnie Banks.

This standard route does make an excellent descent, with its un-demanding path allowing full attention to the views. Route 40 will combine it with the Ptarmigan, a route up on proper ridges rather than that broad slope. Route 42 is a vigorous full day along the loch side and up rough untrodden northern slopes.

The section ends with two must-do midget hills. Conic Hill is well pathed and interestingly rocky. The Kilmaronock Dumpling is as huge as its name suggests, that is to say not at all, but the view from the summit makes it the most compelling 20-minute ascent in Scotland.

40 Ben Lomond: South Ridge and Ptarmigan

Length

Difficulty

Start/finish	Rowardennan Pier (Ben Lomond car park) NS 359986
Distance	10.5km/6½ miles
Ascent	1050m/3500ft
Approx time	5½hr
Max altitude	Ben Lomond 974m
Terrain	Hill paths, steep and mildly rocky on the northwest ridge
Map	LR 56; Explorer 364; Harvey *Loch Lomond*

Ben Lomond is Scotland's most popular mountain, unless perhaps Ben Nevis is even busier. The Ben Lomond Path, straight up and down from Rowardennan, is demanding on the leg muscles but otherwise slightly uninteresting – until it reaches the summit cone at 750m. Then it steepens, and the final 500 metres are along a rather sharp ridge that's exposed to wind and weather. This stretch may disconcert the inexperienced walker who thought it would be as warm as it was down at the loch side.

More ambitious or experienced walkers will take the interesting ascent route by the Ptarmigan. The path is smaller; the approach to the mountain is a ridgeline rather than a slope. Finally, the northwest ridge is real mountain ground, steep and with drops on either side, where the hand will touch rock here and there. That ridgeline may occasionally surprise you with some old, hard-frozen snow. Up the Ptarmigan and down the Ben Lomond Path is the suggested direction, to take the more demanding ridge uphill, and to enjoy in descent the BLP's gentler gradients.

For a considerably higher dose of loneliness and exhaustion, take the roundabout Route 42.

Ben Lomond Path straight up and down
(plus Ptarmigan Ridge descent option)

The Ben Lomond Path needs little description. It **starts** immediately above the swoop-roofed **National Park hut**, waymarked 'Ben Lomond Hill Path'. Wide and well built, it runs up through plantations. These have recently been clear-felled for fine views along Loch Lomond. After crossing a track and then a brief rocky moment, the path reaches a kissing gate at the plantation top, with another gate, 1km later, on open moorland at the 400m contour.

The path runs up the broad slope, with the views behind as the redeeming feature. At 800m the slope steepens harshly, to the final 500 metres of summit ridge. This section is quite airy, around the rim of **Coire a' Bhathaich**, with the wide path slightly below the crest on the left (western) side.

Ptarmigan Ridge descent

The crowds **descend** by the same route. If you impulsively decide to go Ptarmigan instead ▶ then descend the steep northwest ridge ahead to a shoulder at 750m. (This is the first place where the descent stops being steep, and the ridge even rises to a slight knoll NN 3625 0310). Here turn sharply back left, southwest, and follow the small but mostly clear path along the **Ptarmigan** ridge. Below the 600m contour the path eases down onto the right-hand flank, to rejoin the true spur line almost at its foot, below the **Sput Ban** waterfall. It then runs down to the West Highland Way track directly below. Turn left back to Rowardennan.

Ptarmigan uphill is the recommended direction – see below.

Ptarmigan Ridge ascent

From Rowardennan Pier **start** along the shoreline, on a wide path that passes a granite ring war memorial

On Ben Lomond's southeast ridge, overlooking Coire a'Bhathaich

The final steps to the summit on Ben Lomond's southeast ridge, overlooking Coire a'Bhathaich

then joins the track of the West Highland Way. At the entrance track of Rowardennan Youth Hostel this forks right, then keeps left at another fork just above. In another 300 metres the track passes **Ben Lomond Cottage** (actually a large-ish house, 'Rowchnock' on some maps). Immediately afterwards it crosses a wide stream. Turn up to left of this stream on a small path, passing through a gateway and then a kissing gate above.

With a fence on its right, the path eases away from the stream. It is small but well repaired, with well-designed zigzags. (Please don't short-cut as this will create stream lines to erode the path.) At 150m altitude the path reaches a shoulder, with the waterfall **Sput Ban** above. The path slants up to left of this, and runs below (on the left side of) the spur above.

At 600m altitude the path finally reaches the spur line, and follows it as it becomes a pleasant hummocky ridge. This ridgeline bends round to the right, running northeast, to a shoulder at 750m below Ben Lomond's steep northwest ridge.

The small, loose, zigzag path heads up this steep-sided and mildly rocky spur. At 850m the ridge steepening is aided by good handholds in rocks alongside the

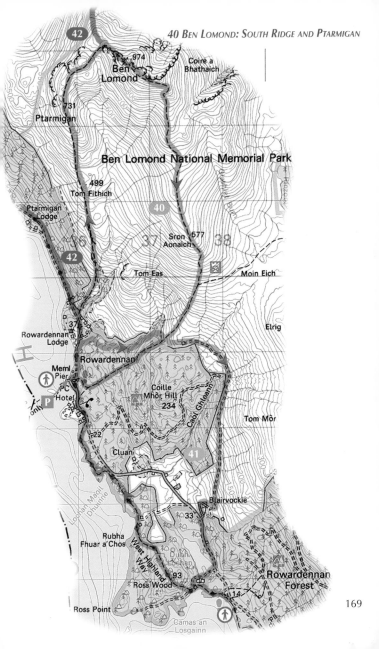

path. The emergence at **Ben Lomond summit** is sudden, with the trig pillar a few metres ahead.

Ben Lomond Path descent is along the almost level ridgeline ahead, with steep drops left into Coire a' Bhathaich, and the wide path just down to right of the crest. After 500 metres the path heads down the steepish slope on the right, to the broad moorland shoulder below.

The well-built and usually busy path descends gentle slopes southwards. At 550m it steepens somewhat, and at 400m it passes through a kissing gate.

At 200m a second gate leads into clear-felled plantations. ◄ The final descent now has fine views up the loch.

Route 41 keeps uphill here for an add-on wander above and beside the loch.

Note If the views aren't sufficient distraction from your battered toes, then the path bed has glacier-smoothed bedrock which in at least one place shows scratch-marks from the stones embedded in the moving ice. Also, above and below the forest road crossing, the path bed is dark, friable volcanic rock quite different from the stripy grey schist of the rest of the walk. That dark rock may well be a basalt dyke extruded by the Mull Volcano, 80km away and 50 million years in the past. By the time you've made up your mind on the plausibility of that one, the car park has appeared below you.

41 Lomond Slopes

Length

Difficulty

Start/finish	Sallochy Wood car park NS 380957
Distance	11km/7 miles
Ascent	400m/1300ft
Approx time	3¾hr
Max altitude	Sheepfold 250m
Terrain	Paths and tracks, with an avoidable pathless wood
Map	LR 56; Explorer 364; Harvey *Loch Lomond*

Loch Lomond shores, a waterfall hidden in the woods, and then a high-level farm track for the wider views – the only drawback to this walk is the clear-felling above Rowardennan, which may have opened out the views but has also broken the old woodland paths. The alternative ascent from Rowardennan is on the well-built and busy Ben Lomond Path (Route 40): this eliminates the difficulty but also the waterfall. Even without waterfall this is a satisfying walk beside and above the loch.

During the first half of the morning, the 1km road section may be busy with cars heading to Ben Lomond. To avoid that traffic – or at least be facing into its afternoon equivalent – you could start and end the walk at Rowardennan (as Route 40).

With Loch Lomond on your left, **start** across a footbridge at the car park corner, on the West Highland Way. After 300 metres it passes a boathouse and small pier, and joins a track. ▶ After 150 metres turn up right on the WH Way path, for a sharp climb over a wooded hill. The path drops through open pinewoods, with views up Loch Lomond, and rejoins the loch shore at **Mill of Ross**, where it crosses a long footbridge.

This is the track from the Scottish Ecology Centre, used at the end of the walk.

In another 700 metres the path almost meets the road on the right, then bends left along the shore-line. In another kilometre it joins the road, to pass the Rowardennan Hotel to the Ben Lomond car park at **Rowardennan Pier**. ▶

Follow the shoreline past the pier, and along a wide path with a granite ring war memorial. The path then joins a track, the WH Way again, towards Rowardennan Youth Hostel.

To avoid the rough woodland paths ahead, you could now head up the Ben Lomond Path to the plantation top (Route 40).

Around 50 metres before the youth hostel, the track crosses a stream at the loch side. Turn up right on a small path to left of the stream, through oak woods. After 300 metres you cross a side-branch of a stream that runs down to the left, where the steam divides. ▶ Here is a red-topped waymarker, and above it the path vanishes into brushwood left by clear-felling. So we shall now leave it.

Such a side-branch of a dividing stream is called a 'distributary'.

Contour to the left, passing a power-line pole, and crossing a short band of brushwood to reach open birchwood. The **Ardess Burn** is now below on your left. Head up in the strip of surviving birchwood between the stream and the clear-felled area; there are paths some of the time. Soon you pass an impressive waterfall in the Ardess Burn.

At the top of the wood cross a fence at its water-gate over the burn. Turn right, up a rough path, next to the fence. Go straight past the kissing gate on the Ben Lomond Path, continuing above the clear fell and a last scrap of the plantation. Ignore a handsome stile on the right at the fence's high point, and instead slant away to the left to a wide gate 50 metres away. Here is the top of a farm track.

Follow the track around the hillside, then gradually downhill above the plantations. It has several gates, which should be refastened carefully (or else climbed over at the hinge end). If cattle are feeding on the track, it's best to avoid them and the resulting slurry by taking to the hillside above. The track leads down through **Blairvockie farm** onto its tarred driveway and the road below.

Turn left for 1km. Past **Dubh Lochan**, turn right on the tarred track to the Scottish Ecology Centre. Keep to right of the buildings onto a dirt track, to reach the loch shore at the small pier. Turn left, back along the WH Way, to the car park.

42 The Back of Ben Lomond

Length

Difficulty

Start/finish	Rowardennan Pier (Ben Lomond car park) NS 359987
Distance	19.5km/12½ miles
Ascent	1300m/4300ft
Approx time	8½hr
Max altitude	Ben Lomond 974m
Terrain	Paths, pathless moor, steep ridge
Map	LR 56; Explorer 364; Harvey *Loch Lomond*

Combine Ben Lomond with a big chunk of Loch Lomond, on the more rugged version of the West Highland Way. This is a long outing over various different sorts of country – woodland, mountain and moor – among which the rough moorland crossing to Cruinn a' Bheinn is a bit of a harsh plod even in summer, and under soft snow will be truly nasty.

For more serious hillwalkers, this is the quiet way onto Scotland's second busiest hill.

Start along the shoreline, on a wide path that passes a granite ring war memorial then joins the track of the West Highland Way. This forks right at the entrance track of Rowardennan Youth Hostel, then keeps left at another fork just above. The track joins the shoreline, then forks up right at the entrance track to **Ptarmigan Lodge**.

After passing above the lodge, look out for a path turning steeply down left to the shoreline: this is the more rugged version of the West Highland Way, the easier way continuing along the track ahead. On the rugged path, a first waymarker is met at the loch shore below. The path follows the shore. It is small and unrepaired, with

Ben Lomond's northern side, seen from Beinn Dubh of the Luss Hills (Route 48)

Map continues
opposite

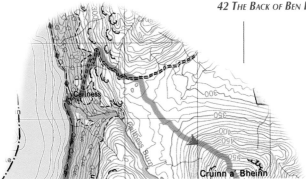

Map continued from p174

boggy bits, and occasional steps on bare rock, which tends to be damp and slippery with leaf mould. So while the going is enjoyable, it will also be fairly slow.

After 3km the Cobbler appears in spectacular silhouette across Loch Lomond, and the path starts to have been improved. It climbs a little away from the loch, and runs through a spruce plantation. Here a short side-path runs down left to **Rowchoish bothy**, a rainproof but probably not midgeproof shelter. The main path runs on for 500 metres to rejoin the track above.

Follow the track ahead, gently downhill, and diminishing to a wide path. It joins the shoreline for a long footbridge over Cailness Burn. Above is the white-painted **Cailness cottage**. Turn up to pass to right of the cottage to the track beyond. Head up this steep rough track with several zigzags, and where it reaches level moorland keep on along it for another 400 metres to its highest point.

Turn off right, taking the highest line across fairly rough and wet moorland towards Cruinn a' Bheinn (pronounced Crinaven, the 'Round Hill'). Join a deer fence arriving from the right, and cross it where convenient (for example at an earthen ramp). The fence then leads you up through a grassy band in the steepening of the hill at 550m.

From **Cruinn a' Bheinn** summit descend south, weaving about to avoid some small outcrops, to the col

Descending the Ptarmigan Ridge of Ben Lomond

Bealach Cruinn a' Bheinn. Head up the mostly gentle spur beyond, crossing a low fence at the shoulder 670m altitude, to reach the knoll (768m) at the foot of Ben Lomond's steep northwest ridge.

As on Route 40, head up the small, loose, zigzag path that takes you up this steep-sided and mildly rocky spur. At 850m the steepening is aided by good hand-holds in the rock alongside the path. The emergence at **Ben Lomond** summit is sudden, with the trig pillar a few metres ahead.

Descend by the main path ahead, as on Route 40 (Ben Lomond Path descent).

Start/finish	Balmaha car park NS 420909
Distance	5.5km/3½ miles
Ascent	350m/1200ft
Approx time	2¼hr
Max altitude	Conic Hill 361m
Terrain	Paths, mostly wide and clear, but some steep and some bare rock
Map	LR 56; Explorer 347

Length

Difficulty

Conic will be appreciated for its small size and its great views of Loch Lomond. It is not a lot less popular than Ben Lomond, and probably gives more aggregate satisfaction than that rather tough trek.

But is it a hill in the Highlands? The answer has to be that it is not. You scramble over the distinctive pinkish puddingstone, or conglomerate, of the so-called 'Old Red Sandstone'. This is a Lowland rock, and despite its name is much, much younger than the Highland schists that start a mile further up the loch beyond Arrochymore Point. In between is the 'Highland Border Complex', and you'll get a look at these odd orange-tinted rocks on the way down.

Start at the large car park, with toilets, at the National Park Centre in Balmaha. To left of the National Park Centre two large samples symbolise the Highland boundary: grey, squiggly schist with quartz streaks, and rounded, reddish-brown Old Red Sandstone.

The West Highland Way runs at the back of the car park. Turn right along its wide, smooth track, and after 300 metres turn left on a wide, smooth path. It runs up through plantations, with steps here and there, to a kissing gate onto open hill. The puddingstone lump of Conic Hill rises above. The path, now more rugged, winds around the flank of **Tom nan Oisgean** (Hummock of the Ewes) to the col between it and Conic Hill. This is Bealach Ard, with a waymark post and a view up Loch Lomond.

At the col a small path zigzags up right, onto the ridge of Conic Hill. Follow the ridge crest, with one steeper section eroded down to bare rock, to the summit of **Conic Hill.**

Note Looking back southwest, you'll see that the ridgeline continues as a line of four islands across the loch. These are often taken as marking the Highland boundary though, strictly, they are the tough puddingstone that forms the extreme northern edge of the Lowlands. In clear weather you can follow the boundary line onwards towards the distant isle of Arran, whose northern half lies in the Highlands.

Conic Hill, from Luss Pier

Descent Return southwest for 20 metres to the first small col, where a well-used path slants down to the right. It joins the WH Way below the steep flank of Conic Hill. Follow it down, along the base of the steeper hill, to **Bealach Ard**.

At exactly the point where you left the WH Way on the upward walk, you leave it again now. Bear right, onto a small path down a small, well-defined ridgeline. This ridgeline lies parallel to, and just to north of, the true downward continuation of Conic Hill's ridge. Follow the ridge path downhill. After 200 metres, the ridgeline is off-set to the right by 20 metres.

Note As you cross the little grassy gully, you may notice the difference in the rocks on either side. On the south side, the ridge you're leaving is the sandstone conglomerate of the Lowlands; on the north side is an orange-black rock with sheared fragments of white limestone in it. This is the Highland Border Complex, which as its name suggests is a messy mix-up, but the dark component is from the deep ocean floor.

Follow the dark-rock ridge down to its steep end, where the path heads down to the right, through gorse then hawthorn. It passes through a muddy wood to emerge through a ramshackle gate onto the road.

Cross diagonally left, thus passing over a small stream. An open field leads down to the shore and the WH Way. Turn left along the shore path. The first rocks you see are Lowland ones, brownish sandstone, though just beyond is a surprise intrusion of grey volcanic rock (with holes that were originally gas bubbles, refilled with white calcite since the rocks were deposited). Follow the wide loch-side path – the WH Way forks up left to visit the viewpoint at Craigie Fort, but staying on the shoreline leads to a footbridge over a bit of the loch and a rocky terrace to **Balmaha Pier**. Follow the lane, and a roadside footpath, to the car park.

ROCK NOTES (SEE ALSO APPENDIX 1)

Three major fault lines run right across Scotland: the Southern Upland Fault, the Highland Boundary Fault and the Great Glen. They were formed at the Caledonian continental collision that brought Scotland into contact with England (400 million years ago, in the Devonian period). England was travelling north, but Scotland arrived slantwise, drifting southwest. Thus various lumps of Scotland slid past each other before everything finally ground to a halt some 50 million years later.

The rounded pebbles in the Conic Hill puddingstone (or 'conglomerate') are whitish quartzite and purplish volcanic rocks. They were probably washed down by flash floods out of mountains that soon afterwards slid away westwards along the fault line.

The puddingstone meets the Highland Border Complex at one of the many fault lines. Movement along the fault line has shattered the rocks, resulting in the little grassy gully crossed on the descent from Conic Hill. This means that the actual fault line has been eroded away and covered over with grass.

The black-orange rocks seen on the descent are not continental at all, but oceanic crust, and so have been squeezed upwards by several kilometres. Contact with the air has broken them down into serpentinite which, when freshly exposed, is greenish and slippery-smooth. That rock is best seen along the loch shore at Arrochymore Point (or on Route 4, above Aberfoyle). It has acted as a lubricant, encouraging the smash and mangle of the Highland Border Complex.

Big view from small hill: Loch Lomond from Duncryne

44 Duncryne

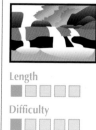

Start/finish	Gartocharn NS 428863
Distance	3km/1½ miles
Ascent	95m/300ft
Approx time	1hr
Max altitude	Duncryne 142m
Terrain	Minor road and earth path
Map	LR 56; Explorer 347

Length
■ □ □ □ □

Difficulty
■ □ □ □ □

A walk of 3km with half that distance being on tarmac; with 95m of ascent; whose single path is an access agreement, so there's not even a different path to come down by; to bag a hill nicknamed the Dumpling. The point of it all is apparent on your final steps to the trig point as there suddenly appears the wide and wonderful view of Loch Lomond. Stretched behind the islands are the Luss Hills, the Cobbler, the Arrochar Alps, Ben Vorlich at the loch's head, Ben Lomond and Conic Hill.

The Dumpling, despite its name, is not made of puddingstone; it is the vent-plug of an ancient volcano. All the basalt lavas that form the flat landscape of the Campsie Fells and Kilpatricks may have emerged out of the earth at this point.

Start at the northeast (Drymen) end of Gartocharn, with roadside parking opposite the end of Duncryne Road. Go up Duncryne Road, with Duncryne rising ahead on the left. A tarred lay-by on the left offers parking for a couple of cars, and here a gate leads into woodland.

181

Duncryne, known as the Dumpling, is the very small hill beyond the loch, with the Kilpatrick Hills behind it

A slightly muddy path leads up through the wood, then crosses a field between two fences to the base of the hill. After a kissing gate, the path winds up through bracken, right then back left, to the trig point at the summit.

45 Bonnie Banks by Boat

Start	Rowardennan Pier NS 359986
Finish	Inversnaid Pier NN 336088
Distance	13km/8 miles
Ascent	200m/600ft
Approx time	4hr
Max altitude	75m
Terrain	Path mostly well surfaced, with 4km (avoidable) rough and awkward
Local transport	Cruise Loch Lomond ferry
Map	LR 56; Explorer 364; Harvey *Loch Lomond*

Length

Difficulty

Cruise Loch Lomond's boat service *West Highland Way Explorer* out of Tarbet takes you to Rowardennan in the morning and recovers you from Inversnaid at teatime. It is timed to allow you 5hr for this walk. The loch views are even better in winter, but in summer the leaves keep out some of the noise of the A82 on the other side. The path is good, though it does have many small ascents and drops. But as 4hr is the calculated time for the walk, the ferry company's 5hr should be plenty.

For a longer hike all the way to Inverarnan – and more complicated connecting services – see Route 46.

Start along the shoreline, on a wide path that passes a granite ring war memorial then joins the track of the West Highland Way. This forks right at the entrance track of Rowardennan Youth Hostel, then keeps left at another fork just above. The track joins the shoreline, then forks

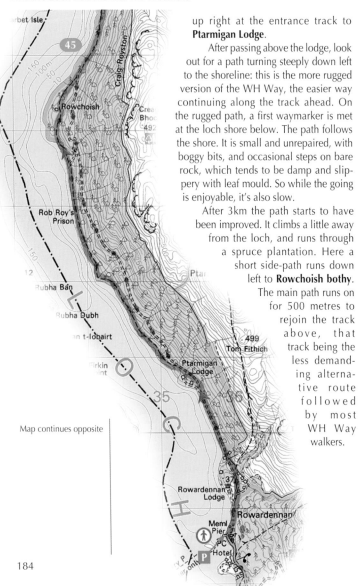

up right at the entrance track to **Ptarmigan Lodge**.

After passing above the lodge, look out for a path turning steeply down left to the shoreline: this is the more rugged version of the WH Way, the easier way continuing along the track ahead. On the rugged path, a first waymarker is met at the loch shore below. The path follows the shore. It is small and unrepaired, with boggy bits, and occasional steps on bare rock, which tends to be damp and slippery with leaf mould. So while the going is enjoyable, it's also slow.

After 3km the path starts to have been improved. It climbs a little away from the loch, and runs through a spruce plantation. Here a short side-path runs down left to **Rowchoish bothy**. The main path runs on for 500 metres to rejoin the track above, that track being the less demanding alternative route followed by most WH Way walkers.

Map continues opposite

On the West Highland Way south of Inversnaid

Follow the track ahead, gently downhill, and diminishing to a wide path. It joins the shoreline for a long footbridge over Cailness Burn. Above is the white-painted **Cailness cottage**.

The following stretch of the WH Way is a particularly pleasant one, on a well-made path that weaves among the oak trees and is occasionally slightly rocky and rugged. After 3km the buildings of **Inversnaid** are visible through trees ahead. The path ascends towards the footbridge above the Inversnaid Waterfall, celebrated in the poem by Gerard Manley Hopkins.

Map continued from p184

185

A windpuff-bonnet of fawn-froth
Turns and twindles over the broth
Of a pool so pitchblack, fell-frowning,
It rounds and rounds Despair to drowning.

To view the falls, descend left before the footbridge. Then cross the high footbridge above the waterfall, and descend to left of the hotel to the ferry pier, which gives a slightly different angle on the waterfall.

If you should have missed the ferry back to Tarbet, the hotel's own small ferry runs to Inveruglas, with a late evening Citylink coach down the A82.

46 The Bonny Banks (north)

Length

Difficulty

Start	Inversnaid Pier NN 336088
Finish	Inverarnan Hotel NN 317184
Distance	13.5km/8½ miles
Ascent	350m/1200ft
Approx time	4–4½hr
Max altitude	RSPB Trail 100m
Terrain	Waymarked path, notably more rugged and bumpy than any other part of the WH Way
Map	LR 56; Explorer 364; Harvey *Crianlarich* and *Loch Lomond*
Local transport	See details below
OS Map extract	See map for Route 26 on pages 123–124

North of Inversnaid, to Inverarnan, the shoreline of Loch Lomond steepens along the flank of Beinn a' Choin. Here Rob Roy lurked below a pile of boulders; here the oakwoods remained undisturbed until such time as the RSPB arrived to construct their short woodland trail. The path here dodges and clambers over rocks and tree roots, and can be a distressing shock to walkers on the West Highland Way wondering if such savagery will continue

Inversnaid Falls, below the footbridge on the West Highland Way

all the way to Fort William. (In fact it ends at Doune Byre bothy, 3km ahead.)

The ruggedness shouldn't bother one-day walkers with light packs and plenty of time. Take the morning coach from Inverarnan to Tarbet (Scottish Citylink, 10.38 on the current timetable) in time for the 'Inversnaid Explorer' (currently departs 11.30). For the full **A' the way** experience (below), take the early morning bus (08.36) and catch the 'West Highland Way Explorer' at 10.00.

Alternatively, for either expedition, park at Tarbet, and once arrived at Inverarnan pass time in the bar or restaurant until the late evening bus (currently 20.43). Note also the ferry Ardleish to Ardlui, allowing the possibility, until 7.30pm (high summer timetable) of pulling out before the final 4km of it all. Bear in mind that the path gets less easy towards the end, and keep going steadily – or else, as the 'Bonny Banks' song itself warns, nightfall may catch you out

> In yon shady glen,
> On the steep, steep side of Ben Lomond,
> Where in purple hue
> The Highland hills we view,
> And the moon coming out in the gloaming.

From Inversnaid to Inverarnan the route follows the lochside and the West Highland waymarkers. **Route details** are the same as for the second part of Route 26 (Beinn a' Choin). See Route 26 map on pages 123–124. Once at the corner of Beinglas campsite, turn left around a field edge beside a stream, then up River Falloch, which is crossed by the campsite track. Turn left on a roadside footpath for 400 metres to Inverarnan.

A' the way, which combines Routes 45 and 46 for a walk of oakwoods from Rowardennan to Inverarnan, is 26.5km/16½ miles with 550m/1800ft of ascent – allow 8hr. Note that the walk passes bothies at Rowchoish and Doune Byre.

PART 7
LOCH LOMOND WEST

The southeast slope of Beinn a' Mhanaich (Route 47)

The west side of Loch Lomond isn't just for looking across at Ben Lomond. The Luss Hills, though technically part of the Highlands, have a character of their own. They're quite unlike the lumps of peat and heather that make up most of Graham's Table of the hills of 2000–2500ft (610–762m). Instead they're go-able grass, from the loch shores right up their steep sides to their gently rounded tops. The place they most resemble is the Howgills of eastern Cumbria – apart from having a whole lot more water all around.

Further north, Cruach Tairbeirt is more typically heathery, and with sides draped in ugly spruce. But because of the plantation paths, the heathery struggle only starts at the 250m mark – and stops again at 475m because that's the top. The final Lomondside mountain is Ben Vorlich which, as an Arrochar Alp, is in the following section.

One day, maybe, there will be ferries on Loch Lomond that really are ferries rather than pleasure cruises for the sedentary. (The National Park Authority might like to inspect the timetable for Ullswater or Derwentwater.) With the boats and buses as they are, it is possible to combine boats and boots along two sections of the lake-shore path – they are listed earlier under Ben Lomond, but the western side is where you get to them from. The oakwoods, lake views and good paths well repay the struggle with the timetable.

47 Luss Hills South

Length

■ ■ ■ □ □

Difficulty

■ ■ □ □ □

Start/finish	Reservoir track foot, Glen Fruin NS 276905
Distance	12km/7½ miles
Ascent	1000m/3300ft
Approx time	5½hr
Max altitude	Beinn Chaorach 713m
Terrain	Grassy slopes and ridges
Map	LR 56; Expl 347

Note Land immediately west of this walk is MoD firing range – see below.

Beinn Chaorach is the hill of the sheep. The Blackface breed was introduced to Highland hills here beside Loch Lomond, and overgrazing ever since has given these ridges their short, walkable grass. These two hills at the western edge look along Glen Luss towards Loch Lomond, southwards to the sea lochs of Cowal and across the Clyde. Downwards there's a view of a different kind, onto the military installations of the Gare Loch.

Very recent OS mapping marks a 'danger area' across the upper part of Auchengaich glen and the valley gap between the two hills of this walk. The range master at Garelochhead Training Range (as well as the warning notices on the hill) reveal that this expansion eastward of the firing range has not, in fact, taken place. **Note though that the west side of the Strone ridge does lie inside the live firing range. It is important not to stray onto this western side of the ridge while descending from Beinn a' Mhanaich.** It would be difficult to do this by accident, as the warning signs at the edge of the range are large, closely spaced and obvious. A red flag flies at the foot of the ridge (NS 270908) near the start of the walk on days when firing is happening. In this case, rather than risk straying off the route you may prefer to descend Beinn a' Mhanaich by the ascent route and return down Auchengaich Burn.

Confusingly, A817 appears on maps as B817, or on old maps as an unclassified minor road. Where it crosses Auchengaich Burn, a tarred track heads uphill. A small parking area is 30 metres up this track.

There is also convenient parking on the old and very small road 400 metres downhill, near its bridge over Auchengaich Burn. From 300 metres to the east, a roughly tarred track leads up to the A817.

Start over a locked gate and on up the track, which leads towards a reservoir. After about 700 metres, as the track levels off, head up to the right. There are gaps in the bracken leading up onto the steeper grass slope of **Auchengaich Hill** (Auchinvennel Hill on Harvey maps).

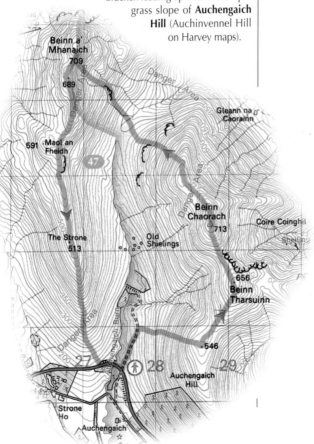

191

Heading north to Beinn Tharsuinn and Beinn Chaorach, over the Luss Hills in autumn brown

The flat grass summit has no cairn. A small path leads northeast across a slight col and up to the cairn on **Beinn Tharsuinn**. The path continues northwest, soon joining a ridgeline fence that leads up to the cairn and trig point of **Beinn Chaorach**.

Descent The fence continues northwest over a minor hump, then briefly down north, before turning down left into the broad col before Beinn a' Mhanaich. The fence zigzags in the low saddle, so before the slope foot bear down right, to cross the saddle and rejoin the fence at its next corner (NS 276938). The fence guides up the spur to right of a stream gully (this is the left-hand of two little gullies in this face of Beinn a' Mhanaich). At the slope top, head up briefly right to the summit cairn of **Beinn a' Mhanaich**. ◄

Ben a' Vannich, 'Hill of the Monk'

A small path leads south, over a gate where the fence crosses the ridgeline, and then along a grassy ridge. After 1km the ridgeline dips right to a wide col. On the hump beyond, **Maol an Fheidh** (the Boggy Hump), you see the first warning notices of the MoD ranges on the western slopes, and Maol an Fheidh itself is out of bounds. The ridge path skirts to left of the forbidden hump. It continues down the long ridge, passing immediately to left of all the range boundary warning notices.

After a level section called **The Strone**, the ridge descends gently, still southwards. Above the A817 it passes a flagpole, then reaches a gate in a fence. Continue directly downhill, or bear down left on coarser, rushy ground, to reach the A817 to right of its bridge over **Auchengaich Burn**. As the burn is in a small gorge, the road bridge is the best way to cross it to the foot of the reservoir track.

48 Luss Hills: Dubh and Doune

Start/finish	Luss NS 359932
Distance	21km/13 miles
Ascent	1500m/5100ft
Approx time	9hr
Max altitude	Doune Hill 734m
Terrain	Grassy ridges and hilltops
Map	LR 56; Expl 364

Length

Difficulty

The Luss hills are grassy-green, and do not even reach the Corbett height of 2500ft (782m). So walkers mostly ignore them. This may be a mistake; the Luss heights have an atmosphere all their own, made up of elegant ridgelines, easy going underfoot, and deep winding hollows sprinkled with oak trees. The views are long (as well as of Loch Long) of both Lomond and Lowlands; and they are as striking visually as they are in their alliteration.

But for baggers of summits, Luss has one unique feature. Here a strong walker can achieve eight Grahams in a day, without any interference from higher Corbetts and Munros. Anywhere else at all, even a three-Graham day is a remarkable tally. The Luss Grahams are a tough day, it's true; but if you do end up doing Beinn Dubh in the dark, the path is good and Ben Lomond is a fine sight by starlight. On this walk we'll do just three, to add to the two in Route 45.

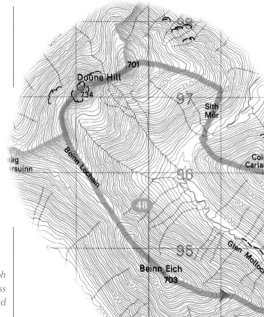

*On Beinn Dubh
above Glen Luss
and Loch Lomond*

Luss village car park is pricey for an all-day ticket (and who carries £7 in coins anyway?). Lay-bys are either side of the village on the A82. A small pull-off is at the start of the Glen Luss road (NS 356932) beside a footpath signpost. **Start** at Luss Pier, which has a beautiful view along the loch to Ben Lomond. Head into the village past rose-covered cottages, then turn right towards the car park. Pass to left of it, and cross the Luss link road (former A82) into a short cul-de-sac with an

ancient signpost for Glen Luss. It ends at steps leading up to a footbridge over A82.

Keep ahead to a kissing gate, and at once turn right over a stile onto the base of Beinn Dubh. Go up to a gate with a stile, where a wide track leads up through bracken. At about 300m the ridge levels off and becomes boggy; the path is now more sketchy. The ridge continues upwards. A fence reaches the ridgeline: the path runs up to left of it, then crosses it by a stile. From the **first**

Beinn Dubh continue along the flat peaty plateau, bending round left to reach the second and main **Beinn Dubh** (657m, named as Coire na h-Eanachan on Landranger maps).

Note As a footnote to the history of hill lists, the 2000 to 2499ft-ers are named Grahams after Fiona Graham who allowed her list of such to be subsumed into a pre-existing list compiled by Alan Dawson. Among her stipulations were that the list be named after her not him, and that Mid Hill be named in Gaelic not English. Normally a nameless hill takes over the nearest bit of writing on the map, 'Mid Hill' being the shoulder to the southwest. Here, though, it borrowed Beinn Dubh from the more distant, but Gaelic, southeastern outlier.

For a shorter day just follow this ridge path down southeast to Glenmollochan farm.

A small path descends southwest for 400 metres onto the shoulder called **Mid Hill**. Here the ridge and path turn left but turn off down to the right, northwest, onto a lower spur. ◀ This steepens with a few peat hags to reach the broad valley col, with a few scattered trees, between Beinn Dubh and Doune Hill.

Slant up to the right, to find a shepherd's path running up Doune Hill's eastern spur. The odd little groove and crag formation, presumably a landslip, is named Sith Mor or the 'Big Fairy'. Once above the bracken of the lowest slope the path is no longer needed and disappears. Head up onto the northeastern top (unnamed, 701m). A path leads down into a col, and up to the trig point on **Doune Hill**.

Various MoD structures in the hollow to the northwest are unmarked on maps. The UK's nuclear submarines are based at Faslane on the Gare Loch, a few miles away.

Descend the grassy ridge southwest to the slight rise of **Beinn Lochain**.

Note Graham-baggers will now divert to the grass hump of Cruach an t-Sidhein, the 'Fairies' Stack'. It's easy enough to contour back round from the Sidhein col to the Eich col, but you miss some of the pleasant ridge-walking.

Follow the charming grass ridge, with path, southeast, with the elegant cone of **Beinn Eich** rising ahead. The ridge becomes still more shapely up to Beinn Eich's summit.

The path continues down the spur eastwards. At 400m the path fades, but converging fences guide you down to a gateway and stile (NS 319942) directly above **Edentaggart farm**. Slant slightly left, to a ladder stile 200 metres to left of the farm. A path leads down to a stile onto the access track below the farm.

Turn left down the track, which at the next stream becomes a tarred lane. (Don't park at this point, which is a turning area: there are a couple of small parking points above Glenmollochan farm.) Follow the lane out for 3km to Luss village.

---

49 Cruach Tairbeirt

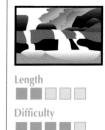

Start/finish	Tarbet station NN 313044
Distance	5.5km/3 miles
Ascent	400m/1300ft
Approx time	2½–3hr
Max altitude	Cruach Tairbeirt 415m
Terrain	Steep hillside, pathed ridge, road verge or rough grassland
Map	LR 56; Expl 364; Harvey *Arrochar Alps*

Length
■ ■ □ □ □

Difficulty
■ ■ ■ ■ □

Cruach Tairbeirt has fine views of Loch Lomond and of the Arrochar Alps (including a surprising take on the Cobbler). Provided there's enough breeze to keep away the midges, its heathery summit makes a magnificent picnic spot. But it's a tough wee hill. The ascent route is steep and rugged. Coming down, if you lose the small path you're in trouble as the surrounding heather and tussocks are strength-sapping, and the descent through the wrong bit of forest would be spectacularly nasty. So carry a compass on this one! ▶

◄ As an easier alternative, use the descent route here for both up and down. It is less steep and rugged as a way up, and eliminates route-finding problems on the way back.

Note The waymarked '**Cruach Tairbeirt Loop**', contouring at 150m in the forest, is a well-surfaced path but its viewpoints have been obliterated by growing trees. When the hill is clear-felled that will once again be a fine easy walk in its own right.

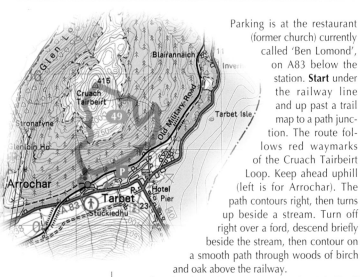

Parking is at the restaurant (former church) currently called 'Ben Lomond', on A83 below the station. **Start** under the railway line and up past a trail map to a path junction. The route follows red waymarks of the Cruach Tairbeirt Loop. Keep ahead uphill (left is for Arrochar). The path contours right, then turns up beside a stream. Turn off right over a ford, descend briefly beside the stream, then contour on a smooth path through woods of birch and oak above the railway.

After 1km the path crosses a stream that I shall call the '**footbridge stream**' on a wooden bridge and slants uphill with the stream on its left. ◄ At a picnic table on the right, maps mark a spur path to a viewpoint, but this has been abandoned and overgrown. The main path turns left, recrossing the footbridge stream. After 500 metres the path turns briefly uphill. Before it turns downwards again, turn sharp right, off the waymarked trail.

Here you might spot crystals of black magnetite in path stones (see Appendix 2).

198

The new path slants up to the right, degenerating into a grassy trod. Where trees have fallen divert to the right under spruce, but then regain the grassy tree gap above. The path crosses the footbridge stream once more and heads up to right of it to the top of the forest.

The path, briefly surfaced with gravel, becomes a narrow way through heather. Keep directly uphill ahead near the stream to just before some scattered larches. Here the path turns up left, steeply through bracken. As the summit dome gets even steeper, the small path is eroded a metre deep. But soon you arrive on **Cruach Tairbeirt**'s heathery summit with its trig pillar.

To **descend**, take a few steps down westwards (towards the Cobbler) to find the start of a small path heading roughly south. This winds down among knolls, passing below a small crag (NN 3119 0538 – a point to rediscover the path if you lost it but have GPS!). The clearer path descends steeply into bracken, to enter the forest (NN 3121 0506). It slants down to the right under trees, to a stream, then descends to left of this to rejoin the waymarked trail.

Ben Vorlich and Loch Lomond seen from Cruach Tairbeirt summit

Turn down right on the steep but well-made path. After rejoining the outward route, the path bends right then turns downhill under the railway.

Up-and-down by the easier southern path

Easier is to use the southern path for both ascent and down again. **Start** by passing under the railway, and at the first path junction turn right on the Red Trail. This contours right for 200 metres, then turns steeply uphill. After a stiff climb to the 150m level the path fords the stream on its right and is about to turn briefly downhill again.

Here turn up left, with the stream on your left, on a sketchy path under the trees. The path emerges onto streamside grass. When it re-enters trees, it continues beside the stream for 50 metres, then turns right at a small cairn. From this point you can see light ahead between the tree trunks. The path follows a gap between the tree trunks up to open hill.

Follow the small path uphill, north, through bracken then heather, occasionally looking back so as to recognise the way again on the descent. The path is continuous all the way to the summit trig point.

Loch Lomond at dawn from Luss pier (start of Route 48)

PART EIGHT
ARROCHAR ALPS

The Arrochar Alps seen from Ben Lui.
From left: Ben Vane, Beinn Narnain, top of the Cobbler just visible, Beinn Ime.

Okay, so if I slipped in a picture of Piz Bernina you'd spot that it wasn't actually Ben Vane in even the most splendid of winter conditions. But the name isn't altogether exaggeration. It does express the vigorous nature of this hill group, the way the mountains rise steeply straight out of the valley, and break out all over in rocky lumps. Explore their unpathed sides, and spend an interesting afternoon on grassy rakes, and waterfalls, and unexpected small overhangs.

In this section are two routes covering Ben Vorlich, Ben Vane and Bienn Ime, plus two more to cover the easier way, and the more interesting one, up Ben Narnain. There are also a couple of low-level walks around the base of the range.

And no, I haven't forgotten the Cobbler. It gets a Summit Summary of its own, with routes that also imply another two lines up Beinn Ime. The Cobbler's overview map is on pages 228–229.

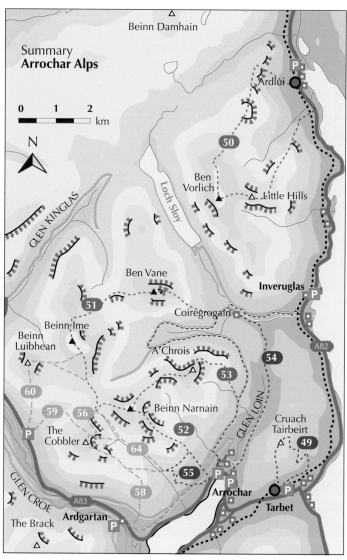

Summary
Arrochar Alps

0   1   2 km

N

Beinn Damhain

Ardlui

50

Loch Sloy

Ben Vorlich

Little Hills

GLEN KINGLAS

Inveruglas

Ben Vane

51

Coiregrogain

Beinn Ime

A'Chrois

54

Beinn Luibhean

53

A82

60

59   **56**

Beinn Narnain

52

Cruach Tairbeirt

GLEN LOIN

49

The Cobbler

64

55

58

GLEN CROE

A83

Arrochar

Tarbet

The Brack

Ardgartan

SUMMIT SUMMARY

Beinn Narnain (Routes 52 & 53) from the slopes of Beinn Ime (Route 51)

ARROCHAR ALPS

Low routes

Arrochar Alps

The Cobbler

Note

For further routes on the Cobbler see the Summit Summary on page 228.

50 Ben Vorlich from Ardlui

Length

Difficulty

Start/finish	Ardlui NN 317155
Distance	11km/7 miles
Ascent	1150m/3800ft
Approx time	6hr
Max altitude	Ben Vorlich 943m
Terrain	Rough grassy hillside, pathless or with small paths
Map	LR 56; Expl 364; Harvey *Arrochar Alps*

With its pair of Ben Vanes, its cluster of Stobs and Beinns a' Choin and a' Chroin, this corner of the Southern Highlands shows more than the usual Gaelic thriftiness with recycled hill names. This is the Ben Vorlich of Loch Lomond. For the other Ben Vorlich that's above Loch Earn, see Route 21.

This Ben Vorlich is a solitary hill, steep on all sides. At first glance there seems little to do with it other than walk up, follow its kilometre of summit ridge, and walk back down again. But it is the Vorlich that's above Loch Lomond, and a second glance shows a pair of knobbly ridges reaching up from the shoreline and offering ground more interesting than the simple steep slog, as well as fine views of the loch. The Little Hills, in particular, have to be a favourite spot for looking along Lomond. (If, however, you do really fancy that simple steep slog, it's usually taken from Inveruglas. Just head up the south ridge – or less simply and even steeper, a southwestern corrie – from the Loch Sloy reservoir road.)

Access to the Ardlui flank of Ben Vorlich is complicated by the railway line. Crossing points are at:

- Garristuck lane, 150 metres south of Ardlui Station
- Bridge 85, midway between Ardlui and Stuckendroin, NN 320149
- Behind Stuckendroin farm.

Parking is opposite Ardlui Hotel (on the west side of A82) or opposite Ardlui Station (on the east side of A82). Also there's some verge parking on the east side of the road just north of Stuckendroin. From Ardlui, **start** south along the A82. It's 1km to the entrance to Stuckendroin – if the road traffic is too unpleasant, after 150 metres you can take the Garristuck lane under the railway, at once turn left over a stile, and follow field bottoms and vague tracks to the gate behind Stuckendroin that's marked 'Access Ben Vorlich'.

Otherwise follow A82 to **Stuckendroin**. Enter the driveway and at once turn right through a signposted kissing gate. Waymarkers lead to right of the farm buildings and round behind them, to a bridge under the railway. Once through, an awkward-to-open gate on the left is marked 'Access Ben Vorlich'.

Descending the northeast ridge of Ben Vorlich, towards Glen Falloch. The unclouded peak ahead is Beinn Dubhchraig

Head uphill on rough pasture, with a stream on your right, towards the foot of the Little Hills ridge, which rises to the left in steep humps. Traces of paths lead up the ridgeline. At the back of the first hump, a crossing fence has a stile at its highest point. After some sharp little rises to start, the going gets gentler.

At about 500m altitude the views open down the length of Loch Lomond, and just get better as you pass the cairned knoll at 640m and reach the first of the two **Little Hills** (NN 308123). (For those descending this route in mist, this is a crucial change of direction; they can identify this lower Little Hill by the perched boulder on its top.) Steep little crags surround it, and it's a great perch for a prolonged pause in the upward progress.

The second Little Hill is grassy and smooth on top, and smooth slopes continue, to Ben Vorlich's trig point and accompanying cairn. Turn right (north) on a path for 300 metres to **Ben Vorlich**'s summit cairn, perched at 943m on a west-facing crag top.

Descent Continue north along the smooth summit ridge for 600 metres, to a slight rise with a large cairn (931m). From here a little care is needed to avoid tumbling into Coire Creagach (ahead right). Descend slightly west of north for 400 metres to an ill-defined puddly col. Now turn northeast, down a humpy ridgeline with a fairly clear path. The ridge, gently angled on the whole, has scattered small crags, and the path heads down, rather than around, a couple of these, giving two scrambly moments.

From the col before Stob nan Coinnich Bhacain, the path heads down to the right. It's aiming for a steep direct descent to Bridge 85 mentioned above, but I prefer the much more scenic continuation over **Stob nan Coinnich Bhacain**. ▶ A gentle grassy ridge descends to a slight rise to **Stob an Fhithich** (419m), which has crags on its right. Stob an Fhithich is 'Peak of the Raven', matching Maol an Fhithich on the opposite side of Loch Lomond.

The name is 'Point of the Mossy Peatbanks', but it's a bit rocky as well.

Descend northeast onto a flat, boggy bit of ridge and at once turn down right (southeast) in a grassy hollow. As a stream develops, keep down to its left to find a little-used but very useful path. It runs down beside the stream, then slants down slightly leftwards through bracken to a gateway in a fence (NN 3111 1563). Head straight down, rediscovering the path about 50 metres left of the stream.

At the foot of a birchwood the path crosses the stream (NN 3125 1547) and joins the next one across to the right. Head down grassland to the houses at **Garristuck** (conspicuous from above and the only buildings above the railway). Turn left along a fence to a field gate. The track back to the right runs past the houses and under the railway, to the south end of Ardlui.

51 Arrochar to Bens Vane and Ime

Length

Difficulty

Start/finish	Succoth car park NN 295049
Distance	19km/12 miles
Ascent	1500m/5000ft
Approx time	8½hr
Max altitude	Beinn Ime 1011m
Terrain	Wide valley path, small steep ridge path, pathless grassland and a good hill path, and descent by a gentle path
Map	LR 56; Expl 364; Harvey *Arrochar Alps*

Including the Cobbler

19.5km/12 miles, 1750m/5800ft Ascent, 9½hr

Between Ben Vane and Beinn Ime is the best sort of Arrochar wild country. High slopes of grass are interrupted by waterfalls, small gorges and black overhanging outcrops. The grass, above about 400m altitude, is short and good to walk on, so that this is go-anywhere territory – provided, of course, you don't fall over any of those overhangs.

The Munro-baggers' path up Ben Vane leads you into this satisfying landscape, while itself being steep and scenic, and equipped with small black crags of its own. And the exit from the wild ground is by another trodden path, down off Beinn Ime to the complex col underneath the Cobbler. At that point you decide whether the day demands to be rounded off by an ascent of the Cobbler, or whether to take the gentle way down by the Buttermilk Burn (Allt a' Bhalachain).

Start from either of the car parks at the head of Loch Long. Just east of the road bridge over **Loin Water**, take a tarred track with a blue footpath marker alongside the river. In about 200 metres turn right on a blue-marked footpath. It crosses the valley floor into woods on the slope of Cruach

Tairbeirt. At a path 'T' turn left, signposted for Inveruglas and Glen Loin.

The path runs up the glen, parallel with two sets of pylons. It joins a track, which soon reverts back to being wide, well-built footpath. This path crosses a col with a small crag above, then another under a pylon, and descends northwards in a wide, boggy tree gap. It runs alongside trees on the left, then enters them for 500 metres. It bends right, across a field, to a kissing gate where it joins a track near **Coiregrogain**. Turn right, over Inveruglas Water, to join a tarred access track at a way-mark post. ▶

Rougher but prettier: turn left, *not* over Inveruglas Water, and pass Coiregrogain to a stone bridge opposite a forest corner.

On the south slope of Beinn Ime, with the Cobbler behind

Turn left up this private road (it goes to Loch Sloy dam). After 600 metres turn left on a track across a bridge and around the base of Ben Vane. After 500 metres, with trees below, it crosses a small stream.

A path sets off to the right just before the stream; but drier is to cross the stream and turn up to the right on a steep path through bracken. It heads up to left of a small wooded crag at the bottom of Ben Vane's steep east ridge. Above the crag, pass round to right of a swamp to rejoin the alternative path.

The path now climbs the steep and bumpy east ridge of Ben Vane. It is eroded in places to bare rock. It wiggles around from side to side of the ridge, passing below dripping crags. At 850m a slightly downhill section is followed by a rock step. The path passes left below this, then slants back up to the right with a few scrambling moves. Above this it slants leftwards along rock slabs exposed by the erosion of the path itself, to the sudden summit cairn of **Ben Vane**.

A small pool is just beyond, and a second cairn. Head down westwards on pathless grass. Pass to right of a swampy plateau at the 700m level. Don't short-cut to the left towards the broad, grassy saddle between Vane and Ime – any such short-cutting leads to crag tops. So keep down west until a broad level ridge with pools leads left (southwest) to the **Vane/Ime saddle**.

Ahead, three streams come down the side of Beinn Ime. The left-hand one is larger, and runs down through a gorge, so ignore that. To right, two parallel streams run down out of the col Glas Bhealach that's between Ime and the almost-Corbett Beinn Chorranach. Follow the right-hand (northern) of the two streams, as it gives an easy passage through the band of broken ground at the slope top. The **Glas Bhealach** col is just above.

Turn left up the fairly steep slope of Beinn Ime. It has broken crag in its lower half. You can slant up to the right onto a grass ledge, pass along it to the left through the crags, and zigzag back right up more grass, to the top of this craggy bit. Stony slopes lead up to **Beinn Ime** summit cairn, perched on a little rock platform. Remains of a trig point are nearby.

Descend southeast on a clear path. As the slope becomes broad and grassy, descend southwards into the wide, complex col between Ime, Narnain and the Cobbler. At the Narnain/Ime saddle, the **Bealach a' Mhaim**, the path across the col reaches a fence, with a stile (NN 2615 0710). It continues south to the **Narnain/ Cobbler col**, where it joins a corner of the Cobbler's well-built ascent path.

Note Here you might decide to take the path onto the Cobbler (Route 56), with a descent by either the rugged East Corrie or the gentle southeast ridge.

Otherwise keep ahead on the smooth, gentle path through the col and down the **Buttermilk Burn**, keeping to left of the stream. After 2km it reaches the two **Narnain Boulders** (scrambled on as Route 63).

Continue down the path to the 350m contour, where the Buttermilk Burn has a small dam and intake. At a white post, keep downhill ahead (not contouring left). The wide, smooth path descends in zigzags to meet a forest road with a mobile phone mast just to the right. Turn left for 50 metres and then down right on the path's continuation, with three-colour waymarks. The path zigzags lazily down to the A83, which it crosses into the **Succoth car park**. A tarred path leads around the loch head to right of the road, to the other, eastern, car park.

Start/finish	Succoth car park NN 295049
Distance	9km/5½ miles
Ascent	950m/3200ft
Approx time	4½hr
Max altitude	Beinn Narnain 926m
Terrain	Rough paths, with a gentle one for descent
Map	LR 56; Expl 364; Harvey *Arrochar Alps*

Including the Cobbler
10km/6miles, 1200m/4000ft
Ascent, 5½hr plus scrambling on
the Cobbler

Length

Difficulty

Many Munro-baggers go up and down Narnain and ignore the Cobbler altogether. Mountain-lovers go up the Cobbler but not the Munro alongside. The Spearhead at the top of Beinn Narnain's southwest ridge is not difficult but is most dramatic, particularly in blowing cloud, almost justifying (for readers of *The Lion, Witch and Wardrobe* series of children's books by C. S. Lewis) the mis-spelling of the mountain as Narnian. Meanwhile the Cobbler is dramatic and, if the true top is reached, difficult as well. So when it comes to choosing between the Munro and the mere (but mountainous) Corbett – I'm broad-minded, and I like to do both.

This route, however, breaks off at the Narnain/Cobbler col, allowing you to make your own choice whether to head down the Buttermilk Burn/ Allt a' Bhalachain (as on Route 51) or go on up the Cobbler (Route 56).

Start from either of the pay-and-display (£1 a day) car parks at the head of Loch Long. They are linked by a tar path between main road and loch, with its own foot-bridge over Loin Water.

From the southwest (Ardgartan) end of the western car park, a path signed for Beinn Narnain and the Cobbler crosses the main road. In a few metres you cross a small stream. Examine this stream, whose bed will form much of the path above. If it is in vigorous flow, choose the alternative described at the end of this route.

If the stream seems reasonably small, continue for another 10 metres and take a path up on the right – deceptively dry for its first few steps before it joins the streambed. After rain, the path is underwater – this does assure clean stones and rock. It is interrupted by giant concrete steps left over from some pipeline.

At the 100m contour you reach a forest road. (Here you could turn left to join the dry route described below; but as your feet are already awash, why bother?) A few steps on bare rock continue the path above, which soon resumes its supplementary duties as a stream. At 300m altitude the angle eases, and the
path runs up for 200

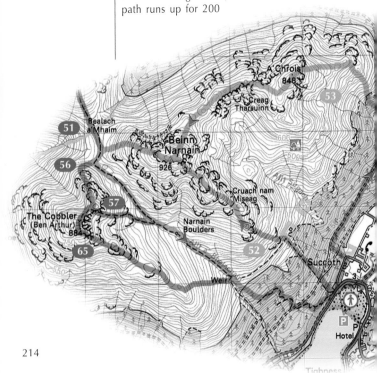

214

metres to the top end of the former pipeline. Here the dry route, described below, contours in from the left to rejoin.

Continue straight uphill on a small path that winds pleasantly among outcrops. The ascent is fairly steep, with a brief levelling at the 600m contour, until it reaches the 813m summit of **Cruach nam Miseag**. Now there is a well-defined ridgeline northwest. After a brief dip the path skirts slightly to left of the crest, above a high steep slope, weaving among rocky lumps. It returns to the crest, dodges past a rocky turret, and is confronted by the high buttress of the Spearhead.

The path goes up to right of the Spearhead in a small gully, to reach the wide summit pla-teau at a preliminary cairn. In about 50 metres a stone-built trig marks the top of **Beinn Narnain**.

Descend northwest past another cairn, onto the clear, eroded path that descends the grassy west-northwest slope of Beinn Narnain.

A' Chrois, looking along the ridge towards Beinn Narnain (on Route 53)

Note that there are two cols (or bealachs) below you now: slightly to your right, the Bealach a' Mhaim (637m) leading to Beinn Ime; and slightly to your left, the Narnain/Cobbler col at 628m. In mist this complex saddle requires attention so as not to climb the wrong hill.

As the slope eases at about 730m altitude, the path bends left, southwest, to the Cobbler/Narnain col. If this is missed you'll drop northwest towards the Bealach a' Mhaim, which is crossed by a fence – so if you meet the fence, find the stile at its highest point, *don't* cross it, but take the path from it back south.

At the **Cobbler/Narnain col** you meet the corner of the well-built Buttermilk Burn path. To the right, it heads steeply up the Cobbler (Route 56); ahead, it passes through the col and descends towards Loch Long (see Route 51).

DRY START FOR ROUTE 52

Start as the main route; from the southwest end of Succoth car park, crossing A83 onto the path signed for Beinn Narnain and the Cobbler. Keep ahead up the wide smooth path, ignoring the small path turning up right as that is the more direct wet way up. At 150m altitude the wide path meets a forest road. Turn left for 50 metres, towards a mobile phone mast, then take the continuing uphill path marked by a red-top post. It runs up through clear-fell and scrubby birch trees.

On open hill at 350m the angle eases, and the small reservoir of Buttermilk Burn is down on your left. At a white-top post, turn right to contour on a firm but wet path around the slope of Ben Narnain, to the top end of the stony pipeline path.

Start/finish	Succoth car park NN 296049
Distance	15km/9½ miles
Ascent	1400m/4600ft
Approx time	7½hr
Max altitude	Beinn Narnain 926m
Terrain	Tracks, paths and grassy ridge, but with very rough steep grass to A' Chrois
Map	LR 56; Expl 364; Harvey *Arrochar Alps*

Without the Cobbler
14.5km/9 miles, 1100m/3700ft
Ascent, 6½hr

Length

Difficulty

A third of the way up A' Chrois I decided this route was too horrible and I'd have to drop it from the book… But at 400m the savage grasses eased slightly and when, on A' Chrois summit, the cloud lifted enough to show the continuing ridge, I realised this was just too nice to miss. On lawn-like grass it wanders around the big craggy corrie on the east side of Beinn Narnain. Perhaps readers of this book will tramp out a small path through the plant life lower down. Perhaps you'll be going up in a month other than July or August which are when the vegetation is at its most vicious.

It's a pointless self-deprivation not to include the Cobbler at the end of the walk. Routes from the following section allow you that choice anyway.

Two inexpensive pay-and-display car parks are at the head of Loch Long. **Start** across the road from the western one, by taking a lane towards Succoth. After 500 metres the lane bends right, over the stream **Allt Sugach**. Take a path up to right of the stream, a bit overgrown with bracken, past some small waterfalls and a concrete water tank.

At a forest road cross a few steps to the right, where the path resumes with a rocky step into a plantation. It continues near the stream up to a higher forest road.

217

Turn right for 2km. At the start of clear-felling on the right a rough track zigzags up to the left (NN 302071). Follow it up to the forest top at 300m (NN 299074). (From here the track runs south along the forest top for another 300 metres, making it easier to hit if descending off the hill.)

Where it first reaches the forest top, leave the track and turn up through a broken fence. The initial slope is steep, on long grass and some bracken, making it very arduous (especially in high summer). Ascend northwest, towards the east ridge of A' Chrois. At 400m the going gets less severe, steadily improving from then on up. Once on the knolly ridgeline turn uphill, west. Quite soon you'll be confronted with the ridge hump at 590m, which has a drop beyond it defended by an overhanging crag. This is disconcerting, but it can be bypassed by taking a few steps down to its left (south) then circling round into the col below.

Behind, the east ridge of Ben Vane (Route 51); in front, the ridge of A'Chrois on Beinn Narnain (Route 53)

The ridgeline steepens, up to the band of broken ground defending A' Chrois. At the base of this broken ground (NN 2905 0778) a grassy gully slants up slightly to the right, its foot divided by a small crag. Pass up to

left of the small crag and continue up the grassy gully, bearing 300° magnetic (2008) to a pointy-topped rock at 777m (NN 2903 0780). Here turn up left, bearing 250°, on grassy slopes between small crags, to arrive at the northern point of the summit plateau (NN 2893 0775). Head south for 50 metres to **A' Chrois** cairn.

The reward for the tough ascent is the grassy wander along the continuing ridgeline. Head southwest for 400 metres, and drop off A' Chrois onto the grassy wide ridge below. The ridge, with its small path, runs west. The path contours round left of the first knoll, and this gives views down into the huge east corrie of Beinn Narnain. Then pass along above Creag Tharsuinn, going over the small knolls to retain your views, rather than following the path as it tries to save effort on the northern flank. The ridgeline turns southwest to the base of the final slope of Beinn Narnain.

Head up the open slope. At its top, a fringe of crag is bypassed on the left, to reach the flat summit plateau of **Beinn Narnain**. The path of the southeast ridge (Route 52) is ahead, the summit trig point to your right. ▶

Descend northwest past another cairn at the plateau edge. A clear eroded path descends the grassy west-northwest slope of Beinn Narnain towards the grassy three-way saddle between Narnain, Ime and the Cobbler. As the slope eases the path bends left, southwest, to the **Narnain/Cobbler col**. Here you reach the corner of a well-built path that runs downhill ahead, or to the right heads up the steep north end of **the Cobbler** on well-built steps.

Here you decide whether to take the path onto the Cobbler (Route 56), with a descent by either the rugged East Corrie or the gentle southeast ridge; or else, to keep ahead on the smooth, gentle path through the col and down the **Buttermilk Burn** (the final part of Route 51).

For a rugged descent route, head back east past another cairn and take the small path down the steep, scenic and rocky southeast ridge (Route 52 in reverse).

54 Coire Grogain

Length

Difficulty

Start/finish	Arrochar NN 297050
Distance	16km/10 miles
Ascent	400m/1250ft
Approx time	5hr
Max altitude	Coire Grogain 300m
Terrain	Tracks and made path
Map	LR 56; Expl 364; Harvey *Arrochar Alps*

Linear route Arrochar – Inveruglas plus Tarbet – Arrochar
11km/7 miles, 300m/900ft
Ascent, 3½hr plus bus or boat time

Despite being marred by forestry plantations and pylons, the walk is worthwhile for its views up to the chunky Arrochar Alps, and it also has some beautiful birches. From the turning point at Inveruglas Water, an extra 2.5km each way would take you out to the café at Inveruglas – or you could start and end there to evade the small pay-and-display charge at Arrochar.

From Inveruglas, a bus (half a dozen a day) could take you back to Tarbet, with a woodland path above the railway station leading back to Arrochar. If the schedules were more helpful, you could make the same link using ferries via Inversnaid on the other side of Loch Lomond.

Two pay-and-display (£1 a day) car parks are at the head of Loch Long, joined by a tar path between the main road and the loch, with a bridge over Loin Water. **Start** from either of them.

Just east of the road bridge over Loin Water, take a tarred track with a blue footpath marker. It runs upstream (to right of the river). In about 200 metres turn off right on a blue-marked footpath. It crosses the valley floor into woods on the slope of Cruach Tairbeirt. At a path T-junction turn left, signposted for Inveruglas and Glen Loin.

The path runs up the glen, parallel with two sets of pylons. It joins a track, which after a footbridge continues as a well-made path. This runs up through the clearing caused by the overhead power lines, and at its highest point passes through a craggy little col. In the wide, flat valley now running north, the path finally enters trees on the left. It passes a board with a trail map, then crosses grassland to a gate onto the Coiregrogain track. ▶

See below for the linear route to Inveruglas.

- **The next section is on rough, wet path** – if you want to avoid this, turn right across Inveruglas Water to a tarred lane. Turn left, up-valley, for 500 metres, then take the smooth unsurfaced track on the left under the steep nose of Ben Vane.

- **For the damp but pretty route turn left**, on the track to left of the river, to the ruined farm of Coiregrogain. Pass round to left of this, and take a rough path upstream to a stone footbridge just where the plantations start on the opposite bank. Cross, and go up to right of the plantation to join the smooth track just above.

Turn left, below the steep nose of Ben Vane, and follow the track as it wanders up into Coire Grogain. Below a waterfall and intake dam the track bends back left into plantations, passing a concrete hut that would be a useful shelter if it didn't already contain an inch or two of water. The track gently descends, then rises to a hill corner where clear-felling has disclosed Ben Lomond ahead and Glen Loin below.

Bridge over Allt Coiregrogain above the ruined farmhouse

The track returns all the way along the side of Glen Loin. Above Succoth village, it crosses **Allt Sugach**. ▸

Immediately before the stream, turn down left on a small path under needle trees. On your right the stream has small waterfalls. A short rock step drops you onto a lower forest road, where the path continues a few steps to the right, still to left of the stream. It arrives at a corner of a tarred lane at the edge of Succoth.

Turn right, away from the settlement, to reach A83 at the head of Loch Long.

If you miss this turn-off, another forest road joins from below, and you reach first a very rough and then a very smooth path down left: descend either of these paths.

LINEAR ROUTE TO INVERUGLAS

Just to the right of the kissing gate near Coiregrogain farm, the track crosses Inveruglas Water, and continues to meet a tarred lane at a waymark post. Turn right, down-valley. After 1km a path down right runs through woods to rejoin the tarred lane below a bend. Exit to A82 just below, and turn left up a roadside footpath to **Inveruglas** power station, car park and visitor centre with café.

Don't be tempted to link back to Tarbet along the road. This section of A82 is bendy, and lacks any footpath or verge. Having found a bus (or boat, or even hitch-hike) to **Tarbet**, follow the pavement of the A83 (Campbelltown) road before turning up right to **Arrochar & Tarbet Station**. Pass under the railway to a footpath board, and turn left on the path for Arrochar. It runs along the foot of woodland above the railway, then down left into Arrochar village.

NOTE: INVERUGLAS TO BEALACH A' MHAIM

From the forest road on the south side of Coire Grogain (NN 277084) a rough track leads up to the top of the plantations and runs along the valley side southwest. It ends about 200m below Bealach a' Mhaim (NN 268075 approx). This newly built track was spotted too late for me to walk it for this book, but it offers a shorter round of Ben Vane and Beinn Ime from Inveruglas (rather than from Arrochar, Route 51) as well as a surprising northeastern approach to the Cobbler. The track's foot is reached by Route 54 from Inveruglas just described; or using the same start as Route 53, from Arrochar.

55 Succoth and See

Length

Difficulty

Start/finish	Succoth car park NN 295049
Distance	4km/2½ miles
Ascent	350m/1100ft
Approx time	2hr
Max altitude	Buttermilk Burn 360m
Terrain	Rough stony path up, gentle paths down
Map	LR 56; Expl 364; Harvey *Arrochar Alps*

With excursion to the Narnain Boulders
6km/4 miles, 500m/1700ft
Ascent, 3hr

This is a ramble around the approach routes to the Cobbler (see Summit Summary below). A tough climb of 300m starts off this walk, but it's worth it for the really fine views on the contouring central section, all along Loch Long and up to the Cobbler. (Well, it's worth it when it hasn't been raining – when it has, that tough ascent path is also under water.) The finish, at least, is easy, down a gentle well-graded pathway.

Start from either of the pay-and-display (£1 a day) car parks at the head of Loch Long. They are linked by a tar path between main road and loch, with its own foot-bridge over Loin Water.

From the southwest (Ardgartan) end of the western car park, a path signed for Beinn Narnain and the Cobbler crosses the main road. In a few metres you cross a small stream. Its bed will form much of the path above.

Continue for another 10 metres and take a path up on the right – deceptively dry for its first few steps before it joins the streambed. After rain, the path is 5 or 10cm underwater. This does mean that after a dry spell, the path's bare boulders are nice and clean. The path is interrupted by giant concrete steps that once supported a hydro-power pipeline.

At the 100m contour you reach a forest road. A few steps on bare rock continue the path above, which soon resumes its extra duties as a stream. At 300m altitude the angle eases, and the path runs up for 200 metres to the top end of the former pipeline. ▶

Here a contouring path turns off left. It follows the line of a buried aqueduct, and though somewhat over-grown and wet was once the well-built main path up the Cobbler; so under the dampness it is firm. It has very fine views, so it's a shame that after 1km, and as you're just starting to enjoy the Cobbler's peaks up on the right, it ends at a junction. A small dam on the **Buttermilk Burn** is just beyond.

Route 52 to Ben Narnain keeps on uphill here.

Loch Long and Arrochar. Route 55 contours the slopes just beyond the village

You'll turn down left here, but if you want to see more of the Cobbler first take the good path up to the right for 1km to the two large **Narnain Boulders**. The lower one has an overhang suitable for eating lunch under. Clambering on them is described at Route 63. Return down the wide, smooth path, to the Buttermilk Burn's dam.

The wide, smooth path heads downhill, to left of the burn. It zigzags down through birchwood and clear-fell to the forest road at 100m altitude. A communications mast is nearby on the right. Turn left for 50 metres, to the continuing downhill path with tricoloured waymarkers. It reaches the A83 opposite Succoth car park.

Schist scrambling on the upper Narnain Boulder (see Route 63) with the Cobbler above

SUMMIT SUMMARY: THE COBBLER

For Munro-baggers it's Ben Lomond; for low-level lovers of the oak tree, it has to be the Trossachs. But for mountain men and women, the true heart of this National Park, and of the Southern Highlands, is called the Cobbler. Its three towers are garnished with excitingly shaped overhangs. One of those rock towers forms the mountain's actual summit, making it the least easy to ascend of any on the Scottish mainland. The North Peak looks even fiercer, though when you get there you can walk right out onto the overhang without even realising just how much empty air there is underfoot. The South Peak doesn't overhang, but even so the climbing of it is slightly harder than the main summit itself. If all that isn't enough fun, on the way down you can try out your fingertips on the Narnain Boulders. And all this mountain stuff hangs above the well-equipped village of Arrochar, and its own shimmering reflection in the waters of Loch Long.

What everybody does today is the Munros; and what we all do it in is a car. But from Victorian times until World War II crowds flocked to the Cobbler by tour bus, bicycle, and steamships out of Glasgow. Scotland's two finest mountain writers, Alasdair Borthwick and W H Murray,

On the Cobbler's North Top, looking to South Peak (left, the Cobbler's Wife) and Central Peak (the Argyll Needle)

227

had their first mountain experiences on the Cobbler within ten months of each other in 1933–34. The first mountaineering club was the Cobbler Club, founded underneath the Narnain Boulders. Even today, late afternoon sees bewildered girlfriends led up the Buttermilk Burn for a summit experience that's the mountain equivalent of a ride in a fast sports car. And for many in the world's greater ranges, the Cobbler remains first in their affections, to come back to again and again. The ten routes here are just the start: the continuation could be the easy rock climbs of the south ridges of the Central and South Peaks.

THE COBBLER ROUTES

Map
LR 56; Expl 364; Harvey *Arrochar Alps*

56 North Ridge from Cobbler/Narnain Col
57 East Corrie (Coire a' Bhalachain)
58 From Ardgartan by the Southwest Ridge
58A Descent via Buttermilk Burn to Ardgartan
59 From A83 by the Back Stream
       (Coire Croe)
60 From A83 via Beinn Luibhean
60A From A83 via Beinn Luibhean and Beinn Ime

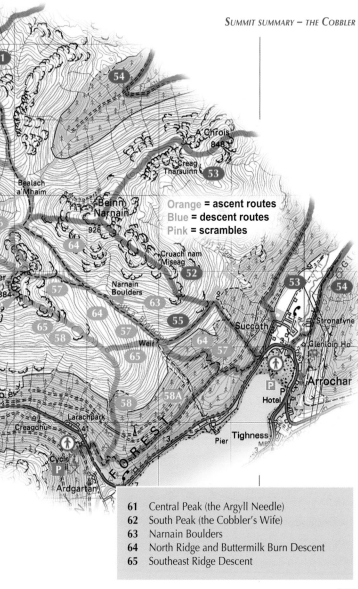

Orange = ascent routes
Blue = descent routes
Pink = scrambles

61   Central Peak (the Argyll Needle)
62   South Peak (the Cobbler's Wife)
63   Narnain Boulders
64   North Ridge and Buttermilk Burn Descent
65   Southeast Ridge Descent

LOAD OF COBBLERS

The Cobbler is, originally, the name of one of the three rocky tops – probably the central peak, though it could be the southern one. The other two peaks then become his wife, and some item of his equipment. If you call the central peak the Cobbler, then the North Peak becomes, very plausibly, his shoemaker's last: the overhanging thing he puts your boots on to hammer in their soles. But some have this peak as his unattractively overhanging wife, the one in the middle as his awl (or needle) and the southern one as him.

Properly, the mountain as a whole ought to be referred to as 'Ben Arthur'. But it isn't, and Arthur isn't even in Gaelic. So I've used the familiar name throughout this book.

By the same token, 'Buttermilk Burn' should be (but usually isn't) referred to, in Gaelic, as Allt a' Bhalachain. The East Corrie is also named sometimes as Coire a' Bhalachain.

56 North Ridge from Cobbler/Narnain Col

Start	Cobbler/Narnain col NN 263065
Distance	1km/½ mile
Ascent	250m/750ft
Approx time up	1hr
Terrain	Path, quite steep to start with but with well-built steps

The well-built path up the North Ridge is the natural way onto the Cobbler when arriving from other mountains. This could be by the route over Beinn Ime (Route 51) or Beinn Narnain (Routes 52, 53) or from A83 by Beinn Luibhean with or without Beinn Ime (Route 60).

When a day started roughly, over A' Chrois or the back of Beinn Ime, the stone steps up the Cobbler are a well-earned relief. When these stone steps are just following the well-built path up Buttermilk Burn the combination is almost too easy (offered as a variant under Route 57). But it's really better to find a tougher way up, and use this North Ridge and Buttermilk Burn (Allt a' Bhalachain) as a descent route. Accordingly, *down* the North Ridge, and then down the Buttermilk Burn, is Route 64 below.

North Peak, known as the Cobbler's Last, seen from the North–Central Col

Start The broad, well-built Buttermilk Path arrives up through the Cobbler/Narnain col to a sharp bend left, which is where the other routes join it. It continues steeply up the north slope of the Cobbler on stone steps. At the top of the steep rise, the path becomes natural, as it slants uphill keeping below and right of the rocky crest. Alternatively, that crest can be scrambled (Grade 1).

The path, still rising, passes below (to right of) North Peak to the col beyond, the **North/Central col**. Here is a large cairn, and a path (Route 57) descending steeply on the left into the East Corrie. ◄

If you don't want the North Peak (but you do, honest!) skip over the next two paragraphs.

A sharp left turn now takes in the **North Peak,** which comes first of the three on this walk but is actually the last (the Cobbler's Last, that is, the pointy overhanging thing he makes your shoes on). It's an easy ascent on a gently sloping slab. It's only after you come down that you realise that what you've been standing on is basically empty air, with a thin shelf of schist sticking out over the top of it.

From **North/Central col** the path leads to the bottom left corner of bare slabs. Continue up these to reach the flat summit: it is less than a scramble, even though what you end up standing on is an overhang. Alternatively, from the lowest slab, a narrow ledge out left reaches broken ground where you can turn up right to **North Peak**.

Return to **North/Central col**, and continue ahead, southwest, dropping a little to pass a slightly lower col 20 metres further on. The wide path then heads up on the right flank of the ridge to the gravel dome beside the **Central Peak**.

Indeed, it's not 'Awl', ie the Cobbler's Needle. See Shakespeare's Julius Caesar *I i line 21.*

The gravel dome may be enough for some. But it's not all. ◄ The true top of the Cobbler is the balanced rocky tower hanging out over the void on the left. It is reached by a scary scramble (Route 61).

57 East Corrie (Coire a' Bhalachain)

Start	Succoth car park NN 296049
Distance	5km/3 miles
Ascent	884m/2866ft
Approx time up	3½hr
Terrain	Good paths, then a rough rocky clamber

After an easy approach right up to the 600m contour this takes an appropriately rugged route into the heart of the Cobbler, below the crags and overhangs. In winter this can feel like a mountain ten times the size. If there has been a thaw-freeze to harden the snow, there will also probably be large steps made by people walking up during the thaw phase – so the ascent may be less challenging than it looks. In summer too the path boulders are firm and clean, to ease the upward clamber.

If doing the Cobbler on its own, without accompanying mountains, this has to be your route.

Start From the southwest end of the western car park cross the A83 diagonally into a wide path marked with a sign for Beinn Narnain and the Cobbler. The wide, smooth path slants up to the left, then has some long, lazy zigzags.

After 400 metres it joins a forest road. Turn left along this to a radio mast, above which the continuing path forks up right with a red waymark. It climbs slantwise then in zigzags through clear-fell and forest, some of which is pleasant wild birch. Once on open hill it joins Allt a' Bhalachain, usually known by its English name of **Buttermilk Burn**. The path runs up to right of this burn to a path junction below a dam.

Keep uphill to right of the burn, still on the well-built path. It threads between the large **Narnain Boulders** (scrambled as Route 63 below). After another 400 metres the path divides. ▸

Turn left, across Buttermilk Burn. The built path ends abruptly as the slope steepens. Ahead is a path that doubles

For the Narnain/ Cobbler col, just keep up ahead, to right of the main valley stream, to its head. Continue to the Cobbler on Route 56.

233

up on wet days as a streambed, as it heads up into the very rocky east corrie (**Coire a' Bhalachain** on some maps) of the Cobbler. The right-hand rim of the corrie is formed by the overhang of the North Peak. The rugged path heads up, just to left of this, sometimes over well-worn bare boulders. The final slope, which is very steep, carries a well-built path to the **North/Central col**. ◀

From here divert right onto North Peak, see Route 56.

Turn left, on a path to right of the crest, to reach the flat gravel summit of the Cobbler. However there is also a sharp summit of the Cobbler, and it's higher! See Central Peak, Route 61.

58 From Ardgartan by the Southeast Ridge

Start	Ardgartan information centre NN 269037
Distance	4km/2½ miles
Ascent	900m/3000ft
Approx time up	3hr
Terrain	Small rough path through plantation gap, then grassy ridge

After a rough haul through the plantations, a ridge route with good views of the Cobbler's three tops. A return route to Ardgartan is given immediately below (Route 58A).

Start From the **visitor centre** head down beside the Croe Water for 400 metres, then turn left on a bike trail with yellow markers. It crosses A83 then rambles above it before turning uphill in zigzags. Just below the top of this climb, one white pole is below the path, immediately followed by another one above it. This one marks a small, rough path directly uphill. At 170m it reaches a forest road. Cross diagonally left, to where another white pole marks the continuing path up.

The path emerges from the trees at a white pole (NN 2749 0420). Three more poles mark the path directly uphill to a slight projection on the ridgeline (NN 2748 0435: in descent, the poles lead down due south from here into the tree gap).

Follow the ridge path over **An t-Sron** then up to the base of the **South Peak**. Pass to left of this below its crag wall to the col beyond (start of the South Peak scramble, Route 62). The rocky path runs up left, to **Central Peak**.

The Cobbler's southeast ridge, looking back to its three peaks

58A Descent via Buttermilk Burn to Ardgartan

If you started from Ardgartan you probably want to return by a different route.

Start Leave the summit down the East Corrie, or via the Narnain/Cobbler col (as on Route 64). Head down the well-made path to left of Buttermilk Burn. Descend past the Narnain Boulders, and continue (still as Route 64) to the forest road above Loch Long.

Turn right, past the mobile phone mast, with a yellow-top marker. After 1km bear down left on a rougher track. Where it ends, the yellow-marker bike path continues ahead, down to Ardgartan.

59 From A83 by the Back Stream (Coire Croe)

Start	A83 bridge (NN 243060) or another pull-in 300 metres uphill
Distance	2.5km/1½ miles
Ascent	750m/2500ft
Approx time up	2½hr
Terrain	Grassy slopes

A back way that rather misses the point. Being the quickest way up, it's favoured by the Mountain Rescue Team.

Start Don't cross the quad bike bridge above the pull-in at the bridge: just cross a stile and head straight uphill to right of the gorge. Continue up the little stream valley above to a concrete dam. There's a stile just above, still to right of the stream. Go up a small path southeast to left of a side-stream, and then directly uphill to the **North/Central col**.

Up left is **North Peak** (more details, if needed, in Route 56). Up right is the wide path to the Cobbler's summit, **Central Peak**.

Start	A83 bridge (NN 243060) or another pull-in 300 metres uphill
Distance	5.5km/3½ miles
Ascent	1000m/3300ft
Approx time up	4hr
Terrain	Grassy ridges and slopes

Beinn Luibhean gives a bonus Corbett considerably less crowded than the Cobbler.

Start Directly above the pull-in at the bridge, cross a quad bike bridge and head up to left of a fence to a gate just above. (Alternatively, you could start at the pull-in 300 metres further up the road NN 242064. A stile leads up between small trees to a fence onto the open hill, but there's bracken to avoid, immediately above.) Go up

Beinn Luibhean from the Narnain/ Cobbler Col

the grassy, rocky south ridge to **Beinn Luibhean**'s mildly rocky summit.

Drop east to a wide col, and contour around the slope of Beinn Ime, rising just slightly to keep above steeper ground. Eventually you join a large path that comes down Beinn Ime's southeast spur. This runs down to the wide **Bealach a' Mhaim** col, where it crosses a fence at a boggy stile (NN 2615 0710). The path heads south along the base of Beinn Narnain to the **Narnain/ Cobbler col,** where you join the big, well-made path up the Cobbler's North Ridge (Route 56).

60A From A83 via Beinn Luibhean and Beinn Ime

Start	A83 bridge (NN 243060) or another pull-in 300 metres uphill
Distance	7km/4½ miles
Ascent	1300m/4300ft
Approx time up	5hr
Terrain	Grassy ridges and slopes

To Route 60's add-on Corbett add also a 1000m Munro. Even so, both count as preliminaries to the main course, which is always the Cobbler.

Start Follow Route 60 over Beinn Luibhean to the wide col to its east.

From the col, slant up east to join Beinn Ime's southeast spur at the 900m contour. Take the path up left to the rock-perched cairn at the summit of **Beinn Ime**.

Return southeast down the same path until the ridge widens and becomes grassy with boggy bits. Head down south then southeast into the wide saddle of **Bealach a' Mhaim**, to cross a fence at a boggy stile (NN 2615 0710). The path heads south along the base of Beinn Narnain to the **Narnain/Cobbler col**, where you join the big, well-made path up the Cobbler's North Ridge (Route 56).

Scramble	Grade 2

The Cobbler's true top is a balanced rocky tower hanging out over the void, reached by a scary scramble. The crucial ramp has smooth, sloping holds; schist is slippery when wet. It's not demeaning to use a rope (15m minimum, plus two long slings) – or if it is, better demeaned than deceased. In true winter conditions you might simply take a few photos of its frosted cakework and continue on your way (it's not a Munro, so it doesn't matter). On the other hand, that frosted cakework would look even more picturesque with you standing on top. If you've got good ice, good nerves, crampons and a rope, you should certainly consider it.

In dry summer conditions it's a scramble that's reasonably do-able by most hillwalkers, and by anybody who is to become chieftain of Clan Campbell.

Start Clamber over boulders to the front left corner of the tower. Pass to the right through a hole (the Eye of the Argyll Needle) to arrive on a ledge above a drop. Walk left along the ledge, which is comfortably wide. At its end a ramp leads up towards the tower's outer end. For the inexperienced it's a good idea to reverse the step onto the ramp immediately after making it, to familiarise yourself with the holds for the descent. Then ascend the ramp on smooth footholds to a nook below the perched

Three stages in scrambling to the Cobbler's true summit

boulder at the tower's outer end. For the roped, here is a secure stance and belay.

Scramble onto the boulder above, and thence to the summit. Given the necessary ancestry, you could now become Chief of Clan Campbell.

Descend by the same route.

62 South Peak (the Cobbler's Wife)

Scramble	Grade 3

Seen from the ridge running down from the Cobbler (or indeed from anywhere else) the Cobbler's Wife looks distinctly unfeminine. The female of the Cobbler is indeed deadlier than the male.

Start At the north (uphill) end of the rock tower, a narrow connecting neck links to the ridge below the Cobbler's main summit. From the end of the connecting neck, step across an awkward gap that is technically the trickiest part

South Peak: the ascent route starts from the connecting ridge at bottom right

of the climb. A ledge path leads round to the right for 20 metres, then a shallow groove with lots of holds leads up to the left, with a short sideways move to the left and then a slightly harder finish past a quartzite lump to a ledge.

Walk round to the left, to a steep but easy climb up to the right in a shallow chimney. At the top of this, walk 2 metres to the right to the base of a well-scratched crack. Jam left leg and arm into this and reach for a high handhold on the right.

Descend by the same route. The crack goes most easily facing inwards with left leg jammed in it. The rest is best taken facing outwards or sideways.

63 Narnain Boulders

Scrambles and climbs

The **upper boulder** is a blocky rectangle, and the more difficult of the two.

Start by examining the descent point, at its north corner. Here the boulder is at its lowest, 3.5m high. You'll have to lower yourself over a rounded edge, with poor

On the upper Narnain Boulder. This scrambler is about to start wandering around the perimeter wondering how the heck... The ascent route is pictured on page 226.

handholds, to drop onto a level, firm ground surface below. Eye this up before attempting the ascent routes.

A short, very steep route with missing handholds is a few metres left of the descent point. Easier are routes on the opposite (south) side. Moderately steep lines have sloping footholds and small rounded handholds. The right-hand edge is least steep, but with poor holds. Alternatively, start at the centre of the face and slant up left onto the arête of the southwest corner. These routes are probably rock grade Severe in wet walking boots, considerably easier in rock boots.

The **lower boulder** is shaped like a plum stone, with overhangs at the east and west corners. The eastern (downhill) end is a rock cave used for lunch breaks.

Start The easiest ascent is from the western (uphill) corner. Its difficulty depends on how tall you are, how large a stone has been left below the overhang, and how long it takes you to work out the left-handed press hold that gets you onto the boulder. Once on the boulder, it's little more than a walk up the gentle slab to the summit.

64 North Ridge and Buttermilk Burn Descent

Descent to	Succoth car park NN 296049
Distance	5km/3½ miles
Descent	900m/2900ft
Approx time down	
	2hr
Terrain	Good paths

The easiest way down, on paths all the way. The steep descent to start has well-built stone steps, and after the Narnain/Cobbler col it's smooth and gentle the rest of the way down.

The well-made Buttermilk Burn path, at the head of its valley (Walk 64)

Start From the Cobbler's summit take the path down northwards to the gap before the North Peak. The lowest point has a small deceptive path down right: 20 metres beyond, a cairn marks the **North/Central col** and the much larger path down to the right (the **East Corrie** route, a rugged short cut to Buttermilk Burn). Up to right is the **North Peak**, which could be ascended by a scrambly walk up well-worn slabs (see Route 56).

For the main descent route head down north on the lower of two paths slanting down the left (west) slopes of **North Peak**. (The upper path leads to scrambling along the crest above the path.) As the path steepens, it becomes well made with stone steps.

At the foot of the North Ridge the slope abruptly eases, and the path takes a sharp bend to the right. Well-built with a gravel surface, it passes through the **Narnain/Cobbler col** and descends the valley of Buttermilk Burn, keeping to left of the stream. After 2km it reaches the two **Narnain Boulders** (Route 64). Continue down the path to the 350m contour, where the Buttermilk Burn has a small dam and intake. ▸

At a white post keep downhill ahead (not contouring left). The wide, smooth path descends in zigzags to meet a forest road with a mobile phone mast just to the right. Turn left for 50 metres and then down right on the path's continuation, with three-colour waymarks. The path zigzags lazily down to the A83, which it crosses into the **Succoth car park**.

Old maps mark a path continuing down to right of Buttermilk Burn, all the way to Loch Long side. This exists and is pretty, but is also pretty steep, boggy and rough.

65 Southeast Ridge Descent

Descent to	Succoth car park NN 296049
Distance	4.5km/3 miles
Descent	900m/2900ft
Approx time down	
	2hr
Terrain	Rough ridge, then grass, finishing down a good path

This descent route takes us past the third and toughest of the Cobbler tops, then onto a gently grassy descent. It is pleasant, scenic, and surprisingly quiet.

Start From the Cobbler's summit follow a path down southeast, to right of the tower of **Central Peak**. The pathed ridge leads down towards the grand tower of the **South Summit** (the Cobbler's Wife, Route 62). A narrow neck leads out to the base of the tower: halfway across this, the continuing downhill path turns sharply back right.

The descent path continues to right of the tower, passing along its base. Once below the rock tower it's possible to descend left into the East Corrie but the path continues along the grassy ridge, with fine views including some back to the three Cobbler summits. It follows this ridge, up a little and over **An t-Sron**, to its final point where it rises to a small knoll at 540m (NN 273050). ◄ Here take the left fork, which descends damp grass to the small dam on the **Buttermilk Burn**.

If you now want to descend to Ardgartan, see Route 58 for tree gap GPS data.

Cross, and take the well-built path downhill to left of the stream. It zigzags down through birch wood and clear-fell to a forest road at 100m altitude. Turn left for 50 metres, to the continuing downhill path with tricoloured waymarkers. It reaches the A83 opposite Succoth car park.

PART NINE

GLEN CROE TO LOCH GOIL

Across Loch Goil to Beinn Bheula and its outliers (Route 69)

The southwest of the National Park is for adventures and exploration. Long sea lochs defend the Cowal peninsula from the casual tourist, and some – not all – of the lower slopes are prickly with impenetrable plantations. The steep sides are surprisingly craggy. The tops above are pathless and coarsely grassy, so that the going is pleasant without ever being completely easy. This could be called the Shostakovich, or the malt whisky, of hillwalking; it's a taste that can take a while to acquire. But once you're accustomed to Cowal, Ben Lomond with its obvious paths may seem just a touch unsophisticated.

This section starts with the comparatively civilised hills around Glen Croe, where there are still paths and people. It then works its way southwest into deepest Cowal.

The section ends in expletives, while Route 72 ("By Eck!") is followed by "What the Puck?". But this odd, almost foreign corner of Scotland will draw forth kindlier words as well.

66 The Brack and Ben Donich

Length

Difficulty

Start/finish	Ardgartan Visitor Centre on A83 NN 269037
Distance	16km/10 miles
Ascent	1250m/4200ft
Approx time	7hr
Max altitude	Ben Donich 847m
Terrain	Steep grass slopes, grassy ridges, track
Map	LR 56; Expl 363 and 364; Harvey *Arrochar Alps*

Glen Croe, Glen Croe, it's the place to go…

Glen Croe is the southern equivalent of Glen Coe, but with the slightly longer name indicating a slightly smaller sort of hill. The six hills around Glen Croe are all of Corbett height – 2500ft but less than 3000ft (762–914m). The circuit of the glen offers the fit hillwalker a unique chance to cover six Corbetts at once (which, if accomplished, is certainly something to 'croe' about).

But Croe Corbetts are also to linger over. Across the valley is the Cobbler with its rock-tower top which, with Beinn Luibhean alongside, was covered in Part Eight. On this walk Ben Brack is superbly rugged, grass giving way to rock in unexpected ways. Ben Donich is smoother, but has interesting rock chasms on the descent ridge.

The walkers' car park is just behind Ardgartan Visitor Centre and across the River Croe. **Start** along the forest road heading up right with a sign 'Walkers Access The Brack'. After 2km this rises to a junction.

Turn right for 100 metres. A tall waymark indicates a small path to left of a stream with waterfalls. The path is steep, especially at the start, and seriously eroded by feet and water. It reaches a stile at the forest's top at NN

253037, 50 metres east of where the stream enters the trees. (The stile has a white-topped pole, not easily seen by descenders from above.)

The rock crevasses on the north ridge of Ben Donich

After 100 metres the path turns right, and crosses the stream. Now head uphill just to the right of the stream on a smaller path. This leads into a shallow corrie under the broken final face of the Brack (NN 249032). One big boulder in this corrie has space under to shelter a couple of people, with a fine view across to the Cobbler.

From here easy slopes lead up left to a col, but a grass gully up to the right offers a more direct and interesting way towards the summit. A small path, weaving among fallen blocks, reaches the Brack's north ridge just below the summit.

From **The Brack**'s summit descend north at first, with steep drops on the right; then swing northwest into the wide boggy col below. A fence runs across the low point of the col. In another 50 metres, a path with white-topped poles also runs across. ▸

For an easy escape bear right on this path, down rough grass to a marked stile into the trees. A well-surfaced path leads down to the forest road below.

For your second hill of the day, head up the wide, gentle ridge westwards. At the 570m knoll (NN 233043) there's a conspicuous cairn on the right among crag hollows and overhangs. The main ridgeline passes to left of this cairn, but it

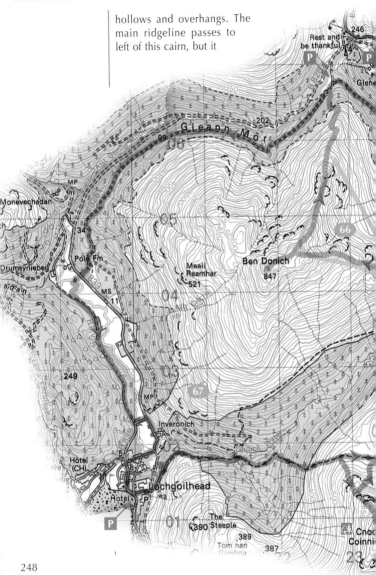

makes a lunch point and a foreground feature for photos in several directions.

The ridgeline continues up to reach a mossy plateau. **Ben Donich** summit is 400 metres to the southwest.

Descent Return across the mossy plateau, and bear left to descend the north ridge of Ben Donich. This has a small path. At the 650m contour the ridge rises slightly in a mass of crag and landslip, with strange deep cracks. The path has a fine moment passing through and over the blocks.

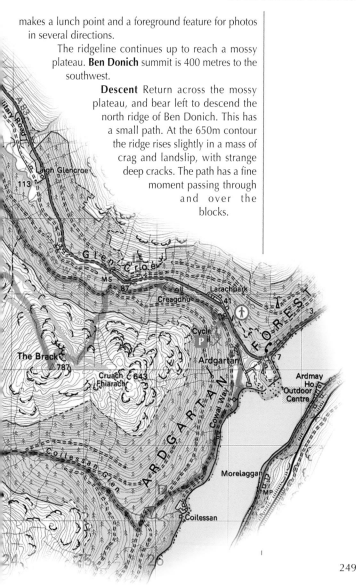

The ridge gets grassy again. Follow its crest down to a shoulder at 500m. Here you drop off the left-hand (west) side of the ridge to a path with white-topped markers. ◄

The path slants down below the ridge crest, then zig-zags below a small crag to a stile. A well-surfaced path leads down to a forest road. Turn right for 200 metres to a junction with a mobile phone mast.

The track to the left would lead down to the Donich access car park beside the B828, and beyond that to **Rest and Be Thankful** and its mobile snack bar. But for a quick return, take the right-hand track. After 1km gently down-hill, fork right into the upper track. In another 3km, you rejoin the outward route and turn down left on the track to the car park.

If you reach a small industrial erection – a 'thingie', like the one on Route 39 – on the ridge crest just above the trees, you have come down slightly too far.

ALTERNATIVE DESCENT

It is also possible to descend by the old road that leaves a corner of the **Rest and Be Thankful** car park. The track of decomposing tarmac is more open than the forest road above and is the old military road used by Wordsworth and Dr Johnson. It runs down to the valley floor, where it enters the planta-tions. As it rejoins the A83, take a bridge on the right to switch into a forest road for 600 metres. When this in turn leads onto the A83, turn back left across a bridge, then right on another section of old road. This rejoins the main road at a car park. A final 1km along the busy road's verge leads to **Ardgartan Visitor Centre**.

Start/finish	Ardgartan Visitor Centre on A83 NN 269037 (or Lochgoilhead)
Distance	26km/16½ miles
Ascent	800m/2700ft
Approx time	8½hr
Max altitude	Argyll's Bowling Green 500m or Cnoc Coinnich 761m
Terrain	Dirt roads, rough track, small moorland path
Map	LR 56; Expl 363 and 364; Harvey *Arrochar Alps*

Diversion up Cnoc Coinnich adds
1.7km/1 mile, 250m/750ft
Ascent, 1–1½hr

Length

Difficulty

This is a long hike around the back of The Brack, mostly on the more scenic sort of forest road, but ending with a wild high crossing of 'Argyll's Bowling Green'. This is a cross-linguistic joke: the ground is not particularly smooth and lawn-like. Instead the name is a misinterpretation of Gaelic Buaile na Griana meaning 'sunny sheepfold' – a commemoration of a May afternoon in the 1690s when the sun came out for two whole hours.

Lochgoilhead as an alternative startpoint is less convenient than Arrochar, but does put the tough bit of the trek at the beginning. On the other hand, Lochgoilhead is a great spot for a lunchtime snack purchased from the Post Office (which also serves cheap and reasonably palatable coffee).

And if you choose a sunny day – not actually all that uncommon – you could reward yourself with a side trip up Cnoc Coinnich. 'Kenny's hillock' is only 250m above the pass, and at 761m (2497ft) is the highest hill *not* to make it into Corbett's list. And this shows J. Rooke Corbett's inspired choice of the 2500ft mark: while Cnoc Coinnich's craglet-perched summit, with its little pool, is a delightful picnic spot, this is not a mountain of such Corbett calibre as The Brack, Ben Donich or the Cobbler.

Start from the upstream corner of the car park, on a broad dirt track (signed for The Brack). After 1km this slants gently uphill, to a T-junction. Turn right, to continue up-valley. There are views between the trees to the slopes of the Cobbler.

After 4km, at the head of Glen Croe, the track reaches a junction with a mobile phone mast. **Rest and Be Thankful** (with, as often as not, a mobile snack bar) is 800 metres down to the right, but keep ahead on the dirt track that runs down the flank of **Gleann Mor**. The forest road gives views out to the surrounding hills over 5km of gentle, fast descent.

Having dropped to the valley floor, the track reaches a junction. Keep ahead to cross the B839 onto a rough track to the **River Goil**. Around 50 metres upstream is a girder bridge, abandoned for wheeled traffic but, when I crossed it, still sound enough for a walker. (The bridge is disused, so make your own assessment of its current condition. There's a road bridge 1km upstream; or else you could continue down-valley on the forest road you just left.) After the disused bridge, cross a field to a rough grassy track. Turn left, down-valley. After 500 metres the

Lochgoilhead, with Beinn an Lochain, Ben Donich and the Cobbler rising behind

252

track enters plantation, and then mixed woodland, to emerge at a corner of the B839.

Turn left, across the river, to a waymarked track on the right. After 400 metres turn right on a track that becomes a riverside path, to a bridge where you rejoin the road into **Lochgoilhead**.

From the loch-side car park, take an uphill lane to left of the Post Office signposted to toilets. It degenerates into a rough wide path. At its top, turn left on the upper of two tracks, with a red waymarker. It runs above forest, then inside it, to cross a footbridge above the confluence of two waterfall streams.

Here a rougher path turns steeply uphill. There are a couple of Cowal Way markers before it emerges at a stile at the forest top.

Now the sketchy path slants left up a grassy hillside, marked with white-topped poles. These poles are too far apart to be visible in mist, so following a compass east is the best way to keep track of the path. After a short climb the path eases into the flat moorland col at 500m altitude.

ASCENT OF CNOC COINNICH

Bear off to the right (southeast) here and ascend the fairly clear ridgeline, past some perched boulders and then with crag drops on the left, to **Cnoc Coinnich** summit cairn. Descend the same ridge until just past the perched boulders, at 600m altitude. Now grassy slopes lead down to the right (north) to rejoin the marked path through the col.

Main route The marker poles and the very small path lead across the moor to a cairned knoll (NN 234018) just east of a small lochan. This cairn overlooks the top of forest – which is being extensively felled – in **Coilessan Glen**. The path is initially steep and rather eroded, then passes to right of a fence corner, to enter the forest at a marked stile. A well-surfaced but uncomfortably steep path leads down to right of a stream. It crosses this by a footbridge to the corner of a forest road.

Head directly downhill, taking care when passing any forest operations (or timing your walk for a weekend or after the working day). Fork right on the main track to stay near the stream. At the next junction keep down right to cross the stream and reach a track T at the slope's foot.

Turn left, recrossing the stream, and passing below a car park onto a tarred lane. After 2km this reaches the loch side. After a short rise, look out for a waymarked path on the right. This leads along the shoreline, passing around the edge of a campsite, then turns inland alongside a stream. It bends right through woods to join a tarred track. Turn left, soon following **Croe Water** upstream. At the first house cross the river on a track bridge reduced to walker-width, and take a path upstream to the visitor centre.

68 Beinn an Lochain

Length

Difficulty

Start/finish	Donich car park on B828 southwest of Rest and Be Thankful NN 227070
Distance	6.5km/4 miles
Ascent	700m/2400ft
Approx time	3½hr
Max altitude	Beinn an Lochain 901m
Terrain	Steep hillside, pathed ridge, road verge or rough grassland
Map	LR 56; Expl 363; Harvey *Arrochar Alps*

Beinn an Lochain was originally classed as a Munro. Early hillwalkers of the Scottish Mountaineering Club reached the 840m south summit and worked out its height by sighting on neighbouring hills; but they then ascended into mist, and badly overestimated the extra ascent to the main summit. The correction came in the 1974 edition of Munro's Tables – 901m Beinn an Lochain being, now, the lowest ex-Munro.

It doesn't feel like a Munro; perhaps because of the 250m start-point, or the way motorcycle noise drifts up the concave east face to the summit. But it is blessed with a very fine northeast ridge, sharpened by landslips on the northern side, so that the path is actually a bit exposed. The route given here uses a very steep ascent of the southeastern flank before descending that good ridge: but a straightforward up and down from the lower car park is popular.

Start by turning left on the B828 for about 30 metres to find some bulldozer wheelmarks which aid the first ascent. Head uphill to right of a plantation. Bear up left above the forest, on a steep slope of wet grass. After a tough ascent, weaving among small outcrops, you arrive suddenly and satisfyingly onto the south summit.

A path runs north along pleasant ridge to **Beinn an Lochain's** main summit. The old one-inch map confirms the impression that the true top is the first one, not the cairned one just behind.

Descent Now the splendid ridge runs down northeast, with crags dropping to the right. On the opposite side you look down into the mass of broken rock where half the ridge has collapsed towards Loch Fyne. A small, rather exposed, path zigzags down.

At the ridge foot the path drops off right, onto moorland. Where it passes between two boulders you can choose between the road route – easy but nasty – and a moorland way which is nasty in a completely different way.

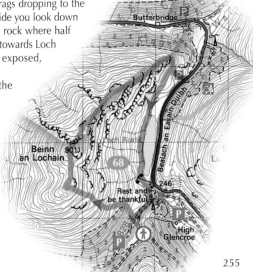

255

Beinn an Lochain and Loch Restil

- **Road route** The path continues straight downhill, crossing a small ruined dam to a **car park** on the A83 (NN 234088). The busy road has a comfortable verge most of the way, but for the last 500 metres you grovel along a sketchy path outside the crash barrier. The narrow B828 leads back to the Donich car park.

- The **moorland alternative** leaves the descent path at the two boulders, and contours to the right with the imposing crags above. The ground is rough but there are traces of paths, leading to a small dam at the outflow of **Loch Restil**. Path traces lead along the loch's western shore to Rest and Be Thankful. The narrow B828 leads back to the Donich car park.

69 Beinn Bheula

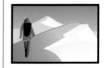

Start/finish	Lettermay NN 187003
Distance	18.5km/11½ miles
Ascent	1750m/5000ft
Approx time	10hr
Max altitude	Beinn Bheula 779m
Terrain	Rough, grassy hillsides, with craggy outcrops
Map	LR 56; Expl 363

Cruach nam Miseag and Beinn Bheula only
14.5km/9 miles, 1100m/3700ft
Ascent, 6½hr

Length

Difficulty

Just because a hill is small doesn't make it any easier – not in Argyll, anyway. Small hills are unwalked. The pathless grassland slows you down, as well as leaving it up to you to work out which way to go. And if you get it wrong (or even if you get it right) there are sudden outcrops to catch you out.

But the important words here are grassland and outcrop. Off-route wandering hereabouts may be slow, but it is still enjoyable. At lower levels there may be some tussocks, bog and bracken, but nowhere is there the thigh-high heather and peat precipices of more easterly areas. The outcrops are small, broken by shelves and gullies, so that there will almost always be a way through or down; plus you learn more hillcraft on such an outing than over a dozen Munros bagged by the well-marked paths.

The four small hills seen across the head of Loch Goil make a tough but tempting day out. They comprise the Corbett, 779m-high Beinn Bheula; two of the lower hill category called Grahams; and Cruach nam Miseag which, at 606m, doesn't exist at all in hill list terms (but as it has over 150m of drop behind it, it is listed among the Marilyns). Useful paths and tracks cover ▶

◄ the ground from sea level to the 300m contour, where the grass 'n' crag fun begins.

Another path, part of the Cowal Way down from Curra Lochan, is a cut-off that offers a shorter day over just the first two of the hills.

Signs at Lettermay ask you to park in Lochgoilhead village. However there are some limited parking opportunities on the verge opposite Drimsynie Estate Office, and 150 metres past Lettermay opposite Ardroy Outdoor Centre. **Start** up a dirt road through the scattered settlement of Lettermay. After 100 metres fork left on a track. After the last house this bends back right through a gate, above an area of small trees, and into tall ones. Still ascending gradually it bends left. In another 150 metres look out for a small, overgrown track turning up left. A culvert with two black pipes marks the bottom of this track (NN 179000).

Under its rushes and moss, the track has a firm stony surface. It slants leftwards (roughly south) to the top of the plantation. Here it slants up left, southeast, to lose itself on the northeastern spur of Cruach nam Miseag. Head uphill, to the easternmost and highest of **Cruach nam Miseag**'s summit knolls. It has a commanding view down Loch Goil.

Leave the summit northwest (because of crags on the left), then turn west over two more grassy summits. Descend southwest. A line of crags, with grassy gaps, separates you from **Lochain nan Cnaimh**. Either go down some grassy gap, or follow the crag tops down almost to the forest top, to reach the outflow of the lochan.

From the outflow a small path is starting to form. Head up southwest, passing above the top end of an incised stream and crossing a fence beyond it, to the wide col southeast of Beinn Bheula.

While there are easier slopes round to the left, the steep end face of the hill can be taken direct. An aeroplane fragment lies at the highest point below the steepening (NS 1578 9734). From here a grassy gully runs up

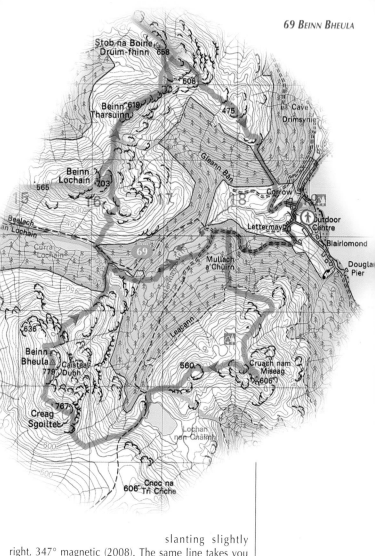

slanting slightly
right, 347° magnetic (2008). The same line takes you
right up through the crags to emerge near the 761m
southeast top of **Creag Sgoilte**. (Creag Sgoilte is unnamed

Beinn Bheula from Lochain nan Cnaimh

on Harvey maps; it's the south top of Beinn Bheula.) (If descending this way, find Creag Sgoilte's southeast top and head 30 metres northeast, to the plateau edge (NS 1572 9761). Turn sharp right and descend on 167°.)

The wide, grassy ridge leads over Creag Sgoilte's nearby northwest top (767m), then through a col to the narrower ridgeline to **Beinn Bheula**'s trig point.

Crags defend the northern and eastern slopes of Beinn Bheula, and the initial descent requires some care. Head down northwest for 200 metres into a col, then turn sharp right and descend east, towards Loch Goil. Zigzag down grass terraces, with a stream gully about 20 metres to your right. After 30m (vertical height) of descent (two zigs right separated by a zag back left) a small path slants down left onto a broad grass shelf below a line of crag. Follow this out onto the northeast-running ridgeline.

Descend this ridge in the direction of Lochgoilhead visible far below. There are two crag bands, each with gaps to pass down through, before you reach the top corner of a plantation. Cross a fence and go down the right-hand edge of the trees, then through their scattered edge, to the outflow of **Curra Lochain**. ▶

The short cut down from Curra Lochain is described at the end of this walk.

Cross the outflow on wobbly stepping-stones (or wade the gravel streambed alongside), and head left along the lochside to cross an equally wobbly old stile. Directly above, now, the slope leads up to a field of large boulders. Slant up steeply left to the bottom left corner of this boulderfield. It turns out to be broken ground from a huge landslip, with ferny hollows and grassy gaps, so that you can go up among the boulders without difficulty – but stay near their left edge so you can escape onto open grass if baulked.

In the hollow above, head up to left of crags onto the ridgeline southeast of Beinn Lochain. The steep face ahead can be taken direct, or make things easier by contouring to the right, north, out of the col, when gentler slopes lead up onto the northern ridge just below the summit of **Beinn Lochain**. ▶ You can now look back and examine the broken ground, grass crevasses, and small

In 2008 I rebuilt its random stonepile into a small but I think shapely cairn.

uphill cliffs of the landslip zone you came up through (see Appendix 1, p280).

A direct descent northwards gets you on the wrong, uphill, side of a line of crag. So leave Beinn Lochain's summit eastwards for 50 metres, before turning down north on grass and bare rock with drops on your right. There's a fence to cross before the col that introduces the short grassy rise onto **Beinn Tharsuinn**. Ben Harsinn, the 'Transverse Hill', is the third so named in this book.

Descend northeast into another col, before slanting up left to **Stob na Boine Druim-fhinn**. It has a steep summit cone with grassy hollows around the trig point.

Descend the summit cone southeast, onto a flat, grassy ridge. Easy walking and great evening views – so don't be distracted by worries about the descent section ahead which, as seen earlier in the day, appeared as an actual overhang! There are indeed serious crags between 600m and 500m contours, but also a straightforward way through. A dip forms to your left in the wide grass ridge, and as the ground steepens downhill this dip develops into a grassy gully that runs right down through the craggy zone (from NN 1730 0223, and down southeast). From its foot work round left onto the grassy ridgeline below the crags.

The ridge is wide, peaty, and almost level, though a further tiny crag drop is split by a continuation of the gully line used higher up. At the ridge end head down southeast, aiming for Lettermay and the far end of Loch Goil. Above a broad tree gap your descent is blocked by a final crag: avoid this on the left. The broad tree gap has a fence, and a grassy path, down to a gate onto a forest road (at about 150m, not on maps). Cross this to another gate, and continue down the tree gap to open ground and a junction of tracks above the ugly green sheds of **Corrow** trekking centre.

Take the track down to the right. Beside a roadstone quarry with piled fragments of stripy schist, turn back left to pass the trekking centre onto the road below. Turn right, across **Lettermay Burn**, to the walk start.

SHORT CUT DOWN FROM CURRA LOCHAIN

From Curra Lochain's outflow, the short-cut path heads downstream for Lettermay. With a fence on its right, the path is grassy and small but marked with white-topped posts. As the slope steepens, it zigzags down boggy shelves among black crag, heading to the right away from the stream, then slanting down left to the foot of the **Sruth Ban** waterfall. Now wider, the path runs down, to right of the stream, to meet a forest road.

From here there are two options. There's a very small and overgrown path running down the right bank of the stream for 1km, when you can take a small forest track to the right. But easier is to turn right along the forest road. This runs briefly uphill, then slants down below a clear-felled area to a bend to the right – here the smaller track of the streamside route rejoins from the left. Keep down the main track, in another 300 metres rejoining the outward route, to Lettermay.

70 Glen Branter Tracks

Start/finish	Glenbranter Forest Walks NS 111978
Distance	10km/6 miles
Ascent	300m/1000ft
Approx time	3¼hr
Max altitude	Glen Branter 250m
Terrain	Paths and tracks
Map	LR 56; Expl 363

Length

Difficulty

This walk combines the two highlights of the forest trails at Glenbranter: the wooded slopes of Creag Bhaogh, and the river gorge of Allt Robuic. In between there's a wander up the clear-felled Glen Branter that adds a little bit of length and exercise.

The car park is just above (northwest of) the Forestry Commission offices and toilets at Glenbranter. **Start** by

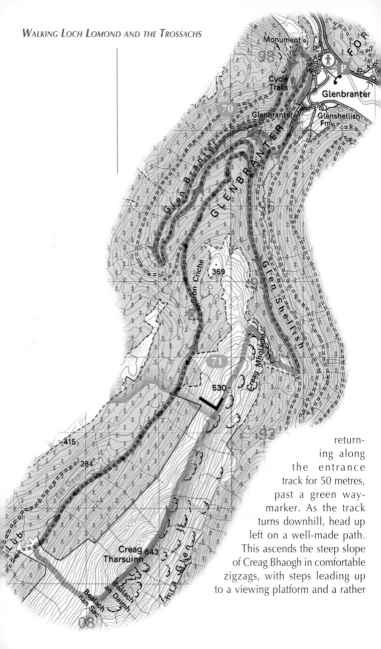

returning along the entrance track for 50 metres, past a green way-marker. As the track turns downhill, head up left on a well-made path. This ascends the steep slope of Creag Bhaogh in comfortable zigzags, with steps leading up to a viewing platform and a rather

Looking back over Glen Branter on a wet autumn morning

gentler path above. This heads left, around the slope, uphill and then descending to meet a forest road.

Cross it slantwise into a wide path descending gently through broadleaf woodland. This path or rough track emerges from the plantations into clear-felled ground and makes its way up **Glen Branter** on the right-hand side of the river. ◄

The margin note:

The return track is visible across the river and you could make your way to it over some rough brushwood.

The track fords the river and turns back down-valley, passing alongside the river's small gorge. On re-entering plantations it makes its way round to the right and slightly uphill to join a wide, smooth track descending from up on the right – the Cowal Way, and return leg of Route 71. Keep ahead for 200 metres, then follow the track as it bends sharply down left.

Just before the bridge over **Allt Robuic** take a stepped path with railing up to the left. This runs above and to left of the wooded stream, descends to cross it, and continues briefly upstream before turning up right to return at a higher level. A path junction has a signpost up left, indicating the start of a track contouring away from the river (northeast). After 500 metres a signpost points ahead for the car park, but take the path up left, signed as 'Forest Walks'. Multicoloured waymarkers guide up to a higher track, along it briefly to the right, and then on a path descending to the car park.

71 Creag Tharsuinn

Length
■ ■ ■ ■ ☐

Difficulty
■ ■ ■ ■ ■

Start/finish	Glenbranter Forest Walks NS 111978
Distance	20.5km/13 miles
Ascent	800m/2700ft
Approx time	8hr
Max altitude	Creag Tharsuinn 641m
Terrain	Grass slopes and ridges, pathless and in places steep
Map	LR 56; Expl 363

Creag Tharsuinn is typical of the likeable and little-visited hills of Cowal. It has the Cowal drawbacks: too many trees around its base, and being in that rather inconvenient corner of the Highlands. But it has also the Cowal advantages: craggy atmosphere, pathless but reasonably comfortable grass, and great sea views. It can also offer smallness (barely over 2000ft) and almost certain solitude.

These hills, like the malt whiskies of Kintyre on the opposite shoreline, are reserved for the connoisseurs prepared to ignore what's popular and easy. So turn up your nose at the Trossachs to enjoy Creag Tharsuinn; and a dozen similar Cowal hills await your further exploration.

Start from the end of the car park, on a multicoloured forest trail contouring south. In 50 metres take the downhill fork. The path runs along the foot of the woodland under beech trees, to meet a track. Turn down left to a wider, smoother track at riverside meadows.

Turn right and follow the track upstream past Glenbranter House. Where it bends up right away from the river, you can take an orange-waymarked path ahead into the Ritual Grove – a clump of impressive full-size Sitka spruce. The path turns uphill alongside **Allt Robuic** and rejoins the track above.

Turn left to cross Allt Robuic and continue on the main uphill track until it turns sharply right. Here keep ahead on a slightly smaller track. This descends at first, then rises gradually to the 200m contour. Almost 3km from the junction the track comes into the open, with clear-fell below and newly planted trees above. It also levels off, and bends right (southwest). A quarry is 200 metres ahead, and just before a slight left bend an overgrown old track sets off uphill on the right. ▶

Head up this once well-surfaced but now unused track. After 200 metres you reach a wet, level area. Here note that the track bends to the left under the rushes for 50 metres before becoming clear and turning once more uphill. At 320m the track forks (NS 105937). ▶ Fork right on a track that leads up to the top corner of mature trees

Credit here to the Harvey map, which alone marks this inconspicuous but very useful path.

I built a small cairn here for the benefit of those using OS mapping.

*Creag Tharsuinn seen
from Beinn Mhor
(Route 72)*

on your right. You must now cross brushwood for 100 metres uphill to reach open hillside.

The slope above is steep grass with small crags. Straight up it looks possible, but the easier way is to slant up to the right along the base of the steeper slope, but above a craggy area called Leacann Ghlas. Soon, crag-less grassy slopes lead up southwest onto the ridgeline of **Creag Mholach**.

Follow the grassy ridgeline southwest over Creag Mholoch, whose summit is unmarked. In the dip beyond you cross a fence, and now a few iron fenceposts guide along the ridge. A second fence crosses the ridge, and then it rises gradually to **Creag Tharsuinn**. The true summit is the second-last knoll, marked by a single quartz stone at the brink of the craggy drops to the left.

Descent After the final knoll, descend southwest into the wide pass Bealach nan Sac, and turn down right (northwest). Cross a fence and follow streams down a wide tree gap to a wide, smooth forest road at the valley floor.

Turn right, following the track all the way up **Strath nan Lub** and then down into Glen Branter. Ignore a first side-track down left, and follow the main track through an open area with views down to Glenbranter. A second side-track joins from down left, and then the main track bends sharply down left at the junction passed on the upward walk. Follow the track down to its bridge over **Allt Robuic**.

You could now continue ahead as on the upward walk, but only do so if soaking wet, blistered, or very tired. Otherwise, just before the bridge, take a stepped path with railing up to the left. This runs above and to left of the wooded stream, descends to cross it, and continues briefly upstream before turning up right to return at a higher level. A path junction has a signpost up left, indicating the start of a track contouring away from the river (northeast). After 500 metres, take the path up left, signed as 'Forest Walks'. Multicoloured waymarkers guide up to a higher track, along it briefly to the right, and then on a path descending to the car park.

72 Loch Eck and Beinn Mhor

Start/finish	Car park at Benmore Gardens NS 144854	
Distance	20km/12½ miles	
Ascent	900m/3000ft	
Approx time	7¼hr	
Max altitude	Beinn Mhor 741m	
Terrain	Track, grassy ridges, pathless grassy plateau	
Map	LR 56; Expl 363	

Length
■ ■ ■ ■ □

Difficulty
■ ■ ■ ■ □

The outward walk is a loch-side track through woods, with a rough little diversion to the Paper Caves. The crossing of Beinn Mhor itself is on grassy ridges and a somewhat soggy plateau above, all surrounded by steep craggy slopes. If this were in the Trossachs, rather than this obscure corner of Cowal, it would be busy with a big path. As it is, you're on your own. ▶

◀ Good Gaelic would say Beinn Mhor as 'Ben Vore', and it is so pronounced by knowledgeable locals. However, the naming of the gardens below suggests that the anglicised pronunciation has been current for at least a century.

Allow time at the day's end for a visit to those Benmore Gardens – I'd suggest two hours, but more if you're a serious gardener. It's one of three official outstations of the Royal Botanic Gardens in Edinburgh, and specialises in trees and shrubs. Its rhododendrons are particularly fine, as are the autumn displays of *Enkianthus*, shrubs related to the bilberry. If you're confident enough of your hill speed to buy your entry ticket at the day's start, you can finish this walk by entering the garden by its upper gates.

Start by crossing River Eachaig on a track marked 'private road', and turning right. Once past **Benmore Gardens** the track bends left past a clock tower to a T-junction. Turn right here. ◀ The small road runs past the foot of Loch Eck to an ugly hydroelectric power station and continues as a stony track along the loch shore.

In another 150 metres a track back left will be the return route.

After 2.5km the level promontory at Coirantee is 200 metres ahead. At this point (NS 137895) the track crosses a stream and bends briefly northwest. On the left is a pull-off for one car, and a rough but clear path heading up under the trees. This is the side trip for the **Paper Caves**. It's about 10 minutes up the rough path to the boulder caves, an ancient rock-slip formation. The caves are narrow, and schoolchildren on courses at the adventure centre at the loch foot get lowered into them on ropes.

The main walk continues along the loch-side track for another 1.5km, until it emerges into open ground just before **Bernice**. Here a forest track turns sharply back to the left. Follow this up for a few metres, then take to rough grassland above to a gate. Follow a fence line uphill, then slant up to the right to the edge of a plantation. Here a rough path runs uphill, letting you avoid all the bracken to reach the plantation's top corner.

Head directly uphill, on rough grass, to the shoulder called Meall an t-Sith (477m, the hump of the fairies).

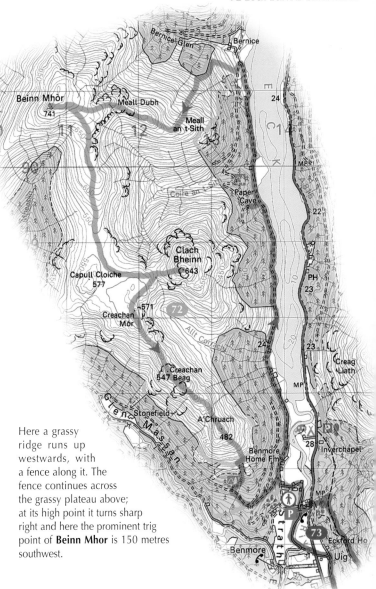

Beinn Mhòr
741

Meall Dubh

Meall
an t-Sìth

24

E

C 14

K

MP

Bernice Glen

Bernice

12

11

Coire an

Paper
Cave

22

Clach
Bheinn
643

PH
23

Capull Cloiche
577

571

72

Creachan
Mòr

Allt Coire

24

23

Creag
Liath

Creachan
547 Beag

Glen Massan

Stonefield

A'Chruach
482

MP

Benmore
Home Fm

28

Inverchapel

MP

Strath

P

73

Benmore

Uig

Eckford Ho

Here a grassy ridge runs up westwards, with a fence along it. The fence continues across the grassy plateau above; at its high point it turns sharp right and here the prominent trig point of **Beinn Mhor** is 150 metres southwest.

The Paper Caves, above Loch Eck

Descent Follow the fenceline back southeast. After 500 metres (NS 112906) an older fence runs roughly south and could be used as a guide; but it's better to take a higher, drier line along the ridge crest to its left. After 1.5km you drop into a wide soggy col. Bend round left into the slightly lower col leading to **Clach Bheinn**. A steep climb on grass among overhanging craglets leads to the first summit, which according to the Harvey map is 1m higher than the one 150 metres northeast.

Return to the col, and head southwest to the cairned knoll of **Creachan Mor**. Now a grassy ridge runs down southeast, with occasional old fenceposts along the crest. It has various humps, the last being **A'Chruach** overlooking Strath Eachaig. Continue southeast following the old iron posts to a fence at the top of plantations. Around 100 metres to left (NS 133862) a gate leads into the small trees. A rough small track runs to the right, then zigzags downhill to join a wide, smooth one.

Turn left, downhill. The track slants down the top edge of Benmore Gardens, with an ornamental hut just above it. Ignore tracks forking off left. The main track slants downhill and joins the tarred lane of the outward route. Turn back sharp right to the corner of Benmore Gardens and the car park.

73 Puck's Glen

Start/finish	Car park at Benmore Gardens NS 144854
Distance	5km/3 miles
Ascent	200m/700ft
Approx time	2hr
Max altitude	Puck's Glen 200m
Terrain	Paths and tracks
Map	LR 56; Expl 363
Local transport	Regular buses from Dunoon ferry and elsewhere: West Coast Motors tel: 01369 707701

Length

Difficulty

Shakespeare was a lowlander who only mentions mountains twice in his 40-odd plays. But as Puck, the fairy spirit of *Midsummer Night's Dream*, put a 'girdle round about the Earth in 80 minutes', then he can plausibly have been everywhere, including here. And if he hasn't, then he's missed a charming little stream ravine.

Strath Eachaig has various Forest Walks and Park Paths (leaflet from Lomond & Trossachs National Park), as well as the spectacular Benmore Gardens. Linked trains, ferries and buses make it conveniently possible to get here as a carless day-trip from Glasgow.

Start by crossing River Eachaig on a track marked 'private road', and turning left. The riverside track has puddles to avoid (some of them deep enough that I'm sure I saw a

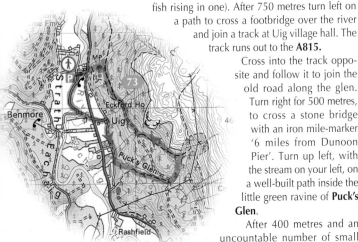

fish rising in one). After 750 metres turn left on a path to cross a footbridge over the river and join a track at Uig village hall. The track runs out to the **A815.**

Cross into the track opposite and follow it to join the old road along the glen. Turn right for 500 metres, to cross a stone bridge with an iron mile-marker '6 miles from Dunoon Pier'. Turn up left, with the stream on your left, on a well-built path inside the little green ravine of **Puck's Glen**.

After 400 metres and an uncountable number of small waterfalls, the path rises up the right side of the ravine to a junction. Continue ahead on a path dropping back into the upper glen. Continue upstream, until the path rises to a forest road.

The **Upper Puck Loop**, ahead, was closed during winter 2008 but should reopen. But if necessary you could just turn left along this forest road. If the upper loop is open, take this rougher path continuing upstream. After 400 metres, and several more waterfalls, it rises up the left-hand side of the stream hollow. Ignore a very rough path continuing upstream, but turn left on a smooth, contouring path signed for Black Gates.

The path passes through open ground with views up the valley, as it descends to rejoin the forest road. Turn right on this track, which runs roughly level up the valley. Two signposted trails down left are short cuts to Benmore Gardens; or continue to a third, with blue/green/red waymarker, that doubles back to the left. It zigzags down to **Black Gates**, directly opposite Benmore Gardens' car park.

THE LONG ROUTES

West Highland Way

The West Highland Way runs 153km (95 miles) from Milngavie on the outskirts of Glasgow northwards to Fort William and is Scotland's most popular long walk. It is wide, well-waymarked, and well provided with accommodation; the scenery it passes through is very fine. However, for much of its length it is within sight and sound of the busy A82, as well as the West Highland Railway, so that for more adventurous walkers its route may seem rather too tame.

It does provide the romantic, and environmentally sound, approach to the area of this book from the edge of Glasgow – or indeed, using footways by Rivers Clyde, Kelvin and Allander, from the city centre. The full length of Loch Lomond, along its east side, is one of the Way's most beautiful sections, as well as its roughest underfoot. Between Walks 42, 43, 47, and 48 you'll visit almost all of this stretch. From Inverarnan northwards, leaving the Lomond National Park, and on to Bridge of Orchy, the Way uses the military road alongside the A82, and this is probably its least rewarding section. Walks 26, 28 and 30 use short sections of it.

North of Bridge of Orchy the Way escapes the main road and crosses wild, remote country: Rannoch Moor, the Devil's Staircase to Kinlochleven, and the Lairig Mor to the base of Ben Nevis. This is bleak mountain scenery quite different from the shores of Loch Lomond.

Cowal Way

The 92km (57-mile) Cowal Way is one comfortable way to explore this odd and undervalued peninsular. While the route has its quirky corners, it also has rather too much forest track and tarred road. That said, the roads are very quiet ones: on the 15km of Glendaruel I recall only a single car passing us. Accommodation and even an occasional shop are well spaced along the way.

From Portavadie, 48km of low-level paths and roads lead to a pass at 300m from Glenbranter to Lochgoilhead by Curra Lochain – see Walk 69. That's followed by a fine moorland crossing at 500m to Ardgartan (Walk 68). The new line of the Cowal Way now follows Walk 54 through to Inveruglas, for a ferry across Loch Lomond to the West Highland and Rob Roy Ways.

Rob Roy Way

This runs northeast from Drymen (south of Loch Lomond) to Pitlochry. It passes through Aberfoyle, Callander, Strathyre, and Lochearnhead, before leaving the National Park towards either Killin or Amulree. The distance is 130–150km depending on which route you choose. The route is low-level, and (like the Cowal Way) has long stretches on dirt roads through Forestry Commission plantations, as well as designated cycle paths. Short sections of it are used on Walk 6 (Menteith Hills, return leg), Walk 11 (Kilmahog, return leg) and Walk 18 (Glen Ogle railway). Apart from these stretches, almost all of it within our area is on forest roads.

APPENDIX 1

Mysteries of the Schist

Schist on Cruach Ardrain summit. The wrinkles are the sign of age and hard living

The mountain rock over the entire area covered by this book is the Dalradian schist. Grey, wrinkly and striped like the hide of some ancient beast, it's what could be called the default rockform of the Scottish Highlands. It's a rock with its own particular personality. As you scramble and walk over the Trossachs and Loch Lomond you'll gradually get intimate with it.

Schist is a metamorphic rock, meaning one that's been bashed about, crushed and folded. The schist of the Scottish Highlands had all that happen to it during the Precambrian, the first of all the geological eras: and then it happened to it all over again during the period called the Silurian, when Scotland's continent chunk crashed into what we now call England and Wales.

It's all this crushing and folding that has given the rock its stripes and crinkles. During the crushing, a platy mineral called mica turns itself around to be across the line of compression. With enough heat, the chemicals start to migrate through the rock and the flat, shiny crystals of mica get larger. This mica gives the schist rock a sparkle and shine, particularly noticeable on a hazy August afternoon. It also makes the rocks rather smooth. If you're used to the grippy volcanic rocks of Glen Coe, Snowdonia or the Lake District, you're going to find the schist slippery, especially in the wet.

Elsewhere in the Highlands the schist gives way suddenly to white, sharp-edged quartzite, rounded speckly granite, or the dark grippy volcanic rocks that are so great for climbers and scramblers. Not here. Over this part of the southern Highlands, it's grey all the way. But on wet days in particular, when there's nothing to look at but the rocks alongside and the stones under your feet, you come to appreciate the subtleties of the schist. Streambeds give clean, unweathered specimens: and every path is also a stream, so there's always something to see...

When the schist received a particularly bad battering, its minerals were able to seethe around in the rock and assemble into interesting crystals. The most distinctive of these is garnet, showing as blood-red speckles. In Gaelic folklore, the faery air-force called the *Sluagh* zooms through the clouds, trying to snatch the souls of the newly dead – and the garnets are the sticky red rainfall that drips from their open wounds. To geologists they are even more exciting, as marking a particular level of heat and pressure achieved by the rocks, corresponding with burial at around 10–20km. And to those born in January, these semi-precious garnets are your birthstone.

Researching this book, I came across garnets on Creag Mac Ranaich (Route 20) and on Stuc a' Chroin (Route 21). But the biggest and most impressive, lying across the boulders like a bad case of the measles, are across Beinn Dubhchraig and Ben Oss, the two outliers of Ben Lui. The rocks that now form Ben Lui itself were slightly less heated and crushed: result, no garnets at all.

The garnet zones are in the north. Along the southern edge of the Highlands the metamorphic rock has been less bashed about: and instead of

the mica mentioned above, there forms a precursor mineral called chlorite. The name means, simply, green, and has

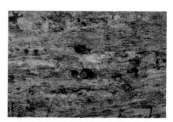

Garnets up to 1cm wide on the ridge of Ben Oss (Route 33)

Phyllite textures on the summit plateau of Stob Binnein. See also Edinample Falls, shown on page 69.

Black magnetite crystals, about 2mm across, in a path pebble from Cruach Tairbeirt (Route 49)

no connection with the element chlorine except that chlorine is also green. Chlorite has a glitter of a different sort, more of a sheen than a shine, and makes a rock called phyllite. The rock surface is wrinkled, and the silvery shine of it is almost like fish skin. Look over the bridge at Edinample at the head of Loch Earn (Routes 12 or 21), and see a small gorge made of this silvery stone.

The schist has been so battered about that, like a well-boiled youth-hostel soup, what it was originally made of hardly matters. Still, a subtle palate can tell the difference between a Scotch Broth and a Mulligatawny. And a schist that started off as limestone will break down into soil that, by the standards of the Scottish Highlands, is especially rich and fertile. Wild flowers flourish on the schist.

Again, when it started off as some sort of underwater rock, water is incorporated into the mineral crystals. Cumin or coriander in that six-day soup makes itself known however long the boiling. And the underwatery sort of schist develops interesting little black crystals. Shiny black specks, up to 2mm across, in the path stone on Cruach Tairbeirt pictured at the bottom of the previous page, are crystals of magnetite, an iron mineral. Through a strong lens the largest crystals can be seen as octahedrons; and if you hold them close, they will very slightly deflect the needle of your compass (but will not affect a compass used normally).

Landslips

The other distinctive feature of these mountains is not down to anything in the nature of the schist rocks, but to the combination of serious faulting (so close to the Highland boundary) and vigorous glaciers (being on the western seaboard, with heavy snowfall and ice formation). Steep slopes undercut by glaciers have, on many mountains, simply slipped downwards. The result is a jumbled, broken-up hillside, with rock crevasses running across the slope, and small crags facing *uphill*. The ridgeline can have a double, a parallel ridge at a slightly lower level, as at the summit of Beinn Challum.

One striking landslip is on the western side of Beinn an Lochain (Route 68); another is on the similarly named Beinn Lochain, 8km further south (Route 69). Once you're aware of this formation, you'll see it on many of the steeper slopes hereabouts.

The Highland Boundary

The Dalradian schists of the Scottish Highlands are what you walk on over almost all the routes described in this book – but not the part of it that's actually in the Scottish Lowlands.

It's usually said that the Trossachs are in both the Highlands and the Lowlands; and that Conic Hill (Route 43) stands on the Highland boundary. But if you look underfoot, you'll realise that neither of these well-weathered assertions is actually correct. The rocks of the Lowlands are Devonian in age, and of the group called the Old Red Sandstone (though that oldness is relative, as they're 200 million years younger than the Highland schists). The ORS rocks next to the Highland boundary all turn out to be conglomerate, or 'puddingstone': big rounded pebbles, bound together with reddish-purple

Conglomerate ('puddingstone') at Lime Craig Quarry (Route 4). The pebbles are made of quartzite and volcanic rocks – see photograph on page 65.

Serpentinite crag, Lime Craig Quarry

Unweathered serpentinite in a broken boulder, Lime Craig Quarry

sand. When Scotland and England collided, huge mountains rose. When these mountains eroded, in flash floods down sandy wadis, these huge pebbles were the result, in seasonal riverbeds, deltas and shingle beaches. This pebbly puddingstone makes up Conic Hill – which,

accordingly, is a hill of the Scottish Lowlands. The same rocks are also seen on the Doon, Callander Craig and the Hills of Menteith (Routes 5, 11 and 4). Walking north from Kilmahog (Route 10), you leave the brown conglomerates as you approach the base of Ben Ledi: Ben Ledi is grey schist, and accordingly a hill of the Highlands.

The boundary between red-brown conglomerates and grey stripy schists is the Highland Boundary Fault. As you approach from the south, or stand on any of these borderline hills, it's easy to spot the sudden rising of the schist into rough knobbly mountains. But look underfoot, and it's a complicated bit of geology.

First of all, when Scotland collided with the England–Wales continent, it did so on a slant rather than head on. Before everything came to rest, chunks of Scotland slid past each other sideways. The Scottish Lowlands have moved westwards across the northern edge of the Southern Uplands; the Highlands have moved westwards across the northern edge of the Lowlands. (And further north again, the Northern Highlands have moved southwest along the Great Glen.) The pebbles that make up the conglomerate were washed down out of mountains to the north: but they are not the grey schist that now makes up those mountains. They are pale grey quartzite, and dark volcanic andesite; and the mountains they came from are now somewhere away in the southwest (or they were, before they eroded away altogether and disappeared).

Everything crunched to a standstill. Two geological eras went slowly past; and the far edge of our 'Old Red Sandstone' continent was being dragged into an ocean trench thousands of miles away to the northwest. The combined Scotland–England continent was, accordingly, being pulled and stretched in that direction. The old fault lines at the two sides of the Scottish Lowlands (the Highland Boundary Fault, and the Southern Upland Fault) cracked open, and the land between them sank into the gap. Yes, Scotland has its own rift valley, just like East Africa (only a whole lot older). And as the ORS conglomerate slid downwards past the schist, it was compressed and bent around. The resulting bent-up puddingstone edge now forms Conic Hill and the islands across Loch Lomond; the Menteith Hills; and Callander Craig.

It was the sinking of the rift valley that brought the younger Lowland rocks down alongside the older Highland ones to the north. Because the Lowland rocks are softer than the well-mangled schists, they have worn down to low, rolling hills, with the contrasting schist scenery overlooking it all from the north.

And so, on wet days when you can't even see the mountains, look down at the stones underneath your feet and see the deep underground of 600 million years ago, when the schist (as it were) *really* hit the fan; the off-white and dark purple pebbles of mountains that vanished long before the dinosaurs; and the sinking scenery of Scotland's Kilimanjaro era.

APPENDIX 2
Access (especially during autumn)

Ben Lomond (left) and its loch, from Inveruglas

Since 2005 Scotland has a legal right of access to almost all open country and farmland (the main exceptions being growing crops and land around buildings). Footbridges are explicitly included in the access rights, as are non-damaging cycling and wild camping – though this doesn't mean roadside camping. Access must be taken 'responsibly', which basically means with consideration and care for other hill-users, land managers and the environment. The full text of the

Scottish Access Code is at www.outdoor access-scotland.com (or from Scottish Natural Heritage).

In parts of this area, from mid-August (sometimes July) to 21 October, responsible access includes avoiding disturbance to deer stalking. Hills managed by Scottish Natural Heritage, the National Trust for Scotland and the Forestry Commission are open to walkers year-round. The northern part of the area is covered by three Hillphones schemes, where recorded phone messages warn you, around 24 hours in advance, of which hills' deer will be shot at. See www.hillphones.info. In the remaining areas, estates request hill-goers to limit themselves to a small number of specific paths and ridges.

For estate boundaries, see the overview map on pages 12–13. Stalking does not take place on Sundays.

Argyll Forest Park, Queen Elizabeth Forest Park (FC)

Forestry Commission (and Loch Katrine, Scottish Water): open access year-round.

Balquhidder

Stalking 15 September–20 October. The routes in this book are within Inverlochlarig Estate. Call Hillphone 01877 384232; alternatively you are invited to call in at Inverlochlarig Farm on your way onto the hill. Eastern parts of the area (not crossed in this book) have different Hillphone numbers; see www.hillphones.info.

Glen Ample (AM)

Commercial stag and hind stalking August–15 February. The glen track (Route 12) is a right of way; otherwise, the estate asks walkers to use the hill path above Glenample Farm (Route 21).

Ardvorlich Estate (ARDV)

Commercial stag and hind stalking August–15 February. The estate requests walkers to use the ridge path Ardvorlich – Ben Vorlich – Stuc a' Chroin (Route 21) and the ridge of Ben Our, keeping out of Coire Buidhe in particular.

Edinchip Estate (EDIN)

Stag and hind stalking September–15 February could affect Walks 19 and 20. Because of the multiplicity of access points, the estate does not post warning signs.

Fyne/Falloch

Glen Fyne/Glen Falloch: stalking mid-August–20 October. Hillphone 01499 600137.

Dochart/Lochay

Glen Dochart/Glen Lochay: stalking mid-August–20 October. Hillphone 01567 820886.

Lui NNR (SNH)

Ben Lui National Nature Reserve is managed by Scottish Natural Heritage but not owned by them, and deer stalking does take placed here. North of Ben Lui is Forestry Commission (open access). West of Ben Lui is managed as part of Glen Falloch Hillphones area (see above) even though not appearing as such on the Hillphones map. East of Ben Lui (in Stirling district and in the National Park) is managed by Cononish Farm (not on Hillphones, so look out for signs locally).

Ben Lomond (NTS)

National Trust for Scotland: open access year-round.

APPENDIX 3
Accommodation and Infomation

Accommodation

Hotels, B&Bs, and general information:
www.visitscotland.com tel: 0845 22 55 121,
and www.visitscottishheartlands.com
(or individual tourist information centres
below; Callander and Balloch are open
all year). See also West Highland Way
information at www.west-highland-way.co.uk

National Park:
www.lochlomond-trossachs.org or National
Park information centres at Balloch, Balmaha
and Aberfoyle.

Scottish Youth Hostels Association:
www.syha.org.uk,
central bookings tel: 08701 55 32 55.

Independent hostels:
www.hostel-scotland.co.uk, or for the free
Blue Guide send stamped addressed envelope
to Scottish Independent Hostels, PO Box
7024, Fort William PH33 6YX.

Campsites: www.UKcampsite.co.uk

Travel

Journey planner: www.travelinescotland.com
tel: 0871 200 22 33

Timetable booklet *Exploring the National
Park by Ferry, Bus or Train* from National Park
Centre, Balloch or download from
www.lochlomond-trossachs.org

Trains: www.firstscotrail.com
tel: 08457 48 49 50

Coaches: Three daily each way Glasgow –
Loch Lomond side – Crianlarich – Bridge of
Orchy, also Edinburgh – Crianlarich
www.citylink.co.uk tel: 08705 505050

Ferries etc: See individual sections below.

Weather and snow

The most useful and accurate Internet forecast
is at Mountain Weather Information Systems
www.mwis.org.uk. There is also a Met Office
mountain forecast at www.metoffice.gov.uk/
loutdoor/mountainsafety/westhighland.html.
One or other is posted daily in youth hostels
and tourist information centres.

The Scottish Avalanche Information
Service issues forecasts for Glen Coe of
snow conditions and avalanche risk daily
December–Easter. Snow conditions in
Lomond & The Trossachs will usually (though
not invariably) be rather less serious. The
forecast is at www.sais.gov.uk/latest_forecast

There is no webcam pointed at any of these
mountains. The nearest is probably Buachaille
Etive Mor at www.kingy.com

Summit panoramas: Computer views from the
Cobbler, Ben Lomond, Ben Lui, Ben More,
Ben Ledi and three others
www.viewfinderpanoramas.org

Trossachs

Tourist Information David Marshall Lodge
tel: 01877 382258; Trossachs Discovery
Centre, Aberfoyle tel: 08707 200 604
www.visitthetrossachs.com

Pubs and restaurants Brig o' Turk Tea
Room: an unpretentious wooden shed with
atmosphere, which also offers evening meals.
Aberfoyle has the Forth Inn (good inexpensive
pub food and real ales), also the Bluebell café
at David Marshall Lodge.

Supplies Co-op Aberfoyle 7am–9pm every
day.

Independent hostels Ledard bothies,
Loch Ard tel: 01877 387219
www.highland-adventure.co.uk

Local transport SS *Sir Walter Scott* on Loch Katrine (Trossachs Pier – Stronaclachar) tel: 01877 376316 or 332000 www.lochkatrine.com

Callander and Loch Lubnaig

Tourist Information Rob Roy Centre Callander tel: 01877 330342 (year-round)

Pubs and restaurants Strathyre has three, including The Inn at Strathyre (good meals, beer, open fire); Lade Inn at Kilmahog, walker- and dog-friendly, awash with real ales, good food, but very busy on Fri/Sats, live music nights. Callander has Crags Hotel, and various chip shops and restaurants.

Supplies Callander is the Trossachs metropolis, with shops including a small Tesco (6am–11pm) and several gear shops. Village shop Strathyre.

Independent hostels Trossachs Tryst, edge of Callander tel: 01877 331200.

Camping Large camp/caravan site at Strathyre – tends to fill up.

Balquhidder and Loch Earn

Pubs and restaurants Kings House Hotel at Balquhidder walker-friendly, bar meals only until 8.15pm; Monachyle Mhor walker-friendly but upmarket. Clachan Cottage Hotel, Lochearnhead does bar meals (until 9pm).

Supplies Small shop on A85 at Lochearnhead (evening opening Fri, Sat until 8pm).

Camping Large camp/caravan site Leitters north of Kingshouse – tends to fill up. Informal camping south side Loch Earn.

Local transport Inexpensive taxibus to Balquhidder is operated by Kingshouse Travel tel: 01877 984768.

Crianlarich and Tyndrum

Tourist Information Tyndrum tel: 01838 400246 (08707 200 626).

Pubs and restaurants Tyndrum has Green Welly Stop (café)

www.thegreenwellystop.co.uk; Tyndrum Lodge Hotel and Paddy's Bar & Grill; and the award-winning Real Food Café (chip shop plus) tel: 01838 400235 www.therealfoodcafe.com; small outdoor and coffee shop at Auchtertyre (closes 7ish pm); Ben More Lodge Hotel Crianlarich (bar meals, Indian takeaway, www.ben-more. co.uk); Station Tea Room Crianlarich.

Supplies Outdoor Store (and food) at Green Welly Stop, Tyndrum until 10pm; Brodie's Mini-mart Tyndrum; small store Auchtertyre; Crianlarich Store (until 6pm).

SYHA Crianlarich tel: 01838 300260 or 0870 004 1112 year-round, but weekends only in January, February www.crianlarichyouthhostel.org.uk

Independent hostels Strathfillan Wigwams (Auchtertyre farm) tel: 01838 400251; By The Way Hostel, Tyndrum tel: 01838 400333 www.tyndrumbytheway.com; Braveheart Backpackers, Killin tel: 01567 829089 www.cyclescotland.co.uk

Camping By The Way Hostel (above); Strathfillan Wigwams.

Ben Lomond

Tourist Information Old Station, Balloch tel: 0845 345 4978; National Park Centre, Balmaha tel: 01389 722100; National Park Gateway Centre, Balloch tel: 08707 200631.

Pubs and restaurants Rowardennan Inn; cafés Balmaha.

Supplies Lomondview Stores, Gartocharn; and Balloch.

SYHA Rowardennan (March–mid-October) tel: 01360 870259.

Camping Cashel tel: 01360 870234 www.forestholidays.com; Milarrochy Bay tel: 01360 870236.

Local transport Loch Lomond ferries: Tarbet – Rowardennan – Inversnaid, tel: 01301 702356 www.cruiselochlomond. co.uk; Rowardennan – Inverbeg three daily

April–September, Rowardennan Hotel
tel: 01360 870273; Inversnaid – Inveruglas
Inversnaid Hotel tel: 01877 386223
www.lochsandglens.com; Ardleish –
Ardlui, Ardlui Hotel April–October, sails
as required 9.30am– 6.30pm, May–August
8.30am–7.30pm, lunch break 2.30–3.30pm.
Hoist ball on pole at Ardleish or tel: 01301
704243. *Maid of the Loch*, Balloch is
currently under restoration and not sailing
tel: 01389 711865 www.maidoftheloch.com

Loch Lomond West
Tourist Information National Park Centre,
Luss tel: 01389 722120; Tarbet tel: 08707
200 623.

Pubs and restaurants Drovers Inn, Inverarnan
('Pub of the Year 1705') has an eccentric
ambiance with stuffed bear and other
ornaments, and serves food until 9pm. Also
bar restaurant at Beinglas campsite. More
pubs all along lochside A82. Ardlui Hotel,
slightly snacky menu but food until 9.15pm.
Inveruglas café, open 9am–5pm.

Supplies Small store at Beinglas campsite (till
8pm); Village Shop, Luss.

SYHA Loch Lomond (Balloch) tel: 01389 850
226 March–October, palatial with ghost.

Independent hostels Bunkhouse at
McGregor's Landing, Ardlui (not really a
bunkhouse, too grand, more bunkpalace
tel: 01301 704205), and at Beinglas campsite.

Camping Beinglas farm (caravan-free,
useful shop etc) tel: 01301 704281 closed
November–February; Ardlui marina
tel: 01301 704 243 (all year); Luss Camping
and Caravanning Club tel: 01436 860658
closed November–Easter.

Local transport Ferries, see Ben Lomond
above.

Arrochar and Glen Croe
Tourist Information Forestry Commission
Visitor Centre on A83 at Ardgartan
tel: 01301 702432 or 08707 200 606.

Pubs and restaurants Village Inn, Arrochar
on A814 towards Helensburgh; Arrochar
chip shop (closes 9pm); and others. Rest and
Be Thankful is not a pub (this deceived Dr
Johnson, among others) but the car park often
has a snack trailer (Famous Bacon Butties).

Supplies Village Shop, Arrochar
(7.30am–7pm Tue–Sat, shorter hours
Mon, Sun). Tighness Stores (on coast road)
8am–8pm, or to 9pm Fri, Sat and 7pm Sun.
Arrochar also has a small outdoor shop.

SYHA None – Ardgartan YH has closed.

Camping Forestry Commission, Ardgartan,
beautiful lochside location tel: 0845
130 8224 closed February; Camping &
Caravanning Club Site is now members only.

Cowal
Pubs and restaurants Lochgoilhead Hotel
(food until 8.45pm); Loch Fyne Oysters at
head of Loch Fyne; Dunoon has all facilities,
but closer to Benmore is Cot House at
Eachaig Bridge (junction of A815 and A880)
which is inexpensive and atmospheric.
Benmore Gardens has its own café.

Supplies Post office and shop Lochgoilhead,
both closing 5.30pm; Inveraray; Dunoon;
Cot House services (small grocer opens to
10pm) at Eachaig Bridge.

SYHA Inveraray tel: 01499 302 454
closed November–Easter.

Camping Cot House (see above) and
Invereck.

Local transport Car ferry across the Clyde
to Cowal: Gourock – Dunoon by Calmac
(tel: 01475 650100 www.calmac.co.uk)
and Western Ferries (tel: 01369 704452
www.western-ferries.co.uk); paddle steamer
Waverley occasionally cruises Gourock to
Lochgoilhead tel: 0845 130 4647
www.waverleyexcursions.co.uk.

APPENDIX 4
Further Reading

Guidebooks
Walking the Munros Vol 1 Southern
by Steve Kew, Cicerone
ISBN 978 1 85284 402 8 (2004)
If you simply wanted the convenient route
up each of the Munros, then you should
buy Kew's book rather than this one.

Arran, Arrochar and the Southern Highlands
by Graham Little, Tom Prentice
and Ken Crocket, SMC
ISBN 0 907521 49 5 (1997)
Climbing guide on summer rock and
winter ice.

*Backpacker's Britain: Central and Southern
Scottish Highlands*
by Graham Uney, Cicerone
ISBN 978 1 85284 527 8 (2008)
Four of the two-day routes are in
Lomond and The Trossachs: Crianlarich
Munros; Ben Vorlich from Glen Artney;
Ben Ledi and Benvane with two hills to
their northwest; Ben and Loch Lomond;
plus many more for in-tents travellers
elsewhere. As you'd expect, route
description is briefer than in this book.

Scotland's Mountain Ridges
by Dan Bailey, Cicerone
ISBN 978 1 85284 469 1 (2006)
Two climbs (Mod–Diff) on the Cobbler,
Ben Lui ridges in winter; with similar
(but mostly more demanding) routes
elsewhere.

The West Highland Way
by Terry Marsh, Cicerone
ISBN 978 1 85284 369 4 (2007)

The Rob Roy Way
by Jacquetta Megarry,
Rucksack Readers
ISBN 978 1 898481 26 3 (2006)

The Cowal Way with Isle of Bute
by Michael Kaufman and Jim McLuckie,
Rucksack Readers
ISBN 978 1 898481 32 4 (2009)

General
Rob Roy Macgregor: His Life And Times
by WH Murray, Canongate
ISBN 978 0 86241538 9
Closely researched but readable;
somewhat partisan in favour of Rob Roy
and Highlanders (apart from Campbells) –
but why not?

Rob Roy by Walter Scott (1817)
The myth rather than the man. One of the
least unreadable of Scott's novels; includes
an ambush alongside Loch Katrine.

Mountaineering in Scotland
by WH Murray, Bâton Wicks
ISBN 978 1 89857 323 4 (Dent, 1947)
the Cobbler should be climbed up! Places
hillwalking in its wider context of rock,
snow and ice climbing. The greatest work
so far of Scottish landscape appreciation.

*Loch Lomond to Stirling: A Landscape
Fashioned by Geology*
SNH/BGS 1 85397 119 7 (2005)
Well illustrated and lucid but a bit brief.

*Granite and Grit: a Walkers' Guide to the
Geology of British Mountains*
by Ronald Turnbull, Frances Lincoln
ISBN 978 0 71122914 3 (2009)
Okay, I wrote it. It's got a whole chapter
on the schist.

*Hostile Habitats: Scotland's Mountain
Environment*
SMT ISBN 978 0 907521 93 8 (2006)
Takes your knowledge a bit further on
everything from ravens to the Romans.

LISTING OF CICERONE GUIDES

BACKPACKING AND CHALLENGE WALKING
Backpacker's Britain:
  Vol 1 – Northern England
  Vol 2 – Wales
  Vol 3 – Northern Scotland
  Vol 4 – Central & Southern
    Scottish Highlands
Book of the Bivvy
End to End Trail
The National Trails
Three Peaks, Ten Tors

BRITISH CYCLING
Border Country Cycle Routes
Cumbria Cycle Way
Lancashire Cycle Way
Lands End to John O'Groats
Rural Rides:
  No 1 – West Surrey
  No 2 – East Surrey
South Lakeland Cycle Rides

PEAK DISTRICT AND DERBYSHIRE
High Peak Walks
Historic Walks in Derbyshire
The Star Family Walks – The Peak
  District & South Yorkshire
White Peak Walks:
  The Northern Dales
  The Southern Dales

MOUNTAINS OF ENGLAND AND WALES
FOR COLLECTORS OF SUMMITS
Mountains of England & Wales:
  Vol 1 – Wales
  Vol 2 – England
Relative Hills of Britain

IRELAND
Irish Coast to Coast Walk
Irish Coastal Walks
Mountains of Ireland

THE ISLE OF MAN
Isle of Man Coastal Path
Walking on the Isle of Man

LAKE DISTRICT AND MORECAMBE BAY
Atlas of the English Lakes
Coniston Copper Mines
Cumbria Coastal Way
Cumbria Way and Allerdale Ramble
Great Mountain Days in the
  Lake District
Lake District Anglers' Guide
Lake District Winter Climbs
Lakeland Fellranger:
  The Central Fells
  The Mid-Western Fells
  The Near-Eastern Fells
  The Southern Fells
Roads and Tracks of the Lake District
Rocky Rambler's Wild Walks

Scrambles in the Lake District:
  North
  South
Short Walks in Lakeland:
  Book 1 – South Lakeland
  Book 2 – North Lakeland
  Book 3 – West Lakeland
Tarns of Lakeland:
  Vol 1 – West
  Vol 2 – East
Tour of the Lake District
Walks in Silverdale and Arnside

THE MIDLANDS
Cotswold Way

NORTHERN ENGLAND
LONG-DISTANCE TRAILS
Dales Way
Hadrian's Wall Path
Northern Coast to Coast Walk
Pennine Way
Teesdale Way

NORTH-WEST ENGLAND
OUTSIDE THE LAKE DISTRICT
Family Walks in the
  Forest of Bowland
Historic Walks in Cheshire
Ribble Way
Walking in the Forest of Bowland
  and Pendle
Walking in Lancashire
Walks in Lancashire Witch Country
Walks in Ribble Country

PENNINES AND NORTH-EAST ENGLAND
Cleveland Way and Yorkshire
  Wolds Way
Historic Walks in North Yorkshire
North York Moors
The Canoeist's Guide to the
  North-East
The Spirit of Hadrian's Wall
Yorkshire Dales – South and West
Walking in County Durham
Walking in Northumberland
Walking in the South Pennines
Walks in Dales Country
Walks in the Yorkshire Dales
Walks on the North York Moors: Books
  1 and 2
Waterfall Walks – Teesdale and
  High Pennines
Yorkshire Dales Angler's Guide

SCOTLAND
Ben Nevis and Glen Coe
Border Country
Border Pubs and Inns
Central Highlands
Great Glen Way
Isle of Skye
North to the Cape
Lowther Hills

Pentland Hills
Scotland's Far North
Scotland's Far West
Scotland's Mountain Ridges
Scottish Glens:
  2 – Atholl Glens
  3 – Glens of Rannoch
  4 – Glens of Trossach
  5 – Glens of Argyll
  6 – The Great Glen
Scrambles in Lochaber
Southern Upland Way
Walking in the Cairngorms
Walking in the Hebrides
Walking in the Ochils, Campsie Fells
  and Lomond Hills
Walking on the Isle of Arran
Walking on the Orkney and Shetland
  Isles
Walking the Galloway Hills
Walking the Munros:
  Vol 1 – Southern, Central and
    Western
  Vol 2 – Northern and Cairngorms
West Highland Way
Winter Climbs – Ben Nevis and Glencoe
Winter Climbs in the Cairngorms

SOUTHERN ENGLAND
Channel Island Walks
Exmoor and the Quantocks
Greater Ridgeway
Lea Valley Walk
London – The Definitive Walking Guide
North Downs Way
South Downs Way
South West Coast Path
Thames Path
Walker's Guide to the Isle of Wight
Walking in Bedfordshire
Walking in Berkshire
Walking in Buckinghamshire
Walking in Kent
Walking in Somerset
Walking in Sussex
Walking in the Isles of Scilly
Walking in the Thames Valley
Walking on Dartmoor

WALES AND THE WELSH BORDERS
Ascent of Snowdon
Glyndwr's Way
Hillwalking in Snowdonia
Hillwalking in Wales:
  Vols 1 and 2
Lleyn Peninsula Coastal Path
Offa's Dyke Path
Pembrokeshire Coastal Path
Ridges of Snowdonia
Scrambles in Snowdonia
Shropshire Hills
Spirit Paths of Wales
Walking in Pembrokeshire
Welsh Winter Climbs

For full and up-to-date information on
our ever-expanding list of guides, please
visit our website:
www.cicerone.co.uk.

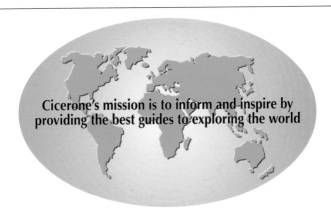

Cicerone's mission is to inform and inspire by
providing the best guides to exploring the world

Since its foundation 40 years ago, Cicerone has specialised in publishing guidebooks and has built a reputation for quality and reliability. It now publishes nearly 300 guides to the major destinations for outdoor enthusiasts, including Europe, UK and the rest of the world.

Written by leading and committed specialists, Cicerone guides are recognised as the most authoritative. They are full of information, maps and illustrations so that the user can plan and complete a successful and safe trip or expedition – be it a long face climb, a walk over Lakeland fells, an alpine cycling tour, a Himalayan trek or a ramble in the countryside.

With a thorough introduction to assist planning, clear diagrams, maps and colour photographs to illustrate the terrain and route, and accurate and detailed text, Cicerone guides are designed for ease of use and access to the information.

If the facts on the ground change, or there is any aspect of a guide that you think we can improve, we are always delighted to hear from you.

Cicerone Press
2 Police Square Milnthorpe Cumbria LA7 7PY
Tel: 015395 62069 Fax: 015395 63417
info@cicerone.co.uk www.cicerone.co.uk

CICERONE